MW00787516

LEGAL LIABILITY

IN RECREATION, SPORTS,

and TOURISM

Fourth Edition

John O. Spengler
Bruce B. Hronek

SAGAMORE
PUBLISHING

@2011 John O. Spengler and Bruce B. Hronek
Publishers: Joseph J. Bannon and Peter L. Bannon
Director of Sales and Marketing: M. Douglas Sanders
Director of Development and Production: Susan M. Davis
Director of Technology: Chris Thompson

ISBN print edition: 978-1-57167-643-6
ISBN ebook: 978-1-57167-644-3
LCCN: 2011936032

10 9 8 7 6 5 4 3 2 1

Sagamore Publishing, LLC
1807 N. Federal Dr.
Urbana, IL 61801
www.sagamorepub.com

For Caroline and Matthew

For Sylvia

Contents

Acknowledgments

The authors wish to thank all those who sacrificed their time and energy to make this book possible—family, friends, colleagues, and associates. Thanks go to Daniel Castellano and Gordon Wilson, who helped with updating and shepherding the cases in this new edition.

Foreword

We practice our professional recreation, sport, and tourism management skills in a different world than we experienced a few decades ago. There is a propensity for people to sue if they are injured or receive property damage. Extensive litigation has resulted in significantly increased insurance rates while organizations and agencies are becoming increasingly unwilling to provide some high-risk recreation and tourism services that they provided in the past.

Recreation, sports, and tourism activities contain all the elements necessary to make those activities subject to accidents and subsequent lawsuits. Sports and recreation activities generally are competitive, fast-paced, use equipment and facilities, and include physical and/or social contact. Tourism places people in unfamiliar locations with varying safety standards.

When these elements are combined, they can result in accidents. This text provides guidance for students to study risk management principles that will increase their management skills. The book provides practitioners the understanding necessary to manage the activities in such a manner that it will minimize the potential of a successful plaintiff suit.

This book provides a legal structure by which students can best learn liability and risk management principles, and professionals can protect themselves and their organizations from those seeking to take advantage of the judicial system for personal gain. In order for recreation, sports and tourism managers and practitioners to be successful in preventing accidents and litigating issues, they must have knowledge of risk management and legal principles.

The authors, John Spengler and Bruce Hronek, not only have a rich legal background, but also have practical on-the-ground experience that provide a no-nonsense approach to the problems associated with legal liability in recreation and sports. They are practitioners, teachers, and researchers in the field of risk management and legal liability.

Tony Mobley, Dean Emeritus
School of Health, Physical Education, and Recreation (HPER)
Indiana University

Efforts have been made to make this book as accurate as possible. This book covers many general facets of legal liability. In order to give the readers a general understanding of the law, the book does not include all aspects of each legal situation. There are differences in the law in various jurisdictions, and there are legal nuances and differing interpretations of the law by individuals and organizations. Application of the principles and statements made in this book may be not be applicable in all circumstances and jurisdictions.

This book is not intended as a substitute for legal counsel. Readers should consult with legal counsel whenever a legal question occurs.

Introduction

The subject of legal liability conjures up thoughts of high costs, fiscal devastation, difficult legal language, attorneys, myriad legal papers, and time-consuming litigation. People generally fear those things that they don't understand. The major purpose of this book is to provide recreation and sports students, practitioners, and professionals in the field with a body of knowledge that will help them manage the legal risks that are an everyday part of their lives.

In the past, the field of recreation appeared to be sacrosanct when it came to people wanting to sue for damages. Prior to 50 years ago, when lawsuits were filed, the courts considered leisure pursuits as frivolous, and therefore counter to the good of society. The social structure and so-called "Protestant ethic" of the time called for hard work, not recreation. Only the very rich were privileged to have "leisure time." In the past decades, the average citizen's opportunity for leisure has increased significantly, and so has the extent of recreation, sport, and tourism litigation. Times have indeed changed!

There was a time when suing someone was not so common in the field of recreation, sports, and tourism. A young forester, graduating with a degree in forestry, reported to his first professional assignment with the U.S. Forest Service. His professional career started in the back country of the Salmon River in Idaho. The mountains of central Idaho were beautiful, the air was clean, and the work was interesting and challenging. There was little else that a young professional forester needed or wanted.

Early one evening a few weeks after he had reported to work, he heard a knock on his cabin door and a rather excited man reported that a woman was "in trouble" at a nearby campground. The man said the woman had entered the campground restroom (a polite name for an old-fashioned smelly single-seat outhouse) and had fallen through the floor into the pit that had been dug beneath the toilet to hold the refuse. The young forester hurriedly loaded the pickup with what turned out to be mostly useless equipment and rushed to the rescue. The site where the accident occurred was an old campground that had been built by the Civilian Conservation Corps in the mid-1930s.

Upon arrival at the scene of the accident, he found a large woman in the toilet pit with only her head above ground level. She was unable to extract herself from the hole, even with people trying to lift her out. The old floorboards and cross supports had been weakened by wood rot, and the floor collapsed under the woman's 250-plus pound weight.

The small group of people appeared to be relieved when "the forest ranger" arrived. Unknown to the campers, he did not have the faintest notion as to what to do. The toilet was built and used in an era when deep holes were dug to hold the waste. Whenever the pit was full of waste it was covered with dirt, and another pit was dug. The toilet building was then skidded to the new location. Pits were sanitized by maintenance crews using large amounts of highly caustic white powdered lye. The lye did little to reduce the unpleasant odor, but it was used anyway for "sanitation purposes."

The caustic lye burned the skin of the unfortunate woman. She had abrasions and was in pain from the downward plunge and was very embarrassed by her predicament. The women graciously awaited her rescue without a complaint.

With the help of some of the people in the campground, the toilet building was sawed down and removed using a deafening power saw that also covered the woman with sawdust and debris. The rescuers then rigged an "A" frame, and a block, and a tackle over the pit. After she was wrapped in rope, the rescuers slowly lifted her out of the pit.

She apologized for all the problems she had caused and walked down to the river to clean up after her ordeal. That was the last time the young forester saw or heard from the woman. The possibility of a suit or damage claim was never mentioned nor was a suit ever filed. The year was 1959.

A serious review of what is now a rather humorous occurrence could result in sleepless nights if it occurred today. An accident of this type today would be highly likely to result in a negligence suit with a potentially substantial court award. Attitudes and the propensity to sue have changed.

The fear of being sued is an ever-present part of American society. A number of years ago, many of these cases would have been considered minor incidents or accidents, and suing would not have been a solution. Today, however, people appear not to want to accept the normal dynamics of living in a world of bumps and mishaps.

In the 19th century and into the 20th century, the courts tried very few cases involving recreation, sports, and tourism. Our culture, especially since World War II, has gradually evolved into a very litigious society. Many, if not most people, feel that someone owes them something if they are injured or have lost property.

Highway billboards, the yellow pages, and newspaper ads encourage and entice people to file suit by advertising legal services with bold headlines that generally state: "INJURED?" followed by statements such as, "IT COSTS YOU NOTHING TO TALK TO US. WE ARE PAID ONLY IF YOU COLLECT." These are tempting statements for someone who has mounting medical bills or is angry about an accident or property loss.

On the other side of the issue of excessive litigation, it should be noted that not all negligence suits are frivolous. The civil courts serve an important service to our society in providing all citizens a means by which disagreements can be settled and wrongs righted without personal revenge and physical violence. The access to civil courts by an average citizen can right a wrong committed by the largest and most powerful institutions, organizations, and individuals. This right to litigate must always be protected and made available to our citizens as part of our democratic form of government.

Because many accidents result from unintentional, but nevertheless negligent and thoughtless acts, a wise and prudent organization or individual should try to settle justifiable legal claims for compensation out of court. Suits should be the last resort for claims and disagreements.

This book was developed to help posture individuals and organizations to prevent accidents and property loss and to counteract excessive legal claims. It is written in an informal manner to enhance the learning process and particularly to facilitate the understanding of a rather complex body of law. General areas of law discussed in the text include a legal foundation, negligence, intentional torts, constitutional law, personnel risk, recreation and event management, recreational sports, playgrounds, and aquatics liability, as well as other subject areas related to recreation and sports legal liability. The authors believe that knowledge of legal liability subject areas is critical to implementing a good risk management program. This book focuses on identification of legal risks, evaluation of the risks, and the implementation of an action plan to manage the risks.

This book is not a substitute for good legal counsel. While the book will cover many general facets of liability, the law may vary among the various jurisdictions. Readers should consult with legal counsel whenever a legal question occurs.

All recreation, sports, and tourism activities have some degree of risk. Legal liability related to parks, events, and recreational sports come in many forms and statistical probabilities. Legal liability is most obvious in terms of physical risk (accidents and injuries), financial risk (loss of property and potential income), psychological risk (mental health and personal well-being), and political risk (public support and financing).

When many individuals think about their personal experiences with recreation and sports, they soon conclude that many of their most memorable recreation experiences included a strong element of personal risk. Activities such as river running, mountain climbing, wilderness use, hiking, bicycling, football, skydiving, baseball, ecotourism, driving for pleasure, and wildlife watching are very popular activities with increasing numbers of participants. And they all contain a relatively high level of risk. Increasing numbers of people participate in high-risk activities because they consider the risks to be manageable.

Kayaking is a popular recreational activity that contains an element of risk.

Implementing risk management plans make all recreation, sports, and tourism activities manageable and more enjoyable, but some element of risk will always be present in any activity. Even a child's swing in a park has some of the factors conducive to an accident: immature physical coordination, speed, and height. Risk management reduces the potential of accidents and lawsuits but it does not eliminate the possibility. Recreation, sports, and tourism observers might conclude that activities without some level of risk are dull and lack excitement. *Taking the risk out of life is tantamount to taking the pleasure out of life.*

The question of whether to warn people of a hidden danger is both legal and ethical in nature. It is very true that you cannot warn people about every conceivable risk. Some legal counsel may believe individuals and organizations should not inform people of a danger that is not obvious. For example, there is an ethical and legal dilemma associated with warning people that there is "thin ice" on a lake. If the danger is known and you do nothing about it, there is an element of foreseeable danger and negligence if an accident occurs. The quick answer to the problem may be protective fencing of the area. However, the reality of fencing an entire lakeshore is likely to be an economic impossibility. The posting of "Danger—Thin Ice" warning signs may be another alternative. However, this type of sign does not adequately warn the very young, those who do not read, or those who do not read English. "How far do I need to go?" and "What should I do to keep people safe?" will always be ethical and legal questions for a risk manager. The courts will decide whether you went far enough. It may be wise to personalize a risk decision by asking the question, *"If my family were visiting the area or engaged in the activity, what warning of danger would I want them to have in my absence?"*

Having a policy of warning people about all hazards is neither wise nor possible. The reason it is not wise is somewhat subtle; when the average person sees a large number of warning notices and signs, dangers lose their significance in the long listings and mere volume of information. Behavioral scientists indicate that more than five information and warning signs in the same location tend to be ignored.

Some managers want to sign the obvious. Within a recreation site, one can find signs and brochures stating "no littering," "stay on path," and other warnings that should be assumed by the visitor in that setting. Signs and printed materials informing or warning about items and hazards that are not obvious may be most useful to the participants and visitors. Signs that inform visitors and participants about hidden hazards, fire regulations, and rules are also helpful and useful for a good recreational experience.

When a risk management program is focused on serving the public interest, then it will likely be ethical and effective. Judges and juries recognize programs that are aimed at providing a safe program for the visitors and participants. When accidents do occur, they are more defendable in a court of law. The risk management focus should always be visitor- and employee-oriented.

When risk management programs are defensive in nature, they lose creativity and broad support. *A good safety and risk management program focused on the visitor or participant is good public policy.*

All employees in an effective risk management-oriented organization must have a common risk management attitude. There are many organizations that designate specific positions within their organizations as "Safety Officers" or "Risk-Management Directors." While it is good to have someone to track safety records or follow up on complex Occupational Safety and Health Act (OSHA) requirements, the designation of a safety officer or risk manager might have the unintended consequence of making employees feel that someone other than themselves is responsible for safety within their work environment. Every individual in an organization, from the president or CEO to the custodian or clerk, should feel a strong obligation to identify and take actions to reduce potential risks. Every member of an organization should be a risk manager or safety officer. Effective risk management requires that all employees be empowered to take actions to prevent accidents from occurring.

Part One

FOUNDATION

Chapter One

INTRODUCTION TO RECREATION LEGAL ISSUES

SECTION 1: TRENDS

Professional managers need to know what is happening around them in regards to trends, risk, and legal liability. It is difficult to keep current in a field that changes with new legislation, precedent-setting court cases, the introduction of new products, and the development of new recreational activities. The emergence of new outdoor recreation activities has resulted in significant risk management concerns and management adjustments. Within the last 25 years, we have seen the appearance of recreation activities that include inline skating, hang gliding, skateboarding, wind sailing (wind surfing), snowboarding, geocaching, mountain biking, and the re-emergence of orienteering, to name a few. Equipment development, such as GPS, has allowed people to access areas that most would not have ventured into a decade ago. Each activity has brought about new concerns related to risk and participant safety. There is reason to believe that new activities and products will be developed requiring prompt responses from professional managers.

Risk management was born of necessity—human, legal, and political. As early as the late 1800s, the American Labor movement, particularly the coal mining unions, saw their union miners endangered by careless mining practices. Underground explosions, collapsed mines, toxic gasses, and black lung disease were common and considered simply a fact of life in the mines.

Factory assembly line work was not much better, with dangerous machines, no medical insurance, and little concern for the fate of the worker. Laws were passed and strikes were called as a result of the mining and factory safety problems. While there are still significant dangers, the combination of safety laws, protective equipment, federal and state safety inspections, and labor demands have resulted in safer conditions in modern underground mining operations and factories. The owners and operators of mines and factories now are faced with expensive litigation if an accident occurs.

During a forestry school field trip in 1957, a group of students heard a timber company executive proclaim that he would rather have a logger killed in an accident than permanently injured. His stated rationale was that the cost of a permanent injury was much higher than "paying off" a death. The students were stunned by the callous remark, but reluctantly realized that the cost factor was correct; however, a significant moral and ethical question remained.

A risk management program must serve three entities: the customer (user/visitor), the employee, and the organization (company).

A good safety and risk-management program is good public policy. Risk management should be part of the training of each employee in the recreation and sports work environment. The home smoke alarm is an example of a limited but important application of risk management. The home smoke alarm senses the presence of smoke and emits a sound, warning the residents that there is the potential of fire, thus saving lives. It does not, however, prevent the fire from occurring. Only an inspection of home maintenance (wiring, heating appliances, etc.) and proper storage will reduce the potential of fire. In the same sense, a risk manager should not only "sound the alarm," but do something to prevent a harmful incident.

For example, the issue of safety is critical in situations where locker rooms are used by recreation and sport participants. There is a duty to provide adequate security and supervision, particularly when children are present. Failure to do so may constitute negligence. The following case provides an example of a situation where a sound risk management and safety plan may have helped avoid a tragic outcome.

In *S. W. and J. W. v. Spring Lake Park District #16* (1999),[1] a 15-year-old girl was sexually assaulted in a girls' locker room adjacent to a school complex swimming pool. She was at the pool to take a swimming test. After the swimming test, she went to the locker room to take a shower and change clothes. It was at this time that she was sexually assaulted. The predator was later caught and convicted of first-degree sexual assault and kidnapping. Prior to the incident, the school secretary, a janitor, and the assistant pool director all saw the man as he exited the girls' locker room. He was neatly dressed and carried what appeared to be flower boxes. They did little in response to the man's presence, given their belief that he was on the premises for a harmless purpose and that he had merely lost his way and ended up passing through the girls' locker room by mistake. The school district had no security policy in place. Additionally, the employees had no official guidance in how to deal with non-students who were on the premises.

The parents sued, claiming the school district was negligent in failing to provide adequate supervision, protection, and security. The court held that the attack upon the girl was foreseeable because three employees were aware the attacker had been in the girls' locker room and understood that he was not a student and did not belong on school premises. Foreseeability, reasoned the court, requires actual knowledge of a dangerous condition which imposes a special duty to do something about that condition. The court found the defendant to be guilty of negligence and not entitled to governmental immunity.

It has been noted that the United States has less than 10% of the world's population and over half of the world's attorneys. In 2010, there were nearly 350,000 civil court cases filed in federal courts alone. Suits related to recreation and sports have increased steadily for three decades and are expected to continue to increase in the future. Society's apparent desire to be compensated for any loss or injury that occurs, attorney advertisements that appeal to a "something for nothing" mentality, and easy access to our nation's courts provide reasons for people to sue. While many of the cases have a just cause, some suits are marginal at best.

Often the media both reflects and influences the values and beliefs of a society. We often hear of cases receiving media attention that pull on our emotions. For example, the famous McDonald's coffee spill case, or more recent suits claiming that "fast food" was responsible for health and weight problems. In the field of recreation, sports, and tourism, types of lawsuits are plentiful, extremely interesting, and quite varied. One lawsuit was brought because a man was bitten by a fish. In another, a baseball spectator was distracted by a dinosaur mascot, then turned and was hit in the face by a baseball. Other suits filed include incidents where people were attacked by cougars in parks, golfers were struck by lightning, and swimmers were attacked by sharks.

Trends in the individual state courts mirror the federal court system. The courts in all jurisdictions are experiencing increasing utilization of resources to litigate civil matters and prosecute criminal cases. Settling disputes and prosecution of criminals is up in most jurisdictions. In 2010, more than 1,950,000 civil, criminal and bankruptcy cases were filed in the U.S. federal courts, approximately one-million more cases than were filed in 1980, mostly due to bankruptcy cases. Likewise, the number of civil cases has more than doubled in that same 30-year time period. The following statistical table shows how the federal court activity has grown in a very short time period.

Table 1.1

Trends in Civil and Criminal Cases Filed in U.S. District and Appellate Courts (1885-2010)

Year	U.S. District Court Civil Cases Filed	U.S. Court of Appeals Civil Cases Filed	U.S. Criminal Cases Filed	Authorized Federal Appeal Judges	U.S. Bankruptcy Cases Filed
1885	2200	200	250	No Data	100
1980	112,734	24,122	38,781	No data	763,072
2001	250,907	57,697	62,708	167	1,437,354
2003	252,962	60,847	70,642	167	1,661,996
2005	253,273	68,473	66,561	167	1,702,693
2007	257,507	58,410	67,851	167	801,279
2009	258,635	61,358	76,655	166	1,202,395
2010	292,307	56,790	78,428	167	1,531,997

Source: Administrative Office of U.S. Courts, Federal Judicial Workload Statistics, Washington, D.C.

The court system, both federal and state, is jammed with pending cases. It is little wonder that there is a tendency to settle claims out of court or through arbitration.[2] Time and patience become important factors in determining what cases come before the courts.

The information in Table 1.1 is from the U.S. Courts.[3] These figures also reflect the trends and general situation that exists in the states' court systems. There are as many as 90,000 product liability cases alone filed in the state courts each year.[4] Seventeen percent (17%) of all product liability cases involve toys or sports and recreation equipment.[5]

SECTION 2: CATEGORIES OF LEGAL LIABILITY

Wrongs committed that violate rules of society are called crimes. When people who commit crimes are identified, they are brought before the criminal justice system.

Through the legal system, wrongs can result in either punishment or compensation by criminal sanction or the imposition of civil liability. Wrongs that are deemed crimes are prosecuted by the government and convicted culprits can be punished through imprisonment or the issuance of fines. However, anyone in this country who is wronged has the opportunity to bring a civil action against the person or persons who wronged them. The primary goal of civil lawsuits is to provide compensation to the victim. The courts are guided by criminal and civil procedure rules, and the classifications of wrongs are governed by statutes[6] and case precedents.[7]

When a wrong occurs, it may become subject to the jurisdiction of the criminal or civil courts, or a special court, such as a court of contract appeals or juvenile court. If the subject area involves federal law, federal land, or federal questions, the case will be heard in a federal district court. If the subject area relates to state statutes or local ordinances, the case will be heard in a state court.

The standard of judgment in criminal courts dictates that if there is "reasonable doubt"[8] as to the guilt of the defendant, the courts must declare the individual not guilty. The standard of judgment in a civil court is a preponderance of evidence.[9]

These two standards of evidence have a significant interrelationship. For example, if a person is convicted of assault and battery in a criminal court, the victim of the attack could be compensated for his/her injury through the civil courts. The question of double jeopardy[10] does not apply if a civil suit follows a criminal conviction.

Once a defendant has been found guilty under the criminal "reasonable doubt" standard, the "preponderance of evidence" standard found in civil courts will be much more easily established. In the vast majority of cases, judges determine that *prima facie*[11] evidence is established as a result of a criminal conviction. This means that a plaintiff has an excellent chance of succeeding on a claim for civil damages.

In our society there is a constant threat of legal entanglements. In developed and civilized countries, all citizens are expected to live within the law. We simply cannot steal that which belongs to others, intentionally injure others, fail to pay our debts, or fail to keep our contractual promises. We must conform to a myriad of rules established by our governing bodies for the benefit of order in society. We must keep our hands out of cookie jars that do not belong to us!

In a broader sense, legal liability goes beyond the categories shown in Figure 1.1. There are risks selecting, supervising, evaluating, and training people; insurance coverage, contracts, concessions, leases, record keeping, waivers, community relations, intellectual property,[12] and many other categories.

Please note that the classifications in Figure 1.1 are not all-inclusive. The categories under each title in bold represent only examples of liability subject areas.

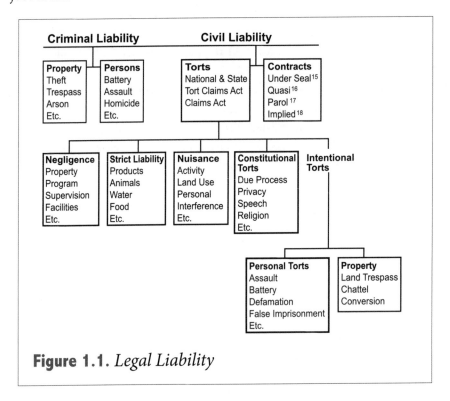

Figure 1.1. *Legal Liability*

Notes

1. *S. W. and J. W. v. Spring Lake Park District*, No.16, 580 N.W.2d 19 (Minn. 1999).
2. Arbitration is the process of resolving a dispute through a third party chosen by both parties to the litigation.
3. Federal Judicial Workload Statistics, 1991, 1992, and 1993. *Annual Report of the Administrative Office of the United States Courts.*

4. Mergenhagen, P. (1995/June). Product Liability: Who Sues?, *American Demographics, 50.*
5. *Rost v. United States,* 803 F.2d 448 (9th Cir.1986).
6. Statutes are acts by legislative bodies declaring, commanding, or prohibiting something. Black, H. C. (1979). *Black's law dictionary* (5th ed.). St. Paul, MN: West Publishing, p. 1264-1265.
7. Precedent is a decision by a previous court used to persuade courts to follow the same rationale to determine future cases.
8. Reasonable doubt is the amount of doubt, based upon the evidence presented, needed to acquit in a criminal case or that needed for a reasonable person to hesitate before acting. Black, H. C. (1979). *Black's law dictionary* (5th ed.). St. Paul, MN: West Publishing, p. 1138.
9. Preponderance of evidence is evidence that is more convincing than evidence offered by the other litigant. In civil cases it refers to greater weight or credibility to the evidence.
10. Double jeopardy refers to Fifth Amendment (U.S. Constitution) prohibition to being tried twice for the same crime.
11. Sufficient evidence to get plaintiff past a motion for directed verdict or summary judgment. Evidence that is sufficient to render a reasonable conclusion in favor of allegation. Black, H. C. (1979). *Black's Law Dictionary* (5th ed.). St. Paul, MN: West Publishing.
12. Intellectual property law relates to copyrights, trademarks, and patents.

SECTION 3: INTERNATIONAL ISSUES

As recreation, tourism, and amateur sports competitions expand in a global environment, more international visitors will participate in international recreation and sports and will utilize park resources. Individuals tend to be apprehensive or fear situations that are outside their comfort levels and cultures where they cannot be understood because of a language barrier. Many international activities involve unfamiliar languages, sights, and sounds that are quite different from an individual's normal environment.

A strong element of risk, both perceived and real, does in fact exist in some international settings. International high risk recreation activities, such as white water rafting in Asia, are becoming increasingly popular among high-risk recreationists. Many developing countries have few safeguards protecting the interest of the customers.

International courts and court systems in most nations serve an important service to our global society in providing people a means by which disagreements can be settled and wrongs righted. Most countries want to protect their economies by protecting the international visitor. They want to assure visitors that they will be legally protected. Recreation programs marketed to international tourists must place a high emphasis on visitor safety and protection. When local laws do not protect the interests of the visitor, those that have suffered loss or injury may choose to file suit against those who arranged the trip or the travel agent.

Each year, the number of recreation-related civil lawsuits filed in various courts throughout the world increases.[1] Most of these cases seek monetary damages for wrongful death, personal injury, or damage to property that occurred as a result of travel, using a recreation facility, or participating in an activity. Regardless of safety measures and risk management activities, accidents will occur. International claims and lawsuits result in a great deal of individual frustration, high cost in personal time, and significant expenditure of financial resources. Because of the unknown aspects of dealing with foreign legal systems, there will always be apprehension and feelings of futility in pursuing claims or litigating in a foreign nation.

There are some basic concepts that need to be understood when dealing with legal liability in an international setting. Nations have significantly different legal systems; some legal systems function to protect both the citizens and visitor. On the other hand, some legal systems benefit the rulers or government of the country. Human or individual rights have secondary importance. Tourism is recognized as an important factor affecting the gross national product of most nations. Nations with thriving economies usually have a significant tourism industry.[2] When nations are involved in civil war, have unsafe travel conditions, lack tourism facilities (infrastructure), and do not recognize that legal recourses and personal protection are necessary, they will not be able to attract visitors. When the government of the small tourist destination island of Aruba, a Dutch protectorate, failed to thoroughly investigate the disappearance of a missing Alabama teenager, passionate appeals were made by governors to boycott the island as a tourist destination. The Aruba tourism industry responded with increased cut-rate travel offers. Some reduction of visits to Aruba, especially by Americans, has been noted.[3]

International cruise ships present a particularly complex legal problem for tourists. Crime on the high seas has been routinely ignored, dealt with by the ship's officers, or with the offender simply expelled on the next port of call. Some claims have been made against local travel agents or those who arranged the trip for failure to warn of a known danger.

Maritime law is a complex area of law. In recreation and tourism activities, cruise ships and ocean fishing activities are under the jurisdiction of admiralty laws unless the incident takes place in the territorial waters of a nation. In the "close to shore" cases, the laws of the nation may apply. The basis for maritime law in the United States is known as the Jones Act. Under admiralty law, the ship's flag determines the source of law that applies to the crime (e.g., property loss or tort on high seas).

In *James and Sheila Mack v. Royal Caribbean Cruises Ltd.*,[4] a customer sued the cruise ship line claiming that the ship's doctor failed to exercise the proper care of an injury and that the cruise line negligently maintained the swimming pool area on the ship. They also claimed that Royal Caribbean Cruises was liable to Sheila Mack for loss of consortium.[5] The defense moved for dismissal of the complaint claiming that under admiralty law, there was no cause of action for negligence (pool area) and vicarious liability caused by the ship physician's negligent treatment of injury. The court had to determine whether or not the state court (Illinois) was bound to apply federal admiralty precedent, precluding vicarious liability claims for the alleged negligence of shipboard doctors or if the state court was free to permit a vicarious liability claim against the cruise line. They also had to determine the validity of a waiver on a ticket where the passenger claimed that he did not read the waiver nor was he given time to read the waiver. The lower court, later sustained by the appeals court determined that the plaintiff could claim vicarious liability as a result of the negligent actions of the ship's doctor. Using a state court, rather than the admiralty court, the plaintiffs prevailed in the case.

Also, in *Spector v. Norwegian Cruise Line*,[6] disabled customers alleged that the cruise line, operating under a foreign flag, violated Title 3 of the Americans with Disabilities Act (ADA). The cruise line's customers claimed that the ship's architectural design violated the "public accommodations" aspects of the act and the cruise line did not make "reasonable modifications in policies, practice, or procures to accommodate disabled persons." The Supreme Court reversed the decision of the Fifth Circuit Court in determining that the ADA does not apply to foreign flag cruise ships in United States territorial waters.

As an example of the basic structure of international law, the following is provided:

English Common Law System

The English common law system forms the basis of the legal system in Australia, Canada, England, Ireland, New Zealand, South Africa, the United States, and other nations that were once part of the British Empire. English common law is a system of laws derived from centuries of experience, study, and traditions. The laws are based upon Judeo-Christian beliefs starting with the biblical Ten Commandments. English common law deals with legal relationships, liabilities of individuals and organizations, and limits the power of government over the people. It recognizes that the power of government is limited and places power in the hands of the people, not an elite or aristocratic group. Under English common law, a judge is an impartial referee of a dispute. A judge is bound to protect the rights of the parties and to follow prescribed procedure in protecting the interests of the litigants and society.

Australia is governed by the English common law system.

Civil Law System[7]

The civil law system is applicable to France, Germany, Belgium, Netherlands, Denmark, Spain, Portugal, Italy, Poland, Czech Republic, Slovenia, Sweden, Norway, Switzerland, and some countries in South and Central America, Africa, and other countries. Additionally, Louisiana in the United States and Quebec in Canada both have civil law systems despite being located in common law countries. Each nation or jurisdiction under civil law varies in its legal structure in some way; however they have a common base that was part of the early Roman legal system. The laws are codified (written). In the civil law system, the law is completely governed by statutes and judges are not free to interpret the law or establish law through case precedent. The non-criminal European legal system protects human rights, property, and allows actions in tort. There are some differences in interpretation, application, and basic law among various nations using the European legal system.

Japanese Legal System

The modern legal system in Japan was initially based on the European legal system, but was significantly modified using the American common law legal system following World War II. The Japanese system includes a bill of rights with 31 articles related to human rights. There is one Supreme Court, eight high courts (appellate) and 50 district courts, plus a number of family courts. The Japanese are not litigious by nature, even though Japan has many codified laws that allow lawsuits. Japanese society is dominated by social mores and traditional ways which value harmony and subjugation. These social conditions have tended to limit suits in tort.

Chinese Legal System

China's legal system is made up of a complex group of custom and statutes concentrating on criminal law with a rudimentary civil code. During recent years, China has passed many new laws and regulations to protect the interest of foreign investors, trade partners, and tourists. This was done to protect their economic interests. Foreign investors appear to have more legal protection than their own citizens. The Chinese constitution (1954) is the basis of the codified legal system. The Chinese system is best described as a "Rule of Law"[8] system and is currently a legal system in transition.

Islamic Legal System

The Islamic legal system (*Sharid*) is based upon rules and requirements found in the Muslim Holy Scriptures (*Quran*). The Sharia system dominates the legal system of the Muslim world. It forms the basis for relations between man and god, and among individuals. The *Hadith* and *Summa* are codified laws and basically follow generally accepted western jurisprudence. The *Figh* includes rulings by Islamic scholars to direct the lives of the Muslim faithful. The Council-of-State (Supreme Court) or *Majlis al-Dawla* is the highest administrative court, usually headed by a leading Muslim cleric.

International Courts of Arbitration

Special international Courts of Arbitration exist to settle disputes where national interests will likely dominate over fair legal decisions regarding the issues. As an example, there are specialty courts for maritime, intellectual property, trade, sports, and other specialized legal areas. The International Court of Justice, also known as the World Court, is located in The Hague, Netherlands.

There is a Court of Arbitration for International Sports (CAS). This court is intended to be athlete oriented. It is an independent court for arbitrating disputes and deals with athletes, sports organizations, or a countries. This court was created in 1993 to bring about the resolution of sport-related disputes which are submitted to it through ordinary arbitration or through appeals against the decisions of sports federations or the International Olympic Committee (IOC).

International sports federations have statutes, practices, and activities that must conform with the Olympic charter. Subject to the authority of the IOC, each international sports federation maintains its independence and autonomy in the administration of its sport.

Notes

1. *International Court News.* (2005, Dec.). Mealy Publications, December 2005, MealyInfo@LexisNexis.com.
2. Tourism and World Economy. (2006, Jan. 17). World Tourism Organization, International Monetary Fund, *Highlights 2004 edition.*
3. "Aruba Tourism Concerns", *USA Today*, Associated Press Article, November 9, 2005.
4. *James and Sheila Mack v. Royal Cruises Ltd*, No.2-0402168, Cook County Circuit Court, Affirmed by 1st District Appellate Court, 4th Division, Illinois (2005).
5. Lack of consortium is defined as the marriage fellowship of husband and wife, and the right of each to company, society, cooperation, affection, and aid of the other in every marriage relation. Black, H. C. (1979). *Black's Law Dictionary* (5th ed.). St. Paul, MN: West Publishing Co., 280.
6. *Spector v. Norwegian Cruise Line Ltd.* No. 03-1388 125 S. Ct. 2169, (U.S. 2005) Court of Appeals for the Fifth Circuit, 356 F.3d 641, United States District Court for the Southern District of Texas.
7. Roman law comprises all the laws which prevailed among the Romans, without regard to the time of their origin. It is sometimes referred to as the "Law of Justin." In the United States, Roman law sometimes refers to the term *Corpus Juris Civilis*, or civil law. Black, H. C. (1979). *Black's Law Dictionary* (5th ed.). St. Paul, MN:West Publishing Co., 1194.

8. Rule of law is a legal principle based upon logical conclusions. It is some-times called the supremacy of law and provides that decisions should be made by the application of known principles or laws without the intervention of discretion in their application. Black, H. C. (1979). *Black's Law Dictionary* (5th ed.). St. Paul, MN: West Publishing Co., 1196.

SECTION 4: LEGAL RESEARCH

A basic understanding of legal research is important to those entering the recreation field. Regrettably, the chances are good that you will experience some legal issue firsthand during your lifetime, possibly through a lawsuit brought against your organization and/or you personally. Even though you will most likely have an attorney handling your case, understanding legal issues relevant to your situation can empower you and hopefully lessen the possible intimidation and stress that you may encounter. Understanding legal research begins with knowing the basic structure of the judicial system. The following figure illustrates the types of courts in which a case might be brought and decided.

As seen in Figure 1.2, there are two important things to remember for the purpose of legal research. First, all published court decisions that you will find in libraries and that you might be using in your class are from either federal court decisions or state court decisions above the trial court

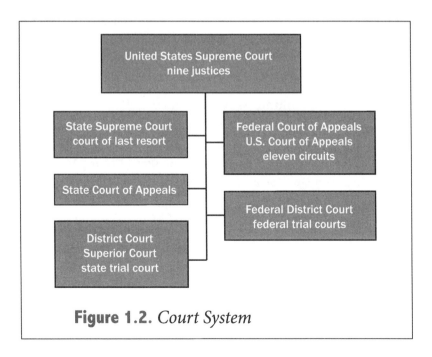

Figure 1.2. *Court System*

The spine of a Federal Reporter.

level. Trial court (also sometimes referred to as district court or superior court) decisions are not published and information from those trials in not readily available.

Second, cases are brought either in federal court or state court. The following chapter provides further detail on the judicial system, but in general, cases are brought in federal court if the parties are from different states (e.g., a person from Iowa is injured while visiting an amusement park in Georgia), or a federal question is involved. A federal question (e.g., federal law) is usually involved in cases where someone is injured on federal park property. Therefore, outdoor recreation cases involving search and rescue of a mountain climber, injury or drowning in a park stream or lake, or an attack on a human by a wild animal in a park would likely be brought in federal court.

Legal decisions from state courts of appeal, state supreme courts, federal district courts, federal courts of appeal and the U. S. Supreme Court, are published in books called reporters. Reporters comprise a collection of state and federal cases, and cases within them are found using case citations. A case citation is the key to locating cases in reporters.

Case citations look something like this: *Doe v. United States*, 38 F.3d 122 (1998). In this citation, *Doe v. United States* is the name of the case. Case names are abbreviated to include only parties to the case. They are also usually underlined or italicized when cited.

Doe v. United States	38	F.3d	122	1998
Case Name	Volume	Reporter	Page	Year

The first number shown in the citation refers to the volume number of the reporter. The middle letters refer to the name of the reporter (e.g., Federal Reporter in this instance), and book series (3d in this example). The last number refers to the page number followed by the year. The system is logical and easy to follow once understood. The process used to find a case by citation is as follows:

1. Find the reporter [Federal Reporter, 3d Series (F.3d)].
2. Find the volume (38).
3. Find the page number (122).
4. Look for the case name and be sure that it is correct (*Doe v. United States*).

Abbreviations for Regional Reporters are intuitive and listed as follows:
Southern Reporter (So.)
Atlantic Reporter (A.)
Northeastern Reporter (N.E.)
Northwestern Reporter (N.W.)
Pacific Reporter (P.)
Southeastern Reporter (S.E.)
Southwestern Reporter (S.W.)

Two states, California and New York, have so many cases that they have their own reporters. They are abbreviated as follows: California Reporter (Cal.) New York Supplement (N.Y.S.) These reporters are sometimes held at a separate location in the library.

Federal court cases also have their own reporters, and as with California and New York, are often located in a separate part of the library. The federal reporters are:

Federal Supplement (F.Supp)—federal district court's cases and Federal Reporter (F.)—cases from U.S. Federal Court of Appeals.

The challenging and often interesting part of legal research comes when you don't have a citation and must begin from scratch with ideas. In that case, for example, if you are given an assignment to research a legal topic and supplement with case law, first you must find sources that will lead you to case citations. These sources are available in books that allow you to search by key terms and topic areas. You can think of them as "encyclopedias of cases." A good place to start is state and federal digests. These books contain information by topic area that explain the topic of interest and provide case citations. Other reference books that allow you to search by topic are *American Jurisprudence* (commonly referred to as *Amjur*), and *Corpus Juris Secundum* (*CJS*).

Another method of finding cases and better understanding legal topics is to research law reviews and law journals. Law journals are usually edited and/or written by law students and legal scholars. They are usually quite lengthy and offer an in-depth discussion of a particular legal topic. Some law schools that publish law journals with topics of interest to our field include *Marquette* (sports law) and *Lewis and Clark* (natural resource law). Other journals such as the *Journal of Legal Aspects of Sport*, and *Entertainment Law* are published outside of law schools and are an excellent source of legal information for those in the field of recreation and sport. Finally, there are publications that offer a discussion of the latest and most relevant cases. The *Journal of Physical Education, Recreation and Dance* (*JOPERD*), and *Parks & Recreation Magazine* both provide very good discussions of recent cases. Citations are also provided so that the reader can find and read the cases for themselves.

You might also find that you have access to online legal research sources through your university or at your workplace. The two most common online sources are Lexis and Westlaw. Both services allow you to research cases by topic, citation, or case name. Online searches are efficient and convenient but also costly once you leave a university or place where you have might have free access. When using these online services, it is important to read and understand the terms and conditions of use.

Legal research is logical and often also interesting and fun. There is much more to be learned about legal research but this brief section should be enough to get you started and on your way. It is important when approaching this subject that you explore beyond any class assignments given to better understand how to navigate your way.

Discussion Questions

1. Briefly describe a case that has received media attention and that involves recreation, tourism, or sport. Give your personal opinion of the case.

2. Why do you think that we live in a "litigious" society?

3. Choose two international legal systems mentioned in the text and briefly compare and contrast them.

4. Briefly summarize a case you have found in *Parks & Recreation Magazine*.

Chapter Two

INTRODUCTION TO THE LEGAL PROCESS

SECTION 1: THE JUDICIAL SYSTEM

The judicial system is necessary to maintain rights and protect individuals in a civilized society. It provides an orderly manner by which people can settle their differences (civil law) and enforce societal rules. The American judicial system also provides for mistakes by allowing contested decisions to be reviewed by a higher court.

The probability of an individual becoming involved in some type of civil lawsuit is very high. It is estimated that four out of five citizens will at some time during their lives find themselves in the court system. The court system is established to resolve conflicts and provide for social justice. It consists of a rather complex system of courts, each with a limited subject area or geographical jurisdiction. Trial courts are divided into two categories—criminal and civil. Civil courts resolve conflicts between private parties, while criminal courts determine the innocence or guilt of those accused of breaking society's rules. Examples of the various courts with limited jurisdiction include magistrate, municipal, probate, family, traffic, juvenile, contract, and justice of the peace.

The federal system includes District Courts, U.S. Court of Appeals, U.S. Customs Court, and the U.S. Supreme Court, as well as some special courts such as Contract, Maritime, Military, and Bankruptcy. The District Courts are the courts where civil (tort) trials are held.

The state court's system may have different names for its various courts; however, the state's court structure parallels the federal system. A court of general jurisdiction (trial court) exists in every state, but may be called a circuit court in one state (i.e., Indiana), a supreme court in another (i.e., New York), and something else in another. All states have some type of appellate system and specialty courts for specific types of subject matter. If a party does not agree with a civil court decision, they may appeal to a higher court.

Not all civil disputes are settled by a trial. Most are resolved prior to trial either by the involved individuals or their attorneys. It is estimated that more than 90% of the civil filings are settled during the pretrial stage. It is important that litigants have signed settlement documents when out-of-court settlements occur.

Pretrial civil procedure generally includes the following steps:

1. Plaintiff files a complaint[1] with the court and a summons[2] is issued to the defendant.

2. Defendants must answer the complaint within a specific time period.

3. Plaintiff and defendant make a motion,[3] usually to seek a judgment on the pleadings or contest allegations.

4. Plaintiff and defendant start the discovery[4] process. They seek evidence through requests for documents, records, interrogatories, depositions, and other sources of information.

5. Plaintiff and defendant have the option of making a motion to dismiss the case, in whole or in part. This motion is called a motion for summary judgment.

6. Plaintiff, defendant, and judge hold a conference in an effort to settle the case without going to trial. At this meeting, the parties will also discuss with the judge how the case will be administered in terms of how much time is needed to try the case and how many witnesses will be called by both sides.

If a settlement is not reached in the pretrial stage, then a trial is held before the judge and/or jury. If the trial is held in front of a judge only, the trial is referred to as a "bench trial."

The trial proceeds as follows:

1. Jury selection (if not a bench trial) with the attorneys trying to select jurors who may be sympathetic to their position. As an example, a plaintiff attorney will try to select jurors who are older, if the client is elderly and was injured as a result of a fall on a snow-covered sidewalk. A young prospective juror who has never suffered a serious accident or pain may not be compassionate toward older persons or not relate to the problems that slick sidewalks present to people who may be unsteady. Federal tort cases do not have juries and are held before a judge. These trials are called bench trials.

2. Opening statements by the attorneys outlining the things they intend to prove during the trial. Opening statements are usually concise and attempt to focus the jury's or judge's attention on specific aspects of the trial.

3. Presentation of witnesses by the attorneys, starting with the presentation of the plaintiff's case. Witnesses can include material witnesses, expert witnesses, and collaborating witnesses. Witnesses are under oath and are cross-examined by the opposing attorneys. Attorneys for the plaintiff always present their case first.

    Expert witnesses are often very important to a case given their credibility as an "expert" and their ability to assist lawyers, judges, and juries in understanding the aspects of a case within their area of expertise. Types of experts in recreation cases range from "sport/ recreation safety experts" to those with expertise in engineering, economics, psychiatry, medicine, emergency medical care, and so forth. An expert is someone with specialized knowledge based upon experience, skill or abilities, education and training. Experts are often instrumental in helping to determine the applicable standard of care in negligence cases. Experts can be found through publications, referral agencies, word of mouth, and Internet sources (e.g., www. findlaw.com).

4. Closing arguments are given by the plaintiff and defense attorneys. The arguments provide the judge and jury a summary of the facts and arguments.

5. Jury instructions are given by the judge to the members of the jury if the case was not a bench trial.

6. Jury verdict or the judgment of the court is given after the trial is held. The final decision and award can be delayed for a significant period of time after the actual trial. In some rare cases, the judge can reject the jury's decision and issue a "judgment notwithstanding the verdict."[5]

The public historically has complained about the judiciary in general and specific court decisions in particular. Depending upon the individual complainer, the court is considered either too conservative or too liberal. Despite all the criticism, the court system stands as the most important means by which wrongs can be righted and the public can find justice. No other system provides the individual protection from government excesses and redress from those with political power and significant financial resources. The courts provide a forum where all voices can be heard at the same level and conflicts can be decided on merit.

SECTION 2: CIVIL PROCEDURE

A basic understanding of legal liability requires an understanding of civil court procedures. While procedures vary considerably among the various states it is important to have a basic understanding of civil procedures. The information contained in this section has broad application. The federal civil procedures constitute the approach used in this section. This section examines the various legal tools available to defend or represent a plaintiff. This section explains in a brief manner how the judicial system functions but does not include differences among the various states and does not detail federal judicial procedures.

Jurisdiction

Jurisdiction refers to the legal right by which courts exercise their authority over specific political subdivisions (cities, states, appellate courts, etc.), over categories of individuals (military, civilians, immigrants), and over subject matter (contracts, tax, bankruptcy, criminal, civil, etc.). Jurisdiction of the courts to try a case is based upon federal and state law. Federal subject matter jurisdiction includes, but is not limited to:

1. Questions arising from the use of federal property.

2. Violations of federal laws or statutes.

3. United States Constitutional questions.

4. International disputes.

5. Conflicts among states or among citizens of different states in claims that are valued at more than $75,000.

Where any of the above conditions apply, the case will be tried in federal court. State and local courts have jurisdiction over most disputes that do not fit into the above categories.

Venue

Venue refers to a particular county, state, or geographical area with jurisdiction to try a case. The location of the court is important to jurisdiction as well as fairness to all the litigants. Cases can be removed from state to federal courts if a federal jurisdiction question existed at the time the suit was filed or if a diversity (citizens of two or more states) question existed at the time the suit was filed. Based upon federal and state laws, courts have long arm Statutes that allow them to serve summons and complaints to persons outside their geographic boundaries into other states or jurisdictions. Venue can also refer to courts specifically designated to hear cases in specific subject areas such as criminal, tort, military, contract, maritime, international, etc.

Pleadings

A civil proceeding starts when a plaintiff files a complaint stating a cause of action (reason) for the suit and names the defendant(s). The defendant then answers the suit denying or admitting to the allegations in the complaint. The defendant answers (responds) to the allegations in the complaint by setting out defenses. The response may include counterclaims or cross-claims (see Parties to the Litigation on the following page). Prior to answering the complaint, the defendant can make a motion to dismiss the case based upon any of the following arguments:

1. Lack of subject matter jurisdiction,

2. Lack of personal jurisdiction,

3. Improper venue,

4. Insufficiency of process,

5. Insufficiency of service of process,

6. Failure to state a claim upon which relief can be granted, or

7. Failure to join an indispensable party

Parties to the Litigation

Parties to litigation can be joined together in a single court hearing if the suit arises from the same transaction or occurrence. Parties must be joined together when they have an interest in the same controversy or it is necessary for the sake of justice. There are various types of pleadings related to proper parties to the litigation. These include:

Counterclaims[6]

An action brought against the plaintiff when injuries or losses occur as a result of the same action or occurrence. If a counterclaim is proven, it will defeat the plaintiff's claim. Counterclaims are either required to be made or made at the option of the defendant.

Third Party Practice[7]

Third party practice occurs when a defendant files a claim against a third party who is not listed as a defendant in the original complaint. This must arise out the same action or occurrence. This complaint alleges that the third party is or may be liable for all or part of the damages that the plaintiff may win from the defendant.

Intervention[8]

A person, not originally a party to the suit seeks to become a party. This is usually done to protect the rights of the third person or impose a claim directly related to the litigation.

Interpleader (stakeholder)[9]

If two or more persons are making a claim on another party, the party who owes something to one or more persons can force them all into court to decide the issue in a single action.

Class Actions[10]

Class actions require a suit to have numerous parties, all with common injuries or loss. They must be typical in injuries or loss, and have adequacy of representation. Under federal rules, each individual in a class action suit must have a claim greater than $50,000.

Amicus Curiae.[11]

The term *Amicus Curiae* refers to a friend of the court. Those who are *Amicus Curiae* are not actually litigants in the case; however, they do have strong interests in or views on the subject matter and their input may help define issues and gain understanding. *Amicus Curiae* usually represent broad public interests and may include individuals, organizations, or government.

Pretrial

Most of the meaningful evidence is confirmed or gathered during the pretrial period of a court proceeding. The vast majority of cases are dismissed or settled during this pretrial period because of the overwhelming evidence established by one of the litigants.

The service (delivery) of a civil summons, complaint, or process must comply with the following guidelines:

1. The summons must be delivered personally to the defendant or delivered by certified or registered mail.

2. A publication notice can be used only as a last resort.

3. The complaint/summons must be delivered to an adult (a person of majority age).

4. The complaint/summons cannot be delivered to a minor (infant), friend, fellow employee, relative, or associate.

If a person does not respond to the complaint/summons in a designated time period or fails to plead or otherwise defend themselves, the court will determine the defendant is in default and render judgment for the plaintiff. This is called a default judgment.

The plaintiff can voluntarily dismiss a case before the defendant answers or files a motion for summary judgment. When evidence is weighted significantly toward one of the litigants, the court can render a decision prior to a trial. This is referred to as summary judgment.[12] Summary judgment relates to the fact there are no genuine issues of material fact (no arguments over the facts of the case) and the party is entitled to judgment as a matter of law. Summary judgment that is rendered without prejudice[13] allows a new suit to be brought on the same cause of action. A summary judgment that is rendered with prejudice does not allow a litigant to sue again on the same issues.

Discovery[14] is one of the most important aspects of pretrail proceedings. Discovery is intended to allow both sides to the litigation the opportunity to identify, determine, and find admissible evidence. Discovery does not allow litigants to explore irrelevant matters, confidential matter (trade secrets, etc), attorney-client communications, mental impressions, opinions, legal theories of attorney, or work products. There are a number of devices attorneys use for discovery. They include:

Interrogatories[1]
[5] Written questions about the case developed by attorneys and submitted by a party to the suit to the opposing party or opposing party witnesses. The answers to interrogatories are usually given under oath and the person answering the questions swears that the answers are accurate and truthful.

Depositions[16]
The testimony of a witness not taken in court that is recorded in the written form and authenticated by the witness. One party asks oral questions of the other party or a witness for the party. The deposition is taken under oath, usually in one of the litigants' lawyer's offices. Depositions may be used to undermine the credibility of a witness at trial.

Request for Production of Documents[17]
Written evidence applicable to the case. The documents can include such items as financial records, letters, instructions, manuals, handbooks, medical reports, and non-privileged investigation reports. Parties to the cases must produce the documents requested and the court will issue a subpoena to produce documents (material) that are not in the control of a party to the suit.

Trial

The general trial process is covered in Section 1 of this chapter. There are some standard rules involving a directed verdict. A motion for judgment as a matter of law (directed verdict)[18] can be made when there is no legally sufficient evidence presented by the plaintiff or the plaintiff failed to present a *prima facie* case[19] for jury consideration. The trial judge may then issue a directed verdict[20] without allowing the jury to consider the case.

The trial judge may reverse or modify the verdict after the jury renders their verdict. This process is referred to as a Judgment Notwithstanding the Verdict[21] (JNOV). This occurs when the judge believes the facts in the case lack substantial evidence and that a reasonable and fair-minded person would differ from the decision of the jury. It is necessary that an attorney for one of the litigants make a motion for the directed verdict.

Attorneys representing the unsuccessful litigants can make a motion for a new trial when the verdict is against the great weight of the evidence. A request for a new trial must be made within ten days of judgment. A motion for a new trial requests a judge set aside the judgment and order a new trial on the basis that the trial was improper or unfair due to specified errors that occurred prior to the verdict.

Post Trial

At the end of a trial, attorneys representing the litigants can appeal the decision of the court. Appeals can only be taken after a final adverse judgment (decision). The appeals court can reverse a final judgment of a trial court based upon:

1. Abuse of discretion in cases involving discretion.

2. Clearly erroneous findings of fact.

3. Mistakes in the application of law (plenary review).

The judgment rendered in one state must be considered as valid judgment in another state.[22] This is referred to as Full Faith and Credit.[23] This rule applies to federal courts as well as state courts.

After the final judgment, a plaintiff is barred from filing further suits against the defendant rising from the action or occurrence. What is referred to as the collateral estoppel d   octrine prohibits re-litigation of issues of fact previously tried in a court.[24]

Discussion Questions

1. Explain why a case would be brought in federal court as opposed to state court.

2. Briefly describe the "discovery process" and explain the written and verbal forms of discovery.

3. Explain what is meant by the acronym JNOV.

4. Describe the order of the trial process (who goes first, second... and what happens first, second...).

5. List the primary components of a case citation (create a hypothetical citation) and explain what each component represents.

Notes

1. A complaint is the original action by a plaintiff to start legal action. The complaint includes a statement describing the grounds upon which the plaintiff believes an injustice has taken place, the reason the court has jurisdiction over the matter, a claim showing that the plaintiff is eligible for relief, and the damages or relief to which the plaintiff believes he or she is entitled.
2. A summons is an instrument issued by the court that commences a legal action and informs the defendant of the alleged charges against him. The summons is given to the marshal (an officer of the law) for delivery to the defendant. Upon receiving the summons, the defendant is required to answer the allegations in a specific time period and is required to appear in court on the day designated in the summons.
3. Motions are proposals made by the litigants requesting the court to take some action, such as a motion to grant summary judgment, judgment notwithstanding the verdict, more definite statement, new trial in bar, dismissal, to strike from the record, to suppress evidence, and so forth.
4. Discovery investigates the facts that have been hidden or unknown. Discovery is a pretrial procedure that includes depositions, written interrogatories, physical (medical) examinations, mental (psychological) examinations, documents, and other information that is known or is in the possession of another.

5. Judgment notwithstanding the verdict is a decision by the judge that changes the original verdict by the jury. A motion for a directed verdict by one of the parties to the suit is necessary before a judge can decide a judgment notwithstanding the verdict.
6. Black, H. C. (1979). *Black's law dictionary* (4th ed.). St Paul, MN: West Publishing Co., p. 315.
7. Black, H. C. (1979). *Black's law dictionary* (4th ed.). St Paul, MN: West Publishing Co., p. 1327.
8. Federal Rule of Civil Procedure (FRCP) 24(a).
9. Black, H. C. (1979). *Black's law dictionary* (4th ed.). St Paul, MN: West Publishing Co., p. 733.
10. Federal Rule of Civil Procedure (FRCP) 23(a).
11. Federal Rule of Civil Procedure (FRCP) 4.
12. Federal Rule of Civil Procedure (FRCP) 56(c).
13. Black, H. C. (1979). *Black's law dictionary* (4th ed.). St Paul, MN: West Publishing Co., p. 1437.
14. Federal Rule of Civil Procedure (FRCP) 26.
15. Black, H. C. (1979). *Black's law dictionary* (4th ed.). St Paul, MN: West Publishing Co., p. 735.
16. Black, H. C. (1979). *Black's law dictionary* (4th ed.). St Paul, MN: West Publishing Co., p. 396.
17. Federal Rule of Civil Procedure (FRCP) 45.
18. Standard Rule 50.
19. *Prima facie* case—A case that will prevail until contradicted or overcome by other evidence.
20. Black, H. C. (1979). *Black's law dictionary* (4th ed.). St Paul, MN: West Publishing Co., p. 413.
21. A verdict is entered by order of court for the plaintiff or defendant although there has been a verdict for the defendant or plaintiff. Black, H. C. (1979). *Black's law dictionary* (4th ed.). St Paul, MN: West Publishing Co., p. 942.
22. Federal Rule of Civil Procedure (FRCP) 59.
23. U.S. Constitution Article IV Section 1.
24. 28 U.S.C. 1738.
25. Federal Rule of Civil Procedure (FRCP) 8.

Part Two

NEGLIGENCE

Chapter Three

THE NEGLIGENCE
CAUSE OF ACTION

Negligence is one of the basic torts derived from English common law. Its application varies from medical malpractice to sports equipment product liability. A person committing a negligent act may not have intended to do wrong, but a negligent act was committed nevertheless. Negligence is either a commission (an act) or omission (failure to act), and, as such, is defined as "The omission to do something that a reasonable man would do, guided by those ordinary considerations which generally regulate human affairs...," or ..." the failure to use such care as a reasonably prudent and careful person would use under similar circumstances."[1]

One of the oldest recordings of a negligence tort occurred in 13th century England. A very angry husband caught another man with his wife and chased the man down the street with an axe. The angry husband threw the axe at the man, missed, and struck a bystander. The bystander sued the man and was awarded a judgment from the court because of the injury. The husband certainly did not intend to injure the bystander, but his negligent act did in fact cause the injury.

If a person is seeking to take someone to court for negligence, the law requires more than just negligent conduct. A negligent action must have all of the following elements to allow the case to be pursued in court:

Elements of a Negligence Action[2]

Duty

A duty, or obligation, recognized by the law, requiring the defendant to conform to certain standards of care[3] to protect others against unreasonable risk.

Breach

A failure to conform to the standards required.

Causation

A reasonable connection between the conduct of the defendant and the resulting injury or loss. There are two forms of causation, Cause in fact and Proximate cause.

Cause in fact. The plaintiff must show that the defendant's conduct was the "cause in fact" of the injury. This usually means that the plaintiff must show that "but for" the defendant's negligence, the injury would not have happened.

Proximate cause. The plaintiff must establish that his/her injury is sufficiently closely related to the defendant's negligence. This aspect of causation is often a policy determination used to limit liability for injuries that are not proximately related to the negligent act. Most states require that the injury be the foreseeable result of the defendant's negligence.

Injury

An injury occurs when there is actual loss or damage to the plaintiff. The concept of negligence may presuppose that there is some standard of conduct or behavior by which negligent behavior can be judged. For example, one would expect that a child's swing would withstand the weight of both the child and a parent in whose lap the child is swinging, and a football helmet would be designed to a standard in which two large football players could come together in a head-on collision and survive the impact without significant damage.

If a defendant recognizes a risk and does nothing to warn another about the risk, reduce the potential hazard of the risk, or eliminate the risk, the plaintiff must still prove that the risk was unreasonable. No person walks without the risk of falling, drives a car without risk of accident, or lives without the risk of contracting a serious disease.

The doctrine of unforeseeable consequences[4] adds another dimension to understanding negligence culpability.[5] Although a serious accident or property loss may have occurred with strong elements of negligence, it may not have been foreseeable in the specific circumstance or situation. As an example, a campground manager who erected a sign warning of a dangerous situation may not have anticipated a foreign visitor to the area who could not read English. The camp director may not have anticipated a child being attacked by nesting birds.

In the case of *Palmer v. Mount Vernon Township High Sch. Dis. 2016* (1995), a student and parent sued the school district for negligence. Palmer was a basketball player on a high school basketball team. He had sustained some minor eye injuries as a result of playing basketball in the past. Palmer borrowed a pair of protective goggles from a teammate to prevent further eye injuries. When his coach saw the goggles, he told Palmer to remove them so they would not interfere with his ability to play basketball. Palmer assumed that the coach meant he could never wear goggles. He asked the coach if he could get eye protection, but the coach said no player at Mt. Vernon had ever worn eye protection. A few days later, during an inter-squad practice game, Palmer was seriously injured in the left eye by a teammate and eventually lost sight in that eye. The trial court jury entered judgment for the defendant school. The Supreme Court affirmed the decision of the trial court.

As proximate cause applies to the foreseeability doctrine, the wrongdoer is not responsible for a consequence that is merely possible, but is responsible only for a consequence that is probable according to ordinary and usual circumstances, which to the average person are foreseeable.[7]

Licato v. Eastgate (1986),[8] is an example of the foreseeability doctrine. In Licato, the plaintiff, Joseph Licato, age 19, was seriously injured on property immediately adjacent to the defendant's motorcycle track. The plaintiff was testing a new motorcycle on the track owned by the defendant. The plaintiff lost control of the motorcycle and traveled 30 feet off the track into the adjacent landowners' property, where he struck an excavation ditch. The ditch the defendant ran into was immediately adjacent (within 30 feet) of the racetrack but not visible from the track itself. The boundary line between the two ownerships did not have barriers or other guard devices or walls to protect cyclists. The defendant Licato was not warned of the hidden danger on the adjacent property. The court determined that the dangerous condition was known to the defendant track owner, and it was foreseeable that motorcycles might sometimes lose control in a testing situation; therefore, the track owner was negligent for failing to warn the cyclists and erect protective barriers in a situation where the possibility of an accident was foreseeable.

The courts determine the standard of care required of recreation and sports activities. The standard of care is usually based upon the normal or established practice common throughout a state or nation under similar circumstances. In recreation and sports cases, the standard of care is usually established by expert witnesses in the fields of sports management, recreation, playground design, recreation risk management, engineering, and other fields related to recreation.

The American Society for Testing and Materials (ASTM) provides standards for helmets used in recreational bicycling.

The standard of care is not always the same standard in every state. Some states, because of their laws and general social attitude, such as New York, California, and Illinois, appear to be somewhat generous in their awards for damages. Certainly, there are specific case exceptions.

The following factors are taken into consideration in determining legal liability

Physical Characteristics

The physical characteristics of the visitor must be considered in the type of activity, facilities provided, level of supervision, and overall design. If a playground is handicapped accessible, but has equipment that is particularly dangerous to use for those in wheelchairs, then the recreation provider did not consider the physical characteristics of the targeted population. When a playground does not meet the standard of care expected for someone with a particular physical characteristic, the organization is exposed to a possible negligence suit if there is an accident. Other categories of individuals that may fall under the physical characteristics classifications include the sight impaired, hearing impaired, and very small or large persons.

Mental Characteristics

Young children, persons with mental illness, and persons with learning disabilities will require special attention by those providing recreation-related services and activities. Many lacking mental maturity or with mental limitations cannot read warning signs or understand complex instructions. The level of supervision may need to be increased when activities are provided for this segment of our population. A deep water warning sign in a children's play area should not be expected to provide adequate protection for children. Not only might they not fully understand the language on the sign, but the water also provides a dangerous attraction for children.

Skill and Knowledge

Many sports and recreation activities require skill and knowledge to be safe. Every year, many mountain climbers are severely injured or killed, and spelunkers are lost and injured in caves. These activities require some specialized equipment and knowledge about how to use the equipment, and practice in using the equipment properly. Certification programs are a primary means by which managers can determine if a person is prepared to engage in high-risk activities.

In *Harmon v. Bench Water Users Association* (1985),[9] a five-year-old boy drowned in an irrigation ditch owned and maintained by the defendant, Bench Water Users Association. The mother of the boy sued the association for negligence and strict liability, and claimed the ditch was an attractive nuisance. Two boys, including the five-year-old Harmon boy, were playing on the edge of an irrigation ditch in the city of Billings, Montana. The canal was dug into the soil and had a vertical concrete wall inside the ditch that contained the water. At the time of the accident, the water level was above the concrete wall, and the water obscured the steep drop off. The Harmon boy, in an attempt to retrieve a stick, fell off the edge of the underwater wall and drowned. The defendant association was granted summary judgment by the trial court after they claimed they were immune from suit under state law. The plaintiff appealed, and the U.S. Court of Appeals, Ninth Circuit, affirmed the lower court's decision related to nuisance and strict liability and reversed and remanded the decision related to negligence and attractive nuisance. The appellate court's rationale was based upon the fact that the drowning of Harmon's son might have been averted had the water level been kept below the steep concrete sides. The court held that the association's actions to overfill the ditch was willful and wanton in regard to negligence, and in fact attracted children to play at the ditch.

Degrees of Negligence

While some courts do not recognize varying degrees of negligence, the court's decisions do consider the relative seriousness of the negligence. Most courts recognize, at least in part, that there are various degrees of negligence[10] as follows:

Slight

A failure to exercise great care. Also defined as an absence of that degree of care and vigilance which persons of extraordinary prudence and foresight are accustomed to using.

Ordinary

The failure to meet the standard of care that a reasonably prudent person would have met.

Gross

An intentional failure to perform a duty in reckless disregard of the safety and property of others. It is an act of omission or commission of an aggravated nature as distinguished from a mere failure to exercise ordinary care.

Willful and Wanton

An act of unreasonable character in disregard of a risk known to the person. It is usually accompanied by a conscious indifference to the consequences. It is highly unreasonable conduct.

In the case of *Muellman v. Chicago Park District* (1992),[11] Dina Muellman was walking through Grant Park with her sister and two friends on her way to a blues festival. Unknown to Dina, there was an open drain pipe on the path ahead of her. She continued walking and stepped into the open pipe, fracturing her ankle. Dina sued the city park department and won. The court held that the park department's conduct was willful and wanton. This conclusion was reached when the evidence revealed that the pipe that Dina stepped into had its lid missing for at least a month. The park department knew the pipe lids were often stolen and knew that the pipes were dangerous. The park department had even painted some of the pipes to warn the equipment operators not to run into them. None in Grant Park were painted to warn visitors of their presence. Because the city park department's conduct was viewed as willful and wanton, the city lost its immunity provided in the state recreation land use statutes.

Discussion Questions

1. Provide a hypothetical scenario from a recreation setting that would illustrate the legal concept of "causation" as an element of negligence.

2. Name and describe four sources that you might consult to help determine the standard of care in a negligence case.

3. List the four elements of negligence. Provide a brief explanation of each element in the recreation context.

4. What is the difference between ordinary negligence and gross negligence? Explain by providing your own hypothetical situation.

Notes

1. Black, H. C. (1979). *Black's law dictionary* (5th ed.). St Paul, MN: West Publishing Co., p. 930.
2. Prosser, W. L. (1971). *Law of torts* (4th ed.). St. Paul, MN: West Publishing Co., p. 143-144.
3. Standard of care is the amount of care that a reasonable man would use if faced with the same circumstances as those presented to the defendant.
4. Unforeseeable consequences are the results or consequences of actions or situations that could not have been predicted or foreseen by a reasonable man.
5. Culpability is determined by showing that a person acted purposely, knowingly, or negligently with respect to the elements of an offense, *Black's Law Dictionary* (5th ed.), p. 341.
6. *Palmer v. Mount Vernon Township High Sch. Dist. 201*, 662 N.E.2d 1260.
7. Black, H. C. (1979). Black, H. C. (1979). *Black's law dictionary* (5th ed.). St Paul, MN: West Publishing Co., p. 584.
8. *Licato v. Eastgate*, 499 N.Y.S.2d 472 (A.D. 3 Dept. 1986).
9. *Harmon v. Billings Bench Water Users Association*, 765 F.2d 1464 (9th Cir. 1985).
10. Black, H. C. (1979). *Black's law dictionary* (5th ed.). St Paul, MN: West Publishing Co., p. 931-932.
11. *Muellman v. Chicago Park District*, 600 N. E. 2d 48 (Ill. App. 1992).

Chapter Four

STRICT LIABILITY.

Strict liability, sometimes called absolute liability, is a category of tort that basically states: If an accident occurs under any of the categories of strict liability—you are guilty; now let's see how much it will cost you. While this concept is not unconditional, strict liability does not depend on actual negligence or intent to harm, but rather it is based on the breach of an absolute duty to make something safe.[1] Strict liability usually applies to particularly hazardous situations, equipment, dangerous materials, or where public protection is paramount. This concept has been extended to the employer/employee safe workplace relationship.[2] Some of the common strict liability categories include:

1. Products
    a. Drugs
    b. Equipment
    c. Product warranty
    d. Appliances, etc.

2. Animals
    a. Zoos
    b. Pets

3. Food and Water
    a. Potable water

b. Food services
c. Dram shop (serving alcohol)

4. Dangerous Activities
    a. Explosives
    b. Aircraft/Automobiles
    c. Applying chemicals, etc.

5. Employee Workplace
    a. Safe place
    b. Safe tools, equipment, appliances
    c. Warning of unsafe conditions
    d. Sufficient number of workers for safety
    e. Enforce rules of conduct for safety

Products

Product Liability

One of the categories of torts under strict liability is product liability. Because recreation and sports managers use a considerable amount of equipment (products) in facilitating recreation and sports activities, professionals must make a special effort to understand product liability.

Avoiding inferior or poorly constructed sports and recreation equipment should be a goal of most managers, especially when they want to protect the users from harm and avoid unnecessary litigation. People have a higher propensity to sue if the accident occurs in a work environment as compared to a leisure activity. Research has shown that 41% of the people considered suing when the accident occurred on the job, while only 20% considered suing in a non-work accident. Sixteen percent of the people involved in work-related accidents actually take action for compensation, while only 7% of those involved in leisure-time accidents take actions to receive compensation.[3]

There have been a number of suits involving stainless steel slides used by children in playgrounds. The metal slides reach very high temperatures when exposed to the direct sun on a warm day. Children have received severe burns on their buttocks, legs, and arms as a result of sitting and sliding on these very hot surfaces. Playground equipment companies have basically stopped manufacturing metal slides and are now making heat-absorbing specialty plastic slides. In order to avoid further litigation, the manufacturers of metal slides are recommending that the sliding surface faces north, away from the direct rays of the sun. Metal slides can also be retrofitted with a tube or tunnel that reduces the temperature on the surface of the slide.

Risk managers should seek a program that meets the standard of care for a particular activity or program. If there is not an established national or local standard of care, the recreation and sports provider should utilize the concept of what a prudent individual should do under the same circumstances. Recreation and sport professionals should recognize that the standard of care varies with age, training, gender, and other characteristics of the participant.

Drugs

We hear of suits against pharmaceutical companies, yet reputable and extensive testing and research prior to marketing drugs has proven to be strong defenses when suits occur. Special care must be taken by organizations, particularly those who serve children, when offering even the simplest of over-the-counter medicines (such as aspirin) to others. Medicine should be taken by the decision of the individual as prescribed by a doctor. If medicine must be provided to a minor by a service provider a signed permission slip must be obtained from the parent or guardian.

Equipment

The strict liability application to equipment is relatively simple: equipment must perform as advertised, cautionary warnings must be posted on the equipment, and operating manuals must be available. Specific safety and operation training for some types of equipment must be given prior to providing the equipment to the user. When equipment is misused by the operator strict liability does not apply.

Product Warranty[4]

When a vendor or contractor provides a warranty on a product or service, that warranty must be honored. Warranties are enforceable under strict liability. Warranties should be in writing; however, many products have implied warrants by their very nature (i.e., expectation of quality and circumstance of sale).

Appliances

Appliances are expected to perform as expected. An old adage related to strict liability regarding appliances states: "the toaster should not toast the toastee." Appliances are expected to be safe. If an appliance is used in a manner that is not intended by the manufacture, the user is not protected under the strict liability doctrine.

Animals

Pets

Strict liability applies to household pets that cause injury or property damage to others. Household pets must be kept securely fenced, leashed, or otherwise controlled. Posting signs that small children may not be able read indicating a dangerous pet on the premises will not suffice. A pet owner whose dog attacks an adult within the pet owner's property is likely subject to a suit under strict liability regardless of whether there was a verbal warning or a sign posted. Pet owners must understand that postal employees, utility meter readers, and so forth, have a right to enter the property without fear of being attacked by an animal. When the mean little boy teases his neighbor's dog and the dog decides to imprint the posterior of the boy with his teeth, the dog owner might be subject to suit under strict liability. Strict liability, however, does not attach to domesticated animals unless the owners of the animals knew or should have known of the animals' dangerous propensities. Domesticated animals can include dogs, cats, bees, bulls, and stallions. Also, people who enter a posted property illegally are not protected under the strict liability doctrine.

Zoos

There is a corollary between dangerous animals and public interest in seeing the animals. Zoos are filled with dangerous animals. Many visitors want to get up close and personal with the animals, and it is a rather delicate balance between allowing clear viewing and not allowing any physical contact with the animals. When wild animals injure zoo visitors, it is a strict liability issue. Animals not only must be separated from visitors, but cages and displays must be secure to such a degree that they cannot be opened or accessed by the public. Access must be limited to zoo personnel only. A loose lion can ruin everyone's day.

Water and Food

Water

A nightmare for campground, special event, and cruise ship managers is the realization that the potable[5] water supply system is contaminated. Notice must be posted immediately and a safe source of water identified and made available. Constant quality testing, chlorination, and filtration of the water system is necessary. When natural waters such as lakes and streams are used for swimming purposes, testing must be made on a regular basis (as determined by state standards) and when contaminants[6] such as fecal coliform[7] are found, the beach must be closed. Poor swimming water quality may cause serious illness, eye irritation, rashes, and other maladies.

Food

Food service is an important enhancement for recreation, sports, and tourism venues. The safe handling of food should be a primary concern for the food service manager. Food poisoning is serious, with the possibility of bacteria such as salmonella[8] and other contaminants causing serious illness and death. Cruise ships have had to return to port and have suffered serious legal and financial problems when contaminated food affected a number of passengers. When food service is necessary for special events it is best to have a licensed and insured caterer provide the food rather than have an organization expose itself to strict liability inherent with food service.

Dangerous Activities[9]

Explosives

Any time explosives are used, special care and intensified safety efforts must be used. Any accident that may occur is the responsibility of the explosives user. A warning of danger, verbal or written, such as calling out "fire in the hole" before igniting dynamite does not absolve the user from strict liability. Commercial fireworks displays also are included in this category. Erratic fireworks are not considered accidental occurrences, but rather qualify under the strict liability doctrine. Firearm testing or target ranges also qualify under this category.

Aircraft and Automobiles

This strict liability category deals with the quality of production and maintenance of aircraft and automobiles. Small reciprocal engine aircraft require a high standard for design, assembling, and maintenance. A number of years ago there was a considerable number of small aircraft manufacturers; however, litigation and other factors reduced the number of active small aircraft producers considerably. It is common for automobiles to issue recalls to modify problems with design or manufacture. Recent recall problems have involved seat belt connectors, brakes, tires, engines, transmissions, air bags, steering, and other design and manufacturing flaws.

Applying Chemicals

Organizations involved in recreation, sports, and tourism use a considerable number of chemicals in the form of fertilizer, herbicides, pesticides, cleaners, sanitizers, deodorizers, and so forth. Chemicals are needed in all aspects of the work and home environment. There is an overriding consideration that must be adhered to when using chemicals, that is—follow the label. If an organization follows the label religiously, there is a better chance the liability for damages is transferred to the manufacturer of the chemical. If the individual or organization decides to exceed manufacturers mixing and application instructions and determines that a little bit more is better the organization or individual might bear the burden of strict liability doctrine.

Employee Workplace

This category of strict liability has been brought about by federal legislation such as the OSHA[10] employee protection laws and other federal, state, and local laws. Workman's compensation legislation is viewed as the application of strict liability in the workplace.[11]

The various laws, regulations, and legal decisions are categorized in the following manner:[12]

1. The duty to provide a safe place to work.[13]

2. The duty to provide safe appliances, tools, and equipment for the work.[14]

3. The duty to give warning of dangers which the employee might reasonably be expected to remain in ignorance.[15]

4. The duty to provide a sufficient number of suitable fellow workers.[16]

5. The duty to promulgate and enforce rules for the conduct of employees which would make the workplace safe.[17]

Discussion Questions

1. Explain what is meant by the term "strict liability."

2. Explain how the concept of "duty" relates to strict liability.

3. Explain the relationship between product liability and strict liability.

Notes

1. As defined in *Black's law dictionary* (8th ed.), 2004, St. Paul MN: West Publishing, p. 934.
2. Prosser, William. (1980). *Law of torts* (4th ed.) St. Paul, MN: West Publishing, p. 526.
3. Warranty is a promise by the grantor as to the quality or serviceability of a product or is free of defects.
4. Potable water relates to that water that is fit to drink.
5. Contaminants can include any natural substance that finds itself in the food supply. The can include pathogenic substances (bacteria, etc.), cleaners, detergents, insecticides, herbicides.
6. Fecal coliform is transferred to water through human waste.
7. Salmonella is a pathogenic bacteria genus that can contaminate a number of foods. It usually is spread through the mishandling of food.
8. Nelson, T., & Wechsler, H. (2003). School spirits: alcohol and collegiate sports fans. Addictive Behaviors, 28(1), 1. Retrieved from ScienceDirect database on November 2, 2006.
9. Stewart, S., & Kushner, M. (2005). Introduction to the special issue on relations between gambling and alcohol use. *Journal of Gambling Studies, 21*(3), 223. Retrieved from EBSCOHost database on October 24, 2006.
10. Helmuth, E. (2003). Study: underage, heavy drinkers consume half of U.S. alcohol. Join Together. Retrieved from www.jointogether.org/news/features/2003/study-underage-heavy-drinkers.html.
11. National Highway Traffic Safety Administration, Department of Transportation (U. S.). Traffic safety facts 2002: zero tolerance laws. Washington (DC): NHTSA. Retrieved from http://www-nrd.nhtsa.dot.gov/ pdf/ nrd-30/NCSA/TSF2002/2002oldfacts.pdf on November 2, 2006.
12. Smith, R. (2000). A comparative analysis of dramshop liability and a proposal for uniform legislation. *The Journal of Corporation Law, 25*(3), 553. Retrieved from LexisNexis database on October 31, 2006.
13. Saltz, R. (1993). The introduction of dram shop legislation in the United States and the advent of server training. *Addiction, 88*(supp), 95s. Retrieved from EBSCOHost database on October 24, 2006.
14. Saltz, R. (1993). The introduction of dram shop legislation in the United States and the advent of server training. *Addiction, 88*(supp), 95s. Retrieved from EBSCOHost database on October 24, 2006.
15. Lian, L., Sloan, F., & Stout, E. (2004). Precaution, compensation, and threats of sanction: the case of alcohol servers. *International Review of Law and Economics, 24*(1), 49. Retrieved from ScienceDirect on October 30, 2006.

16. Levine, H. (1984). The alcohol problem in America: from temperance to alcoholism. *British Journal of Addiction, 79*(1), 109. Retrieved from EBSCOHost database on November 16, 2006.
17. Saltz, R. (1993). The introduction of dram shop legislation in the United States and the advent of server training. *Addiction, 88*(supp), 95s. Retrieved from EBSCOHost database on October 24, 2006.
18. Levine, H. (1984).   The alcohol problem in America: from temperance to alcoholism. *British Journal of Addiction, 79*(1), 109. Retrieved from EBSCOHost database on November 16, 2006.
19. Davies, L. (2005). 25 years of saving lives. Mothers Against Drunk Driving. Retrieved from www.madd.org on November 16, 2006.
20. Smith, R. (2000). A comparative analysis of dramshop liability and a proposal for uniform legislation. *The Journal of Corporation Law, 25*(3), 553. Retrieved from LexisNexis database on October 31, 2006.
21. Holder, H., Janes, K., Mosher, J., Saltz, R., Spurr, S., & Wagenaar, A. (1993). Alcoholic beverage server liability and the reduction of alcohol-involved problems. *Journal of Studies on Alcohol, 54*, 23.
22. Sloan, F, Reilly, B., & Schenzler, C. (1994). Effects of prices, civil and criminal sanctions, and law enforcement on alcohol-related mortality. *Journal of Studies on Alcohol, 55*, 454.
23. Gottlieb, H. (2005). Jury dons stadium beer vendor $105M for injuries caused by drunken fan. *New Jersey Law Journal*. Retrieved from Legal-Trac via Thomson Gale on October 30, 2006.
24. The overriding case involved abnormally dangerous things and activities is the old English case of *Fletcher v. Rylands*, 1865, 3 H.& C 744,159, Eng. Rep 737 reversed in *Fletcher v. Rylands*, 1866, L.R. 1 Ex. 265, Affirmed in *Rylands v. Fletcher* 1868, R.R.3 H.L.330. *Rylands v. Fletcher* has been accepted in most American courts.
25. OSHA means employee safety standards set by the Office of Safety and Health Administration, in the U.S. Department of Labor.
26. See Prosser, William L., *Law of torts*, Employer's Liablity, Section 80, p. 525.
27. Ibid, p. 526.
28. See *Armour v. Golkowska*, 1903, 202 III. 144, 66 N.E. 1037.
29. See *Petrol Corp v. Curtis*, 1948, 190 Md 652, 59 A.2d 329.
30. See *Engelking v. City of Spokane*, 1910, 59 Wash 466, 110 P. 25.
31. See *Flike v. Boston & A.R.Co.*, 1873, 53 NY 549.
32. See *Tremblay v. J.Rudnick and Sons*, 1940, 91 N.H. 24, 13 A2d 1

Chapter Five

LEGAL PROTECTIONS

SECTION 1: DEFENSES TO NEGLIGENCE

In the field of recreation and sports, it is only a matter of time, even under the best of circumstances, before a suit will be filed for negligence. There are a number of recognized defenses to negligence. Defenses are discussed below.

Comparative Negligence

Many states have statutes that require the plaintiff to prove that the defendant was at least 50% to blame for the property loss or accident. This is referred to as comparative negligence. When the plaintiff does not meet this requirement, he or she will not prevail before the court. The comparative negligence doctrine also applies to the proportion of damages awarded to a successful plaintiff. This is referred to as pure comparative negligence. As an example, in a pure comparative negligence state, a court may award a plaintiff $100,000. If the court determines that the defendant was 60% at fault and the plaintiff was 40% at fault, the actual award would be $60,000.

In *Mesick v. State* (1986),[1] the 17-year-old plaintiff fell into rocks while attempting to swing on a rope at a park owned and operated by the state of New York, a comparative negligence state. Mesick received a serious back injury that left him a permanent quadriplegic. The state knew of the danger and previously had a serious accident at the same site. The state failed to warn the users of the danger and failed to remove the rope that was used to swing over the rocks. Mesick sued the State for $6.5 million. The trial court found the State to be 75% at fault and awarded him $4,537,500. The state appealed the decision to the Supreme Court of New York, claiming that the plaintiff assumed the risk of injury when he swung over the rocks. The Supreme Court affirmed the lower court decision; however, it determined that because of Mesick's contribution to the accident, they would only award him 50% of the claim ($3,025,000).

Contributory Negligence

Contributory negligence is conduct by the plaintiff that falls short of the standard expected of a person in similar circumstances. The conduct is based upon what a prudent person would do in the same circumstances for his or her own protection. If a person is driving too fast on a poorly maintained road, the court will determine if the driver contributed significantly to his or her accident. If it was determined that the plaintiff contributed significantly to the accident, the defendant would not be held liable for the harm done, even though the road was poorly maintained. This defense is in fact a "proximate cause"[2] argument. Did the excessive speed of the automobile contribute significantly to the accident? This defense is limited, due to the fact that it exists in only a few states.

In the case of *Smith v. North Carolina DNR* (1993),[3] the Smith family had visited Stone Mountain State Park. While at the park, they decided to have a picnic on the stream above a waterfall. The family had been to that location a month earlier and had noticed the sign that warned "Danger, Falls Below." Mrs. Smith was awakened from her nap by the screams of her son. Her husband had slipped on a rock above the falls and had fallen to his death. She sued the state for failing to warn of a dangerous condition. Mrs. Smith lost the case. The court concluded that the danger of falling from the waterfall was open and obvious. Since Mr. Smith knew of the danger from his previous visit and the presence of the warning signs, the court held that Mr. Smith did not act reasonably and contributed to his own negligence. Since North Carolina is a contributory negligence state, any fault on the part of the injured party precludes recovery. Mr. Smith's family therefore recovered nothing.

Statute of Limitations

States have statutes that establish a maximum time period between the time of the accident and when the suit can be filed. In most states, there is a one to three-year time limit between the time of the accident and the filing of a lawsuit regarding injury or property loss. In the case of wrongful death, there is usually a one- to five-year period of time.[4] The time limit protects the interests of the defendant, since as time passes, evidence and reports are often lost or discarded, and/or people with knowledge of the case may have died or moved away.

In *Teiffenbrun v. Flannery* (1930),[5] the plaintiff's husband, from North Carolina, was killed as the result of being hit by an automobile by the defendant Flannery in Miami, Florida, on August 30, 1925. The plaintiff instituted the suit on August 29, 1926 one day short of the statute of limitation for wrongful death in North Carolina. Flannery argued that the accident occurred in Florida, and therefore the one-year statute of limitation for wrongful death in Florida should apply. The trial court decision for the plaintiff was then appealed on jurisdictional issues.

Failure of Proof

The plaintiff has the responsibility to prove the allegations and must show that the defendant has violated one of the elements of negligence. This defense should be raised at the pleading or initial stage of the litigation process. The plaintiff must prove that there was a legal duty, that the duty was violated, there was a causal relationship between the violation and the accident, and there were actual damages sustained. As an example, when a person is injured on a walkway, the plaintiff must prove that the landowner had a legal duty to protect the visitor, the walkway did not meet the standard of care or construction standards expected, the violation of the standard of care was the cause of the accident, and that the accident resulted in damages. Failure to prove all the above factors would result in dismissal of the case in a court of law.

In *Sajkowski v. YMCA* (2000),[6] a participant was injured in a YMCA-sponsored Wellness for Life obstacle course. The course was a single activity called the Nitro Crossing that involved swinging on a rope from a log over an imaginary pit of flat, bare dirt to another log on the other side. The rope hung only a foot and a half above the ground in the center of the imaginary pit. As the plaintiff swung across the pit, she lost her grip and fell to the ground, injuring her ankle. She then sued the YMCA for negligence in failing to put shock-absorbing materials below the crossing. The defendant YMCA prevailed in the case since the plaintiff failed to prove (failure of proof) that playground safety standards were inappropriate for this event, or that the event was analogous to gymnastics where higher standards were required (e.g., having a spotter).

Assumption of Risk

Assumption of risk is an important legal doctrine/defense for sport and recreation providers. The doctrine's premise is to place responsibility on a participant or spectator for their actions when they choose to voluntarily encounter a known and appreciated risk in a sport activity. Sport and recreational activities often involve an element of risk that is essential to the activity. However, the risk also provides the potential for injury and subsequent lawsuits. The risks assumed are often referred to as risks inherent to an activity. Inherent risks are those that are a natural part of a recreational experience, such as submerged rocks in a white-water river or trees lining the edge of a ski slope. Inherent risks are often presumed to have been accepted by participants, either orally (e.g., being told of the risks prior to a rafting trip) or written (in a document read prior to participation that lists the potential risks), or risks can be accepted implicity (i.e., knowledge is implied by the circumstances or the knowledge and skill level of the participant).

In the case of *Morales v. New York City Housing Authority* (1992)[7] Jose Morales had decided to play football with two of his friends on a grassy area behind a building owned by the New York Housing Authority. Water that flowed from the building made the ground wet and muddy. Although the footing was bad, they decided to play anyway. On one play, Jose went out for a pass and slipped on the wet grass. He fractured his right ankle and sued the New York Housing Authority for negligence. Jose lost the case. The court held that Jose had assumed the risk of falling, because he knew that the field was wet, muddy, and slippery. He had voluntarily chosen to play on an obviously dangerous playing field. Since he had a choice whether to play or not and nothing dangerous was hidden from him, the Housing Authority was able to win the case by saying he had assumed the risk of playing there.

Notice of Claim

In many state and local jurisdictions, a plaintiff with a claim against a public entity must first present a claim (bill) for damages to the proper agency prior to filing a lawsuit. The claimant has from 30 to 120 days, depending on the jurisdiction, after an injury to present his claim, depending upon the applicable statute or ordinance.[8] These laws were enacted to allow governments to make a decision to immediately pay legitimate claims or to gather evidence to defend themselves against frivolous or improper claims.

In *Van v. Town of Manitowoc* (1989),[9] the Vans claimed that their property was damaged as a result of the town's maintenance of roads. The Vans claimed that their property was flooded when the town constructed a new road that restricted the natural flow of water on the land. The trial court judge issued summary judgment in favor of the defendant, Town of Manitowoc, because of a state statute that required injured parties to file a notice 90 days after the alleged damage. The appeals court agreed that the Vans had failed to give the city a "notice of claim" in accordance with the statutes and affirmed the judgment for the defendant.

Some risks are often assumed, such as collisions with trees lining a ski run.

Governmental Immunity

Governments (local, state, and federal) can be sued for negligence but enjoy some limited immunity. It is sound public policy that the people and organizations that represent public interests (government) should not be subject to litigation every time a citizen is upset with governmental actions and decisions. Governmental immunity allows government entities to be free from liability except where they consent to be sued. Consent is granted by the Federal Tort Claims Act and the individual state tort immunity laws.

In the past, government entities enjoyed what was referred to as sovereign immunity. In essence, this meant that one could not successfully sue the government for negligent acts. In 1946, the U.S. Congress passed the Federal Tort Claims Act (FTCA).[10] This act allowed individuals for the first time to sue the federal government and its individual agencies in certain categories of a tort that included injury, death, and property loss. Section 2674 of the Federal Tort Claims Act provided that the government would be liable in the same manner "as a private individual under like circumstances. ..." Some types of damages are excluded from claims under the FTCA in that government shall "not be liable for . . . punitive damage."[11] The FTCA bars suits not begun within two years from the date of injury[12]—a time period considered a statute of limitation for federal tort cases.

The federal government does not have a body of tort laws; therefore, tort liability for the federal government and federally owned lands and properties within the several states are determined by the tort laws of the individual states in which the accident, negligence, or property loss occurs.

Following the lead of the federal government, most states enacted tort law legislation that waives some categories of state government immunity. As a result of statutes and case law, states and their subdivisions no longer enjoy complete immunity from suits. An example is the Indiana Tort Claims Act[12] that was passed in 1974 and amended in 1981. The amended act exempts 15 different categories from suits, including unimproved property, state natural resource lands, and governmental discretionary functions. Most of the individual state tort claims acts were passed by state legislatures in the 1970s and 1980s. Because of the rather recent history of the tort claims laws, case law, legal interpretation, and application of the law are presently in the developmental stage.

The Federal Tort Claims Act and various tort statutes of the individual states exempt public employees and their agencies from suits related to budget allocation and discretionary decision making. This is generally referred to as governmental immunity. In other words, the government and the individual government employee are immune from suit when an agency employee makes a decision that is mandated by a rule, regulation, or funding situation. The discretionary function exception, as it is called, is needed to preclude excessive suits when people don't like administrative decisions. Public discontent over the government decision-making process is pervasive, natural, and normal in our society. If there was no immunity, the government would be constantly sued over its primary purpose and would simply be unable to function.

In *Faulkner v. Patterson* (1994),[13] a six-year-old child broke his leg while ice skating on a field trip sponsored by the school district and supervised by defendant Patterson. The child had enrolled in a day camp sponsored by the school when the accident occurred. Plaintiff Faulkner claimed that Patterson, an employee of the school district, had negligently supervised the students. The trial court decided in favor of the defendant Patterson. Faulkner appealed the decision, claiming that Patterson was obtaining snacks and skates for the other students when he should have been supervising the skating. The appeals court agreed with the decision of the lower court that Patterson was immune from suit under the Alabama Constitution (Article I §

14) which states "that the State of Alabama shall not be made a defendant in any court of law or equity."

Under some circumstances, government immunity from suit is not available to government employees. For instance, when government employees take actions that adversely affect others and the action is outside the scope of their duties or job description, when they take actions based on their independent judgment outside of the existing policy, and when decisions are considered willful and malicious negligence by the courts, they are held accountable. When government employees are working within the scope of their duties, they may make mistakes that result in lawsuits, but are protected from personal suits.[14]

The case of *Fahl v. United States* (1992),[15] illustrates how the discretionary function exception works. In the Fahl case, a child fell from the south rim of the Grand Canyon. The child's parents sued the National Park Service for negligence in failing to warn of a dangerous condition and failing to provide a guardrail to protect visitors. The primary issue on appeal was whether the decision of park employees not to post warning signs was based on their independent judgment or whether they acted under a mandate from a rule or regulation.

If the decision not to place warnings or guardrails at the site of the fatal fall was mandated by a park regulation, or if the decision was grounded in political, social, or economic policy considerations, then the government and its employees would be immune from suit. If however, the decision not to warn visitors of the dangers of falling from the cliff or not placing a guardrail at the site was based on independent considerations of safety, then the park service would be liable.

The court found that social and economic policy considerations were at the heart of the decision not to warn or place guardrails. The court decided in favor of the National Park Service. The social and economic policies were summed up by the court, which stated that "requiring the Park Service to place guard rails and warnings at every conceivably dangerous place in the park would certainly conflict with the avowed policy of attempting to interfere as little as possible with nature in addition to being an extremely costly undertaking." Also, see *Childers v. United States* (1993).[16]

Governmental functionaries must have the flexibility and right to make decisions based upon their own judgment, conscience, and circumstances.[17] When suits are successful, plaintiffs are usually awarded compensatory damages (direct damages), pain and suffering, consequential damages, and continuing damages. Following the pattern of the federal government in the FTCA, most states do not allow plaintiffs to collect punitive damages from public entities under the provisions of their state tort claims act.

State Tort Claims Acts

Each state[18] has enacted legislation that encourages outdoor recreation through recreation land use statutes. In addition to these statutes, every state provides limited immunity for state and local government. There is a great variance in the protection provided by the various state tort claim acts. The statutes limit both private and public landowners' liability when no fee is paid for the privilege of using the land. The statutes, directly aimed at rural landowners, encourage landowners to open up their lands to hikers, campers, hunters, fishermen, bikers, equestrians, and other recreationists for noncommercial purposes.

In *Commonwealth Department of Environmental Resources v. Auresto* (1986),[19] the plaintiff was injured when his snowmobile struck a snow-covered tree stump in a state forest. The State Recreation Land Use Act states:

> (A)n owner of land owes no duty of care to keep the premises safe for entry or use by others for recreational purposes, or to give any warning of a dangerous condition, use, structure, or activity on such premises to persons entering for such purposes. The preceding immunity extends only to owners of land who hold their property open to persons entering for such purposes. The property is open to the public free of charge. The purpose of this act is self-evident. It encourages owners of land to make land and water areas available to the public for recreational purposes by limiting their liability toward persons entering thereon for such purposes.[20]

Auresto argued that the state did not intend that state lands be protected under this act. The Supreme Court of Pennsylvania determined that "... the conclusion is inescapable that since a private citizen would have been protected from the present suit so must be the commonwealth." The court decided in favor of the defendant state. In most states, the recreation land use statutes apply to private, local, state, and federal lands. However, some state statutes and subsequent case law does not provide the privilege of limited immunity to any land ownership other than privately owned lands.[21]

State recreation land use statutes provide for special protection for the land owners, and in most jurisdictions this special protection is also available to publicly managed lands.

In most jurisdictions, public agencies, local, state, and federal managing recreation areas are liable only for willful and wanton acts of negligence.[22]

Willful and wanton misconduct is wrongful conduct, done either with a knowledge that serious injuries to another will probably result or with wanton and reckless disregard of the possible results. The essential elements of a wanton and reckless act are:

1. Actual or constructive knowledge of the peril.

2. Actual or constructive knowledge that injury is probable, as opposed to a possible result of the danger.

3. Conscious failure to act to avoid the peril.

In *Hall v. United States* (1986),[23] a 17-year-old Boy Scout was hiking in a national forest in southern Illinois and was injured when he fell off a cliff when attempting to cross a natural waterfall. Hall was crossing the falls in an area that did not have designated paths or improvements. Hall argued that he was an invitee, and the United States Forest Service advertised and promoted the areas for recreation, and failed in its duty of care for his safety in failing to warn and guard the visitors against known dangers. The defendant, United States, claimed that the national forest lands were covered under the Illinois Recreation Use Statute.[24] Under the Illinois statute, the plaintiff had to prove that the defendant's conduct was willful and malicious. In its decision, the court said that "…there is nothing in the evidence which would support a finding of willful and malicious conduct on behalf of the United States." The court further stated that "the extreme risk of falling from the face of this sheer rock cliff, if you attempted to cross it, was something any person of ordinary sensibilities would have recognized. An urban dweller would have recognized it as akin to walking across the face of a building on a wet ledge two floors above the ground level. There is no duty to warn against such an open and obviously perilous condition." The court declared the applicability of the Illinois Recreation Use Statute to this case.

Waivers

Waivers are either effective or useless, depending on the circumstances in which they are used and the skill of the writer. Written and signed releases and waivers can be used as a positive defense when they involve adults and are specific to the dangers being assumed by the participant. See section 2 for an expanded discussion of waivers.

Other Limited Defenses

Last Clear Chance Doctrine

This is part of and an extension of the strict rule of contributory negligence. The doctrine emphasizes that the injury or loss was the result of the plaintiff's actions. The plaintiff had knowledge of, or should have had knowledge of, the potential for injury or loss, and had the last clear chance to avoid it.

In *Way v. Seaboard Air Line Railroad Company* (1967),[25] a man was killed by a fast-moving train while sitting on the railroad tracks. The deceased's wife sued the railroad for failure to keep a look out under the last clear chance doctrine. The train was traveling 75 miles per hour at night and the train's headlight had a visual range of 400-600 feet. Two members of the crew were watching the track at the time of the accident. The plaintiff's deceased husband was dressed in dark clothes and had been drinking heavily prior to the accident. The train was equipped with a rotating light, bells, and sounded a whistle just before the accident occurred. Both train crew members initially thought the object on the track was just one of the numerous pieces of debris adjacent to the railroad tracks. The two crewmen identified the object as a man when it moved and immediately applied the emergency brakes. The train did not stop in time and struck Way. The court decided in favor of the defendant railroad company stating:

> The last clear chance will not apply to a person who was injured or killed while intoxicated, unless there was sufficient time after his/her perilous position was discovered, or should have been discovered, within which it was possible for the other party by the exercise of reasonable care to have avoided the accident.

Act of God

An act of God is an unpredictable natural circumstance or occurrence (e.g., earthquake, tornado, etc.) that causes injury or loss. It is usually unpredictable and unforeseeable to the land owner or provider of services. While we have daily weather forecasts, the physical ability to warn all dispersed outdoor recreation visitors on a short notice that a weather event (e.g., a tornado) is imminent, is usually not practical or possible. The science of meteorology has resulted in an accurate hurricane forecast that can predict storm wind velocities and paths; however, these predictions are not infallible. Naturally occurring events, such as lightning, earthquakes, and shear

winds are much more difficult to predict. Truly unpredictable naturally occurring events provide a strong defense for negligence suits.

In *Hames v. State* (1991),[26] a golfer was killed by lightning on a state-
operated golf course in Tennessee. The golfer was killed while taking shelter
under a large tree during the lightning storm. His widow brought a wrongful death action against the state, claiming that the state failed to provide
lightning-proof weather shelters or utilize lightning warning devices. The
state claimed that the accident was an act of God and did not contain an
element of negligence. The plaintiff argued that the golf course was operated
under the U.S. Golf Association rules, where lightning warnings, shelters,
and signs are required. The trial court ruled in favor of the state while the
appeals court reversed that decision in favor of the plaintiff Hames. The state
Supreme Court determined that the situation was indeed an act of God and
decided in favor of the state of Tennessee.

Unforeseeable Circumstance

When events occur that cause an accident, yet are not foreseeable by a
normal, rational person, a negligent culpable act may not have occurred. For
example, if a person is injured as a result of a large bird's nest falling from a
tree, the circumstances would not have been foreseeable.

In *Wamser v. City of St. Petersburg* (1976),[27] a swimmer was seriously
injured when he was attacked by a shark while swimming in the Gulf of
Mexico adjacent to a beach operated by the city. The plaintiff, a minor, was
swimming approximately 25 feet from shore and approximately 35 feet from
the lifeguard stand when the attack occurred. The plaintiff claimed the city
was negligent by not warning the swimmers of sharks. The defendant city
argued that sharks had never come that close to the beach before, and just
a few minutes prior to the accident a loudspeaker warning was given to all
swimmers to be careful because a shark had been spotted south of the city
beach. The beach did not require that a fee be paid. The appellate court confirmed the lower court's decision in favor of the defendant city, validating
the defense's position that the facts of the case indicated unforeseeable circumstances.

Unforeseeable Plaintiff

An injury or property loss to someone who would be reasonably considered an unexpected plaintiff could act as a defense against successful suits.
For example, if a citizen of France is injured as a result of burns in a natural
hot pool in the United States because he could not read the English language
warning on the sign, he would be considered an unforeseeable plaintiff.

In *Grant v. City of Duluth* (1982),[14] a group of young people trespassed into a city amusement park when the park was closed at night after observing a No Trespassing sign and climbing a high security fence. The group decided to slide down a 30-foot slide that was normally a children's ride. The slide was posted with a sign stating "Danger: This slide is chained and locked nightly for your protection." There were security lights in the park at night. Grant, after drinking a quantity of beer, was first to slide. He slid into the chain blocking the slide and suffered injuries that resulted in his death three days later. The trial court decided in favor of the plaintiffs, stating that the chains were placed negligently on the slide. The defendant city appealed. The appellate court reversed and remanded the lower court's decision, stating that the facts of the case indicated an unforeseeable plaintiff.

Doctrine of Respondent Superior

If an employee acts at the insistence or direction of his or her employer, the employer can be held liable for the wrongful acts of an employee. As an example, if an employer told a maintenance employee that the repair of a dangerous slide in a playground was not a priority item, and the unrepaired equipment caused an injury, the employer would be liable for the accident. Further extension of the doctrine of respondent superior may include a number of "wrongdoer" defendants. The organization, manufacturer, board of directors, and others directly connected or within the line of authority may be listed as defendants in a lawsuit. See *Boucher v. Fuhlbruck* (1965).[29]

Legislative Authority

Certain laws restrict or prohibit suits that result in property loss or injury. In most states, Recreation Land Use Statutes require the proof of gross negligence rather than simple negligence when a recreational user of the land or property has not paid a fee. As an example, Indiana has specific legislation related to the use of state lands managed by the Department of Natural Resources. The Indiana statutes[30] restrict suits against private landowners, governmental entities, and public employees. The immunity includes discretionary functions, natural conditions, unimproved property, and unpaved access ways. The exception to the statutory immunity is payment of use fees and willful and wanton conduct by the defendant landowner.

In *Barbre v. Indianapolis Water Co.* (1980),[31] a 17-year-old boy dived into a water company reservoir, striking his head on the bottom, resulting in quadriplegia. Barbre stated that he saw no signs prohibiting swimming, fences, or no trespassing signs prior to his dive. The water company agreed that there was no warning, but argued that they were immune from suit by state law unless willful and wanton negligence could be proved. The plaintiff claimed that the water company was negligent in not warning of the danger, and that act alone constituted willful and wanton negligence. The trial court determined that the water company owed no duty of care because of the protective legislation (legislative authority) for public lands in Indiana. The plaintiff Barbre appealed. The appellate court affirmed the lower court decision in favor of the defendant water company.

Consent by Plaintiff

This defense must show voluntary and reasonable consent by a person with the mental capacity to make a rational decision. As an example, if a person decided to play football on a school team and was injured as a result of a tackle, he would not likely be successful in a lawsuit.

In *O'Neill v. Daniels* (1987),[32] a softball player sued his teammate to recover for injuries he received when he was hit in the eye by a softball during warmup exercises just prior to an amateur softball game. O'Neill accused Daniels of being careless and throwing the ball when the plaintiff's attention was diverted. Daniels argued that O'Neill should have been paying better attention to the events on the playing field rather than watching extracurricular activities. The defendant Daniels was granted summary judgment by the trial court, and O'Neill appealed. The appeals court agreed with the lower court decision in favor of the defendant, stating that:

> It is clear that plaintiff's participation in the game warmup was voluntary, and thus our concern is only with the scope of consent. It is well established that participants may be held to have consented by their participation to injury-causing events which are known, apparent, or reasonably foreseeable, but are not reckless or intentional.

Recreation and sports administrators must be able to understand the basic defenses to tort liability. Understanding the defenses, particularly the application of legal defenses, will result in implementing a more meaningful risk management program. A knowledge of negligence defenses can help the recreation and sports professional investigate accidents, inspect facilities for safety, administer programs, and implement a meaningful risk management program. While it is important to know legal defenses, it is equally important to consult competent legal counsel when faced with potential litigation.

Notes

1. *Mesick v. State,* 504 N.Y.S.2d 279 (A.D. 3 Dept. 1986).
2. Ibid.
3. *Smith v. North Carolina Department of Natural Resources,* 436 S.E. 2d 878 (N.C. App.1993).
4. As an example, Indiana's statute of limitations establishes a two-year period for property damage, personal injury, and wrongful death.
5. *Tieffenbrun v. Flannery,* 151 S. E. 857 (N.C. 1930).
6. *Sajkowski v. YMCA,* 269 A.D.2d 228 (N.Y. App. 2000).
7. *Morales v. New York City Housing Authority,* 187 A.2d 295; 583 N.Y.S.2d 456 (A.D. 3 Dept.1992).
8. Black, H. C. (1979). *Black's law dictionary* (5th ed.). St. Paul, MN: West Publishing Co., p. 1173.
9. *Van v. Town of Manitowoc Rapids,* 442 N.W.2d 557 (Wis. App. 1989).
10. 28 U.S.C.A. § 2674.
11. 28 U.S.C.A. § 2674.131.
12. Act of 1974, P L. 142 and Act of 1981 PL. 290. Also see Indiana code, Title 3416.54.
13. *Faulkner v. Patterson,* 650 So.2d 873 (Ala. 1994).
14. See Federal Employees Liability Reform and Tort Compensation Act of 1988, Public Law 100694.
15. *Fahl v. United States,* 792 F.Supp. 80 (D. Ariz. 1992).
16. *Childers v. United States,* 841 F.Supp. 1001 (9th Cir. 1993).
17. Black, H. C. (1979) *Black's law dictionary* (5th ed.). St. Paul, MN: West Publishing Co., p. 419.
18. All states except Alaska and North Carolina have enacted legislation referred to as recreation land use statutes. Alaska and North Carolina have case precedents that essentially protect the landowner from outdoor recreation-related suits on lands used without fees.
19. *Commonwealth Department of Environmental Resources v. Auresto,* 511 A.2d 815 (Pa. 1986).
20. Pennsylvania Recreation Use of Land and Water Act § 4661 through 4668 and the Snowmobiles and All-Terrain Vehicles Act § 7701 and 7722.
21. As an example, the states of Michigan, New Jersey, and Wisconsin have not applied their recreation land use statutes to publicly owned lands.
22. As an example see California Code, Section 846.
23. *Hall v. United States,* 647 F.Supp 53 (D. III. 1986).

24. Illinois Recreational Use Statute, Illinois Revised Statutes Chapter 70, Paragraph 34.
25. *Way v. Seaboard Air Line Railroad Company,* 270 F.Supp. 440 (D. S.C. 1967).
26. *Hames v. State,* 808 S.W.2d 41 (Tenn. 1991).
27. *Wamser v. City of St. Petersburg* 339 So.2d 244 (Fla. App. 1976).
28. *Grant v. City of Duluth 673* F.2d 677 (8th Cir.1982).
29. *Boucher V Fublbrack,* 26 Conn. Sup 79, 213 A. 2d728 (1965).
30. See Ind. Code Ann. §141318 and §14263 (private land immunity) and lnd. Code § 41631 to 3 (publicly owned lands).
31. *Barbre v. Indianapolis Water Company,* 400 N.E.2d.ll42 (lnd. App.1980).
32. *O'Neill v. Daniels,* 523 N.Y.S.2d 264 (A.D. 4 Dept. 1987).

SECTION 2: CONTRACTUAL PROTECTIONS (WAIVERS)

Waivers (exculpatory agreements[1]) are intended to release or reduce the recreation or sport provider's liability exposure from their users, guests, patrons, visitors, clients, and participants. Waivers need to be considered in sport and recreation activities because of the litigious nature of society. Recreational sport and natural resource managing agencies provide recreation experiences that tend to be risky. Whitewater canoeing, mountain climbing, spelunking, contact sports, and so forth, provide separate and significant risk possibilities. Waivers, releases, and agreements to participate tend to inform the participant, justify the activity, warn of danger, and clear the agency from fault or guilt arising from an accident or damages.[2] There is a common misconception that waivers are not worth the paper they are written on. The idea that waivers are never upheld is simply untrue. The court's response to the validity of waivers and releases varies from state to state, but waivers are upheld when they meet certain legal requirements.

Waivers are consensual agreements to accept the normal risks associated with recreation- or sport-related activities. A waiver is therefore a contract, since it is an agreement where both parties have something to gain from the deal. As such, a waiver is valid only if it holds up to the same scrutiny a court would give a contract.

There are six basic points to remember about waivers:

1. A waiver must be clearly written and easy to understand.
The law requires that a valid contract can only be made when both parties agree to its terms. In legal terms, this is called "a meeting of the minds."

An offer is made by one party and it is accepted by the other. A court will generally find that the terms of a waiver have been accepted only when it is also found that the participants fully understand these terms. It is obviously difficult to have a mutual agreement when one of the parties does not know what is going on. Therefore, a waiver needs to be written in plain English and not in the convoluted language to which many lawyers have grown accustomed.

2. It must be made obvious that it is a waiver.

Just as it is impossible to have a meeting of the minds when a document is written in a way that it cannot be understood, it is impossible to agree to the terms of a waiver when the participant does not understand that he or she is signing a waiver. This point seems obvious, but it is surprising how often this issue arises. Waivers are sometimes found in the strangest places. They are sometimes written on the back of tickets, medical forms, sign-up sheets, or as the following case illustrates, the bottom of a softball roster. They are also often tucked away in the text of some long and boring document, or written in print so small that a magnifying glass is needed to decipher it. The courts often frown upon waivers constructed in this manner. Not many people, for example, read the backs of their ticket stubs.

A waiver needs to be situated at a location in the document where it will put the participant on notice that they are signing a waiver and giving up an important right. Waivers should be located on the front page of the document where possible and written in bold, capital letters (e.g., WAIVER OF LIABILITY). The following case illustrates the problems that can arise when waivers are not located front and center on the document.

In the case of *Johnson v. Rapid City Softball Assoc.,* (1994)[3] Darci Johnson had signed up to play in a softball league. During one of the games, she had rounded second base, and anticipating a close play at third base, decided to slide. She injured her ankle in the play. She claimed that the city who owned and operated the field was negligent because they had failed to put the base in the correct position and keep it in good shape. Darci sued the city for negligence. She lost her case in the trial court and appealed.

Prior to playing in the league, Darci was required to sign a roster and she did. As it turned out, at the bottom of the roster, there was a waiver. Darci claimed that she didn't see it, even though it was highlighted in red ink and written in bold letters. Therefore, her attorneys argued that from a legal standpoint, she could not have consented to the waiver terms since she didn't know she was signing a waiver in the first place.

The court stated that one of the essential elements of a contract is that both parties consent to it. If a waiver is written at the bottom of a roster beneath the signature lines, as was done in this case, it becomes uncertain whether consent to agree to the terms of the waiver is fairly and knowingly made. Therefore, the court sent the case back down to the lower court so that a jury could determine whether Darci consented to the terms of the waiver.

In the case of *Dombrowski v. City of Omer* (1993),[4] Gregory Dombrowski had decided to participate in a rope-climbing event at an annual summer festival. In this event, participants climb hand over hand on a rope strung across a river. Gregory had almost made it across the river when he lost his grip, fell headfirst into the river and was seriously injured. He sued the city for negligence and lost. The primary reason he lost the case was he had signed a waiver. The city required each participant in the rope-climbing event to sign a waiver before entering. The words WAIVER OF LIABILITY were clearly and boldly displayed at the top of the form. Also, the waiver terms were written in a clear and straightforward manner, and the document was not misleading. The waiver was held valid and the city was released from liability.

3. A waiver must be signed by one of majority age.

For many types of contracts to be enforceable, they must be written and signed. This is the case with most waivers. The participant must sign the waiver form. Signing the waiver offers proof that you have read and understood the terms. The participant, however, must be competent to perform the task of signing. In other words, he or she must be able to understand the terms of the contract. Most states will not allow those who are mentally disabled or of a young age to enter into a binding contract, because they cannot fully understand its terms. Minors, in most states, are classified as those people under the age of 18 (in other states, minors are classified as those under the age of 21). A waiver signed by a minor is not enforceable.

Also, a waiver signed by a parent on behalf of a minor might not be enforceable against the minor. The outcome depends on the state with jurisdiction over the case (states are split on the issue so it is important to know the law of your state). The same is generally true when a guardian signs a waiver on behalf of a minor or someone with a disability that makes him incapable of entering into a contract. When the parent or guardian signs a waiver, they usually give up their own right to sue but have not given up the rights of the minor to sue. The following case illustrates what happened in the state of Washington when a parent signed a waiver for her child while on a ski vacation.

In the case of *Scott v. Pacific West Mountain Resort* (1992),[5] a 12-year-old boy was on vacation with his parents at a western ski resort. He had been skiing for two years, so his parents decided to enroll him in ski racing lessons. His mother filled out and signed the application for the ski school that contained waiver of liability language. With that, the boy was enrolled and began his lessons. A race course was set up by the ski school owner for the students to use for practice.

He was cruising down the course on one of his practice runs when he missed a marker and lost control. He headed off the course directly toward a small shack. The shack was elevated by wooden support beams. When he attempted to turn his skis to avoid the structure, he was thrown forward and underneath it, hitting one of the supports in the process. He had severe head injuries. The boy's parents sued the ski school for negligence. The trial court found that the waiver was valid, and therefore the ski school was not liable.

The case was appealed. The state Supreme Court reversed the decision of the trial court. One of the issues addressed was whether a parent could sign away the rights of her child to sue for negligence. The court held that parents do not have the authority to sign away those rights. The court felt that it would be against public policy to allow parents to sign away those rights, because there are times when parents might not have the financial means to provide care for a seriously injured child. In such cases, the child would have no recourse against a negligent party to get the money he or she would need to deal with the incapacity. Additionally, the court held that although the child's suit is not barred, the parent's suit is barred by the waiver agreement.

4. A waiver must be specific as to what it covers.

Drafting the waiver document is usually the job of a lawyer. It must be done, however, with the help of the client, so that all of the bases are covered. Everything that could possibly go wrong should be considered first. Then the waiver can be tailored to cover those areas that the client and attorney agree need the greatest attention. Often a waiver will only free the recreation provider of liability from natural occurrences that are beyond everyone's control. At times, however, it might be wise to include language in the waiver that relieves the recreation provider of liability for situations over which they do have control. In the following case, for example, the ski operator's waiver might have relieved them of ordinary negligence had specific language been included in the waiver.

Waiver language, however, can generally not relieve the provider of liability for acts that are willful and wanton. Willful acts include acts that are committed when a dangerous condition is known and nothing is done to correct it. Wanton acts occur when there is a great chance that someone will be hurt due to a dangerous condition and no care is taken to warn or protect people from it. An example of a willful and wanton act might be when a mountaineering outfitter supplies climbers with a rope that they know is badly worn and unsafe, and a climber is subsequently injured in a fall resulting from the faulty equipment. A waiver could not be written so as to protect the outfitter from such willful and wanton conduct.

In the case of *Sirek v. Fairfield Snowbowl, Inc.* (1990),[6] Veda Sirek had rented skis at a commercial ski resort. She had her own boots, so all she needed was the skis and bindings that would fit properly. Before she could rent the skies, however, she had to read and sign a rental agreement. In anticipation of an exciting day on the slopes, she quickly read the agreement and signed her name. She was then off to the lift for some action. On her way down the slope, she turned and fell hard. Her bindings, which should be set to release the boots from the skis when enough pressure is applied, did not release the boots. Since the bindings did not release, her legs were twisted and she was injured. She sued the ski resort, claiming that they were negligent in failing to set her bindings properly. The ski resort claimed, however, that they were released from liability since she had signed the waiver. The trial court agreed with the ski resort. Veda appealed the case to a higher court.

The higher court, the court of appeals, reversed the decision of the trial court. The court held that the waiver did not release the ski resort from liability for its own negligent acts. The waiver read in part: "I understand that the bindings furnished on said rental equipment are release-type, designed to reduce the risk and degree of injury from falling, and that these bindings will not release under all circumstances and are no guarantees of my safety." This language does not address whether the ski resort is liable for the actions of its employees in not properly setting the bindings or selecting the appropriate skis. It only gives a general warning and says that there is a possibility that the bindings will not always release. The court therefore held that the ski resort failed to release itself from liability for its own negligent conduct, since this was not stated in the waiver. The case was reversed and remanded.

Another case where the waiver language was at issue was *Swierkosz v. Starved Rock Stables* (1993).[7] In this case, the plaintiff, an adult horseback rider, was injured after a rented horse bolted under her, throwing her to the ground. The plaintiff claimed that because the horse's actions caused her injuries, the stables were responsible under the principles of strict liability. Swierkosz, the plaintiff, had signed a waiver prior to taking the horse. The waiver Swierkosz signed stated in part:

Section II. Warnings and Assumption of Risk Agreement

I/We understand that horseback riding is classified as ADVENTURE RECREATIONAL SPORT ACTIVITY and that there are inherent elements of risk always present in any such activity, despite all safety precautions. I fully accept such risk, some examples of which are listed as follows:

1. It is not possible for any person or establishment to predict exactly how a horse will behave when it is frightened, angry, or under stress; it may react according to it natural instincts, which are to jump sideways, forward or backward.

2. Upon mounting a horse and taking up the reins, the rider is in primary control of the horse. If a rider falls from a horse to the ground it will be a fall of from 3 to 5 feet and the impact will be according to physical law, possibly resulting in injury to a rider.

Section III. Release Agreement

1/We understand and agree that except in the event of this stable's gross negligence, I/We accept full responsibility for bodily injury which is sustained by any member of my ground so listed above, on or in relationship to the premises and operations of this stable and/ or while riding or handling horses or other animals owned by the same; and I/We hereby, for myself, do hereby release and discharge the owners, operators, sponsors of the premises and their respective servants, agents, officers and all other participants of and from all claims, demands, actions and causes of action for same injuries.

The trial court decided in favor of the defendant stables. The decision was appealed by the plaintiff. The appeals court affirmed the decision of the trial court stating that "where a person rents a horse and understands and expressly accepts (signs the waiver) the risk of using the horse, he cannot recover damages from the person who rented the horse to him..." The appeals court further found that the waiver fully described the dangers involved in horse riding. The decision was for the defendant stables.

It should be noted, however, that although waivers that attempt to release extreme forms of negligent conduct may be deemed to violate public policy in most states, there are some exceptions. For example, some state courts (e.g., in Florida, Illinois, Kentucky, and Pennsylvania) have upheld waivers that release liability for gross negligence. Other states (Colorado, Texas, and West Virginia) have upheld waivers that protect against liability for reckless conduct.

5. A waiver must be signed voluntarily.

As mentioned, for there to be a valid contract, both parties must give their agreement. The law calls this mutual assent. Also, this mutual assent must be voluntary. A voluntary act is one made with freedom of choice. Therefore, a voluntary act must be made without duress. Duress consists of threats or physical force that would make someone do something contrary to their free will. Threats could consist of words intended to scare or embarrass an individual, or physical acts that one might perceive as a threat to his physical well-being. Physical force could consist of holding someone against his will or injuring him physically. Obviously, waivers signed while under duress are not valid.

Another way for a waiver to be made involuntarily is to take away the participant's choice. For example, what if a male skier is taken to the top of a very steep mountain with the only safe way off being to ski down it? He is then told that he will be given a pair of skis only if he signs a waiver. This lack of choice would defeat the effectiveness of the waiver. A more common example would be when a patient goes to the hospital for emergency surgery. She is given a waiver form to sign before the operation will begin. In such a case, the patient has little choice. Either she signs the waiver or they will not do the necessary surgery. Therefore, as it relates to recreation, always be sure that the participant has a choice whether or not to sign a waiver. Do not ask the person to sign it once participation in the activity has begun, and never use any form of duress to force a participant to sign a waiver form.

6. A waiver must not be against public policy.[8]

Some courts have held that a waiver can only be against public policy if a public duty is involved. A service that involves a public duty is one that deserves public regulation, is of great importance to the public, and is for some a practical necessity. A provider of a service that involved a public duty, therefore, would stand in such a position of power that the participant would have no choice but to agree to the terms of the waiver. This would create very unequal bargaining power, between the participant, who must have the service, and the provider of that service.

It would therefore be against public policy for the provider of an essential service to take away the participant's right to sue when he has no choice but to accept the terms of the agreement. The following case illustrates a situation in which the plaintiff loses the argument that the waiver was against public policy. Most recreation providers do not provide services that are a public necessity and therefore would not have waivers that were against public policy.

In the case of *Boyce v. West* (1993),[9] Boyce had enrolled in an advanced scuba diving class at his university. He was able to take this course because he had passed the prerequisite beginning diving course and had become certified the previous summer. He signed a release similar to the one he signed for the beginning course that named the university and the Professional Association of Diving Professionals (PADI) as those released from liability.

One of the dives that Boyce participated in while taking the course was a dive in a deep-water lake. During the dive, Boyce and another diver began to run low on air while they were 100 feet below the surface. The instructor noticed this and guided them to begin their ascent. As they moved toward the surface, one of the students ran into trouble. The instructor came to his aid and assisted him to the surface. While this was happening, the instructor lost sight of Boyce. He was next seen floating on the surface. He had died from an air embolism that forms in the blood stream when one tries to come to the surface too quickly after a deep-water dive. His parents, as representatives of his estate, sued the university and the instructor. They lost the case in the trial court and appealed.

Boyce's estate argued that to release the university from liability would violate public policy, so it should therefore not be enforced. The court reasoned that for a public policy to be violated, the activity must be one where a service of great importance to the public is performed; a service that is often a matter of practical necessity for some members of the public. The court concluded that it did not take much to find that scuba diving, though a popular sport in the area, did not involve a public interest. There was no practical necessity for Boyce to take the scuba class. He took the class voluntarily at a private school. Therefore, the court held that upholding the validity of the waiver did not violate public policy, and the decision of the trial court was affirmed.

SECTION 3: THE AGREEMENT TO PARTICIPATE

Even with certain limitations placed upon waivers, recreation providers should still not be hesitant to use them to limit liability with their adult participants. When they are specific, they provide the participant with a strong reminder as to the dangers involved with the activity. That reminder of dangers, accompanied by a signature representing understanding, forms a basis whereby a specific waiver or release invokes the assumption of risk defense.

The best instrument to limit the liability for minors (children) is the agreement to participate. This document must be specifically worded to cover the risks and dangers involved in the activity in detail. It must also include all the rules of conduct required for safety and organization purposes so the children/minors and their parents/guardians understand what is expected of them. This agreement to participate documents the fact they (the parents) understood the dangers involved in the activity, and agreed to let their children participate and to instruct their children to abide by the rules.[10]

An effective agreement to participate document places the parents in the key role of making decisions on behalf of their children and the responsibility to inform their children of the precautions and rules for participating in the activity. In order for the assumption of risk defense to hold in court, the risk of any activity must be described in detail in the agreement to participate.

Recreation managers should understand that it is less risky to provide recreation activities for adult participants than young participants. That may be a legal fact; however, public recreation agencies have an obligation, both ethical and social, to serve that segment of the population that is most vulnerable to accidents and that needs to be protected from harm … the nation's youth. The following is an example of a case where assumption-of-risk language succeeded in limiting the liability of the recreation provider.

In *Saenz v. Whitewater Voyages, Inc.* (1990),[11] the plaintiff wife of a man who drowned during a whitewater rafting trip on the American River in California brought a wrongful death suit against a commercial river outfitting and guide company, Whitewater Voyages, Inc. The 280-pound, 28-year-old decedent had paid a fee to participate in the raft trip and read and signed a "Release and Assumption of Risk Agreement" (waiver). The release read as follows:

> I am aware that certain risks and dangers may occur on any river trip with Whitewater. These risks include, but are not limited to hazards of and injury to person and property while traveling in rafts on the river, accident or illness in remote places without medical facilities, and the forces of nature.

> I hereby assume all of the above risks and, except in the case of gross negligence, will hold Whitewater harmless from any and all liability action, causes of action, debts, claims, and demands of every kind and nature whatsoever which I now have or which may arise out of or in connection with my trip or participation in any activities with Whitewater.

The agreement further stated it operated as a release and assumption of risk for the participant's heirs. As part of the orientation process, the decedent was given extensive safety instruction and was fitted with an adult large/extra-large life jacket. All trip participants were given the option of either walking around difficult rapids or entering and traversing the rapids on a raft. They were warned of the dangers and the best ways to avoid problems while on the river. The decedent fell out of the raft in a particularly hazardous part of the river and drowned. The decedent's wife claimed that Whitewater conducted their operation in a willful and wanton negligent manner and the release that was signed violated public policy. The trial court issued a summary judgment in favor of the defendant Whitewater. Saenz appealed. The appeals court affirmed the summary judgment of the trial court stating that the decedent expressly assumed the risk that led to his death.

A well-drafted and soundly planned waiver can be a useful part of a recreation manager's risk management plan. The cases and principles discussed in this chapter should give you a good understanding of a waiver's uses and limitations. You are encouraged to read as many waiver cases as possible, particularly in your state of interest, to best understand their use and validity in different situations and sport settings.[12]

As with all legal documents and contracts, it is important to know that the courts in each state interpret the laws somewhat differently. Some courts are favorable toward waivers while others are not as much so. You must seek advice from competent legal counsel in your state prior to using a waiver or other legal agreement.

Given what you have learned about waivers, how many flaws can you find in the following waiver that would make it invalid? What are they?

LITTLE SLUGGERS SOFTBALL LEAGUE

Team Roster
Sign Your Name in the Available Spaces Below

_____	_____
_____	_____
_____	_____
_____	_____
_____	_____

Contract of Indemnification

In consideration of City Park furnishing services and/or equipment to enable me to participate in softball games and practices while on city property, I agree to the following:

I fully understand and acknowledge that outdoor recreational activities have (a) inherent risks, dangers and hazards and such exist in my use of City Park equipment and my participation in activities while on City Park property; (b) my participation in such activities and/or use of such equipment may result in injury or illness including, but not limited to bodily injury, disease, strains, fractures, partial and/or total paralysis, death or other ailments that could cause serious disability; c) these risks and dangers may be caused by the gross negligence or reckless conduct of the owners, employees, officers or agents of City Park, the forces of nature or other causes.

Unconscionable acts inherent to but unforeseeable to said game having arisen from or with same, include but are not exclusive to said activity and include, but are not limited to: harmful impacts with rapidly moving spherical projectiles, inclement atmospheric conditions which serve as a contraindication to human health and safety, irregular conditions inherent to the loam or turf, or other dangerous conditions arising therefrom or heretofore on said premises, (d) by my participation in these activities and/or use of equipment, I hereby assume all risks and dangers and all responsibility for any losses and/or damages, and agree not to sue City Park for any injuries which I may incur. I specifically understand that I am releasing, discharging and waiving any claims or actions that I may have presently or in the future for the negligent acts or other conduct by the owners, agents, officers or employees of City Park.

I understand that if I do not sign this indemnification agreement I will lose my right to participate in this Softball league and all future leagues in this or any other sport sponsored by City Park. I further understand that by not signing this agreement, I give up my right to ever eat ice cream again for the rest of my life.

Discussion Questions

1. Explain the difference between negligence and an intentional tort.

2. Describe the elements of "battery" and provide an example of how battery might occur in the recreation setting.

3. Describe the elements of "defamation" and provide an example of how defamation might occur in the recreation setting.

Notes

1. Exculpatory clause—a statement clearing another party for alleged fault- or guilt. *Black's law dictionary* (5th ed.), St. Paul, MN: West Publishing Co., p. 508.
2. Exculpatory clause—a statement clearing another party for alleged fault- or guilt. *Black's law dictionary* (5th ed.), St. Paul, MN: West Publishing Co., p. 508.
3. *Johnson v. Rapid City Softball Assoc.,* 514 N.W. 693 (S.D. 1994).
4. *Dombrowski v. City of Omer,* 502 N.W.2d 707 (Mich. App. 1993).
5. *Scott v. Pacific West Mountain Resort,* 834 P.2d 6 (Wash. 1992).
6. *Sirek v. Fairfield Snowbowl, Inc.,* P.2d 1291 (Ariz. App. 1990).
7. *Swierkosz v. Starved Rock Stables,* 607 N.E.2d 280 (Ill. App. 1993).
8. Kaiser, R. A. (1986). *Liability and the law in recreation, parks, and sports.* Englewood Cliffs, NJ: Prentice-Hall, Inc., p. 92.
9. *Boyce v. West,* 862 P.2d 592 (Wash. App.1993).
10. van der Smissen, B. *National Safety Network Newsletter* Volume 1, Number 4, March 1985.
11. *Saenz v. Whitewater Voyages, Inc.,* 226 Cal. App.3d 758 (1st Dist. 1990).
12. For an excellent discussion of waivers in sport and recreation settings, see Cotton & Cotton (2000), *Waivers & Releases,* IHRSA.

Part Three

INTENTIONAL TORTS

INTRODUCTION

In the past, intentional torts were not a problem that concerned managers of recreation and sports facilities and activities. The litigious nature of the public and the general breakdown of behavioral norms, particularly among youth, have led to aggressive and antisocial behavior that results in criminal prosecution or civil litigation. Intentional tort law provides the legal basis of non-criminal dealings among members of our society. While criminal laws restrain us from certain acts against societal order, our liability derived from dealing with others is often decided through civil actions.

Many people have experienced the pain, frustration, and financial loss associated with personal injury and property loss as a result of the intentional actions of others. Managers and staff engaged in recreation or sports management have been subject to injury or property loss as a result of verbal threats to do bodily harm, actual unwanted touching or striking, extreme mental stress resulting from the actions of others, unwanted intrusion of people or objects on property, people using personal possessions without the permission of their owners, and people publishing or telling lies about others. All these experiences could qualify as intentional torts and may result in some type of litigation.

Intentional torts are those committed by a person who intended to do that which the law has determined to be wrong, as contrasted to negligence, where a person fails to exercise an acceptable degree of care and no harm was intended.[1]

For many managers, it is difficult to understand how their organization or their individual employees become defendants in an intentional tort case. Experienced managers recognize that intentional torts are common in our society and care must be taken to avoid having employees, their organization, or themselves involved in a lawsuit. Those individuals employed and participating in recreation and sports represent a cross-section of society. It is important to recognize that employees are subject to the same emotions and reactions to the dynamics of day-to-day living as the people they serve. After facing angry people all day who castigate their management, honesty, and integrity, is it little wonder that employees, and therefore organizations, periodically have problems with intentional torts.

Recreation and sport participants can and do assault employees. There are instances when public or private employees have committed intentional acts that have resulted in harm to visitors or participants. These acts often occur during the last hours of an employee's shift. One of the significant factors is a high likelihood of fatigue, both physical and mental. Wise managers train employees to recognize behavior and situations that can lead to personal torts. Working shorter shifts in exceptionally hot weather, recognizing difficult work environments, and working in pairs, can reduce the incidents of personal torts.

In the case of *Frank v. Orleans Parish School Board* (1967),[2] a 14-year-old boy was injured when physically disciplined by a coach in a high school physical education class. The class was practicing lay-ups on the basketball court. The 14-year-old was being disciplined for his behavior and was sitting on the sidelines, not allowed to practice with the rest of the class. Frank tried to rejoin his classmates in the shooting line, but was stopped from participating by the coach. The third time Frank tried to enter the class, the coach chased him down, shook him, lifted him off the floor and dropped him, causing his arm to break. The coach claimed that Frank was trying to hit him and he was simply protecting himself from assault. The coach was 5'8", 34 years of age, and weighed 230 pounds. The plaintiff was 4'9" and weighed 101 pounds. The trial court ruled against the school district in favor of the plaintiff, stating that the coach "went beyond that degree of physical effort necessary to either protect himself or discipline the boy, and that this lack of judgment on the part of the coach in injuring Frank in the course of disciplining him and subjected the defendant to liability." The appeals court affirmed the judgment of the lower court.

When conflicts or differences in opinion occur, the arguments appear to develop in well-defined stages as follows:

Stage 1—They argue on present facts and debate the merit of the individual positions. If this process does not convince one of the antagonists, then

Stage 2—The debating sides solicit political or technical allies to force the other to yield to the influence rather than the merit of the argument. If this process does not convince one of the antagonists, then

Stage 3—The two sides attack the character and integrity of the opposition, rather than deal with the subject matter.

As a result of this evolution of disagreements, many arguments that start as a presentation of facts and logic sadly turn to verbal assault, defamation of character, or invasion of privacy.

It is important that all managers and supervisors in recreation and sports recognize the potential for intentional torts within their organizations. They need to protect themselves, their fellow workers, and their organizations from being subject to and from committing intentional torts.

Notes

1. Black, H. C. (1979). *Black's law dictionary* (5th ed.). St. Paul, MN: West Publishing Co., p. 1335.
2. *Frank v. Orleans Parish School Bd.,* 195 So.2d 451 (La App. 1967).

Chapter Six

HARM TO PERSONS

There are two broad classifications of torts—voluntary and involuntary. Voluntary torts are deliberate and are intended to do harm, while involuntary torts are the result of a careless or negligent act by an individual or organization. The intent of the defendant is the most critical factor in determining whether the injury resulted from a voluntary or involuntary act. Negligent acts can be the result of simple negligence, with no intent to do harm.

Battery

Battery is the intentional infliction of harmful or offensive touching of another without that person's consent. The battery does not have to cause physical damage. The act of physical touching may be offensive and result in mental damage as well, as is the case of unwanted or unsolicited touching between males and females or in molestation situations.

The elements of battery include:

1. An act by a defendant,

2. intended to result in actual touching or the apprehension of imminent touching,

3. which act does cause such (harmful and offensive) touching.

The law of battery is intended to protect the personal safety and security of people and to recognize an individual's right to be free from physical intrusions. Sometimes, particularly in contact sports, both assault and battery are legal and expected. Contact sports such as boxing, football, rugby, and

to a limited extent, basketball, soccer, and baseball, constitute categories of limited legal battery. Children's games such as tag or hide and seek also represent a form of acceptable battery.

When an individual has knowledge that a person is particularly offended by a specific act of touching that is accepted as normal by a reasonable person, but nonetheless touches in a manner offensive to that specific person, there are reasonable grounds for a civil suit involving battery. As an example, a person does not want to be hugged and tells the offender that she does not want to be hugged. When the offender ignores the individual and hugs her, a battery has likely been committed.

Battery against sport officials is of increasing concern in all levels of sports.

Not all types of touching constitute a battery. Physical contact as a result of crowded subways and streets will always result in unwanted touching, but not necessarily battery, because the contact is often not intentional, harmful, or offensive. The courts will decide if touching went beyond that which would normally be expected. The decision to play a contact sport is a decision to be touched within the bounds set by the rules of that specific sport.

Battery against sport officials is of increasing concern in all levels of sports. In the case of *Baugh v. Redmond* (1990),[1] an umpire, Jimmy Baugh, was punched in the face by Marice Redmond following an incident in a city league softball game. During the game, umpire Baugh called a runner out for leaving a base before a fly ball was caught. Redmond was very angry as a result of the call and verbally harassed Baugh the rest of the game. As Baugh was leaving the game, Redmond confronted Baugh and hit him in the face with his fist. The blow broke his glasses and caused extensive damage to Baugh's mouth and teeth, resulting in four root canals as well as oral surgery. Baugh sued Redmond for battery. The court awarded Baugh medical damages, attorney fees, and compensation for his pain and suffering. Redmond appealed the case, and the appeals court upheld the ruling of the lower court, stating that the battery was flagrant, and no sports official should be subject to such a situation regardless of whether a call was accurate or inaccurate.

Assault

Assault is the intentional creation of an apprehension of imminent harmful or offensive contact without consent.[2] An assault can be committed without actually touching anyone, just by threatening an act of violence. An act, without words, such as brandishing a knife or displaying a gun, may constitute an assault. In some jurisdictions, the word "assault" is defined to include both threatening and harmful touching. For the broad purposes of this text, assault does not include harmful touching. Additionally, there is a general rule that words not accompanied by some overt act, will not constitute an assault. However, there may be some situations where the surrounding circumstances are such that words alone may suffice. For example, a threat delivered by a notorious gangster.

The elements of civil assault consist of:

1.   An act by a defendant *intended* to

2.   cause an *apprehension* of an *immediate battery* (harmful or offensive touching),

3.   with the *apparent ability* to commit the battery.

The status and circumstances surrounding the assault have a great deal to do with meeting all the elements. Suppose a recreation supervisor is called to break up a disturbance on a playground and finds two adults fist fighting. When he or she attempts to break up the fight, one of the protagonists threatens the peacemaker, shouting, "You are going to get beat up as soon as I finish with this guy." The angry adult then approaches the supervisor in an aggressive manner. An assault has been committed by the very threat of violence. Threatening words need not be used in an assault if the defendant brandishes a weapon.

In *Hackbart v. Cincinnati Bengals, Inc.* (1979),[3] Dale Hackbart, a seriously injured professional football player playing with the Denver Broncos, brought suit against Charles Clark, an offensive player with the Cincinnati Bengals. In the suit, Hackbart alleged that Charles Clark intentionally hit him with his forearm in the back of the head and neck while he was on his knees, causing him to sustain a serious neck fracture injury. During the trial, Charles Clark admitted that he acted out of anger and frustration resulting from an intercepted pass. Clark further admitted that the blow was not accidental.

The trial court decided in favor of the defendant Cincinnati Bengals and Charles Clark, when the court determined that the very nature of football is violent and players know or should know they are subject to serious injury. The trial judge stated that due to the vicious nature of the sport, they could not apply the normal laws and principles of assault and battery to the game of football. The plaintiff Hackbart appealed the decision of the trial court. The appeals court concluded that the lower court's emphasis on the violent nature of the game should not be the primary reason for their decision. The appellate court indicated that the plaintiff was entitled to an assessment of whether his rights had been violated. The question of intent was the primary issue. The lower court's decision was reversed and remanded[4] for a new trial in accordance with the views of the higher court. The case was finally settled out of court.

False Imprisonment

A person should have the right to move about freely and without constraint unless he or she has been formally and officially arrested. The tort of false imprisonment protects individuals from being incarcerated without cause and due process. False imprisonment can take place by restricting a person's movements by (1) locking a person in a confined space such as a jail, room, or enclosure, (2) physical force, handcuffs, physically holding a person, tying with ropes, and so forth, or (3) duress that threatens a person with physical force or violence, pointing a gun toward him, or other threatening acts.

The elements of false imprisonment are:

1. An act by a defendant intended to

2. confine the plaintiff

3. within definite physical boundaries

4. with an awareness of the confinement, and

5. without the plaintiff's consent.

The defendant must take some action and/or speak words indicating that the plaintiff is being forcibly detained. Verbal threats only are usually not accepted by the courts, because the lack of provable actions makes verbal threats difficult to prove. Some exceptions, accepted by the courts, relate to orders from an officer of the law (police), threats related to destroying the plaintiff's property if the plaintiff does not comply, threats of physical violence by a larger person, males threatening females, and adults threatening children. In all of the above situations, the courts are likely to consider such conduct as forceful detainment.

The intent of the defendant requires only that the defendant intended to do the act that gave rise to an intentional tort. It does not require the intent to harm. If the actions of the defendant were intentional, and also resulted in the illegal confinement of the plaintiff, then false imprisonment may have occurred.

For example: A park ranger managing a remote picnic area makes his evening patrol of the area and informs the picnickers that the area closes at 10 p.m. All the recreationists leave the area by 9:30 p.m. except for one group. The leader of the remaining group indicates that "we will leave when we feel like it." The park ranger returns to see if they have left the area at 9:50 p.m. The leader of the remaining group indicates again they "will leave when they feel like it." A very irritated park ranger leaves the picnic area immediately, locking a large iron gate across the roadway. The group is left in the remote area the entire night, unable to leave with their vehicle because of the gate and unable to walk out or call for help on a telephone because of the remote location. Members of the stranded group sue the park ranger and the natural resource agency for false imprisonment, claiming that they were "just kidding around with the ranger, and the ranger overreacted." The group said they were packing up and planning to leave when the ranger came for the last time. The ranger admitted locking the gate five minutes before the 10 p.m. deadline. The leader and his group may have grounds for a false imprisonment suit, even though the ranger believed that they refused to leave at the 10 p.m. closing time.

There are two categories of torts that fit under the category of false imprisonment but are not false imprisonment. They are false arrest and malicious prosecution. False arrest can be defined as an arrest without proper authority. If ill will or malice is proved by the plaintiff, then punitive damages may be awarded to the plaintiff. The tort consists of illegal constraint on a person's personal liberty.

Intentional Infliction of Emotional Distress

The tort of intentional infliction of emotional distress has been developed in the last few decades. It protects people from being subjected to extreme conduct that affects them mentally but not necessarily physically. Assault and battery damages a person physically, and infliction of emotional distress affects people psychologically. Certainly, assault is a threat of physical harm and has psychological effects; battery results in physical harm and also has mental implications.

Intentional infliction of emotional distress may or may not be accompanied by a verbal or written threat. The tort consists of extreme conduct by a defendant resulting in psychological damage. This tort validates and adds credence to the argument that many times words can be more damaging than physical force.

A particularly successful coach said that he felt no stress in his work because his job was to create stress in others. Most of life's challenges are stressful, and when the challenges are met, they provide for life's significant satisfactions. Most recreation and sports management professionals and athletes know that their physical and mental senses are keener and work best under some level of nervous stress. Stress is a tool that can be used for our benefit, yet each of us can only tolerate so much stress before it turns into distress. Psychologists contend that most of the negative aspects of stress are self-inflicted. However, when extreme stress (distress) is created by another person, is outrageous in nature, and causes damage, a plaintiff may have a case of intentional infliction of emotional distress.

The elements of intentional infliction of emotional distress are:

1. An *intentional* or *reckless* act by the defendant,

2. constituting *extreme* or *outrageous* conduct,

3. causing *severe* emotional distress to the plaintiff,

4. resulting in damages.

It is important to note important words (italicized above) in the elements of this tort: intentional, reckless, extreme, outrageous, severe. The words are important in determining if a suit is valid. Just because a coach makes an athlete feel bad, or a supervisor disciplines an employee for something that the employee feels is unfair, the resulting severe emotional distress does not constitute a valid case unless the words intentional, reckless, extreme, and outrageous also apply.

There can be no case or recovery for profanity, obscenity, or verbal abuse without circumstances of aggravation, or for insults, indignities, or threats that are nothing more than annoyances. The plaintiff cannot recover merely because he or she has had his or her feelings hurt.[5]

While we are all entitled to some level of tranquility in our lives, in a court of law the plaintiff will normally have a difficult time proving a case of intentional infliction of emotional distress. The plaintiff must make certain that the circumstances of this case are indeed intentional, outrageous, and constitute extreme conduct.

The following are examples of extreme and outrageous conduct that resulted in a successful intentional infliction of mental distress suits: Cruel prankster who tells a family that their son was killed in a football game, a rejected suitor who tells his ex-girlfriend that her new boyfriend is HIV positive, and a businessman who pretends to be a federal tax auditor and harasses a competitor with threats of fines, jail sentences, and public disgrace. The examples illustrate that suits for intentional infliction of mental distress must have an element of obvious extreme and outrageous conduct element.

Defamation of Character

Our personal reputation is important to our self-esteem, our family, and our profession. Defamation is the invasion of our good name and reputation by untruths. Defamation requires that the lie be spread to a third person. The difference between infliction of mental distress and defamation of character is defined by the fact that the derogatory words and insulting remarks are made to a third person in defamation.

Defamation is divided into two distinct and important categories: libel and slander. Libel relates to written statements, and has expanded to include pictures, signs, statues, motion pictures, and public media broadcasts (radio and TV). Libel is considered the more serious of the two categories.[6] Slander is false oral or spoken words. As such, truth is an absolute defense to defamation.

The elements of defamation are:

1. A false and defamatory statement about another,

2. intentionally published to a third party,

3. which causes injury to another.

The separate torts of defamation and invasion of privacy tend to overlap in the area of right to privacy, but each tort defines a separate right. The right to be left alone relates to the right to privacy, while defamation protects a person's reputation from false statements.

In *Bauer v. Murphy* (1995),[7] a standout female basketball star from the University of Wisconsin sued her coach for defamation of character. The coach allegedly stated at a team meeting that Bauer was "a disgrace to the team and the university." The basketball star Bauer, had been accused by the athletic department of having an "inappropriate relationship" with a male assistant coach. The assistant coach had been dismissed from his position at the university because of the relationship. Bauer emphatically denied that she had an inappropriate relationship with the assistant coach, and the allegations of the athletic department were a lie. She subsequently attacked the professional skill and ability of the coach at a team meeting and resigned from the team. Some time after the incident, the head coach (Murphy) advised a member of the basketball team and a potential roommate of Bauer not to room with a player who had resigned from the team. Bauer, who had filed a defamation suit, amended her complaint accusing the coach of "denying her income by discouraging the player from subleasing part of her apartment." The lower court decided in favor of the defendant coach. Bauer appealed. The appellate court affirmed the decision of the lower court, stating that the statement by the coach, if true or not true, was not per se defamation, because it was a statement of opinion rather than a statement of fact. The appellate court also determined that because Bauer was able to immediately sublease her apartment there was no pecuniary loss.

There are three categories of defamation that the courts have found to be particularly serious:

1. Crime,

2. Loathsome disease, and

3. Business, trade, profession, or office.

Accusing another of a crime imputes a person's reputation and may subject him or her to criminal prosecution. The crime a plaintiff is accused of must violate accepted moral standards of the community. If a coach or recreation manager is accused of child molestation, the results can be devastating to the professional. The simple public pronouncement by a defendant that, "I know enough to put him in jail" may be sufficient to prove a defamation of character case.

While we may think that the loathsome disease category of defamation is an outdated concept, consider the social life of a person unjustly accused of having AIDS. Or if a person is rumored to have a venereal disease or another highly communicable disease, not only is he socially rejected by society, but the stigma of the disease (herpes, syphilis, etc.), particularly in a community with conservative attitudes, casts doubts on his or her character.

Our free enterprise (commercial) system allows individual businesses and professions to compete against one another for customers and profit. The heat of competition sometimes results in degrading other businesses or professions in an inaccurate and dishonest manner. For example, if one health club started a rumor that its competition was about to go bankrupt, the end result could be no new customers and a mass exodus of existing patrons. Lies about businesses can cause a lack of public trust and significant loss of profit and customers. Lies about shortchanging customers, shoddy merchandise, and dangerous facilities could turn customers away.

Some statements may not be defamatory in most circumstances, but under certain conditions be considered damaging. As an example, the statement, "He is all thumbs" is not considered malicious, unless the statement is directed toward a surgeon.

In *Maidman v. Jewish Publications, Inc.* (1960),[8] a newspaper publisher was accused of libel by the plaintiff Michael Maidman, when they reported the prominent politician "was unworthy of his high position, of knowing less about his religion than an adolescent child and of causing all members of his religion to look ridiculous." The editorial appeared in a weekly religious newspaper, the *B'nai B'rith Messenger*, and circulated principally within the Jewish population of Los Angeles, California. The plaintiff claimed that because Maidman was a prominent individual in his community and chairman of the board of a competitive newspaper, the *B'nai B'rith Record*, that the alleged libelous editorial had a divisive and ill will context. The California civil code describes libel as "a false and unprivileged publication by writing, printed picture, effigy or other fixed representation to the eye, which exposed any person to hatred, contempt, ridicule, or obloquy, or which causes him to be shunned or avoided, or which has a tendency to injure him in his occupation." The defense contended that their editorial was simply fair comment, and "it is not only the privilege, but the duty of every citizen and every newspaper in the community to fairly and impartially criticize the faults and misconduct of public officers." Trial court decided in favor of the defendant newspaper. On appeal, the Supreme Court of California determined that the editorial was published primarily because of "hatred or ill will towards the plaintiff" and reversed the decision of the lower court in favor of Maidman. The case was later overruled.[9]

Discussion Questions

1. Explain the difference between negligence and an intentional tort.

2. Describe the elements of "battery" and provide an example of how battery might occur in the "recreation setting."

3. Describe the elements of "defamation" and provide an example of how defamation might occur in the "recreation setting."

Notes

1   *Baugh v. Redmond*, 565 So.2d 953, (La. App.1990).1
2. Black, H. C. (1979). *Black's law dictionary* (5th ed.). St. Paul, MN: West Publishing Co., p. 105.
3. *Hackbart v. Cincinnati Bengals, Inc.*, 601 F.2d 516 (10th Cir. 1979).

4. Remanded means to return to the lower court for further action. The action may include a complete retrial or other specific court considerations.
5. Prosser, W. L. (1971). *Law of torts* (4th ed.). St. Paul MN: West Publishing Co., pp. 54-55.
6. Prosser, W. L. (1971). *Law of torts* (4th ed.). St. Paul, MN: West Publishing Co.
7. *Bauer v. Murphy*, 530 N.W. 2d 1 (Wis. App. 1995).
8. *Maidman v. Jewish Publications, Inc.*, 355 P.2d 265 (Cal. 1960).
9. *Brown v. Kelly Broadcasting Co.*, 48 Cal. 3d 711 (1989).

Chapter Seven

TRESPASS

SECTION 1: TRESPASS TO LAND

The sanctity of property rights has been the center of many personal controversies, feuds, and to a great extent, wars. The right to own, protect, and find security on one's land has been a major tenet of English common law and American jurisprudence since their very inception. Trespass to land involves the invasion of the sanctity of real property. It is a tort where the defendant enters the plaintiff's land, or causes another person or object to enter the plaintiff's land.

The elements of trespass to land are:

1. An intentional act by a defendant,

2. to enter or cause a third party or object to enter,

3. the land in possession of another or causing the act to occur.

The following case illustrates several forms that trespass can take. Trespass is not merely the act of physically stepping onto the property of another.

In *Mantle Ranches v. United States* (1996),[1] the government counter-claimed against Mantle Ranches for damages due to trespass. Mantle Ranches, Inc. owned ranches that were private inholdings within the boundaries of a national park. The Park Service claimed that Mantle was dumping waste into a river running through the park and that contained a critical fish habitat. The government also claimed that Mantle allowed their cows to graze on park property, built private roads on park property, and ran their snowmobiles illegally on park property. The National Park Service relied upon the National Park Service Organic Act as authority to bring the trespass claim. The purpose of the act is to preserve the scenery and natural resources in a protected state for the public to enjoy. The court held that Mantle could continue to enter a portion of the park on snowmobiles where they had been going for many years because they had created "an historic right of access" through many years of use. However, Mantle was ordered to discontinue and clean up its dump along the river on park property.

The act of trespass also affects the standard of care owed to the person entering the land of another as the following case illustrates.

In *Rowland v. City of Corpus Christi* (1981),[2] the plaintiff swimmer broke his neck when he dived from a seawall into a marina breakwaters. He brought suit against the defendant City of Corpus Christi for damages, alleging that the city knew or should have known of the danger and failed to give him proper warning. The defendant city maintained that Rowland was a trespasser and the area was not maintained or advertised for swimming, let alone designated as a diving area. The plaintiff argued that he was an invitee and the city was negligent in its warning of possible dangers. The trial court decided in favor of the plaintiff Rowland, based on the fact that the city maintained dangerous conditions, and the sign "Caution: Deep Water Lower Steps Slippery When Wet" failed to give adequate warning of a dangerous diving condition.

Signs are useful only when they can be clearly seen and understood.

The defendant's attorney made a motion that the court (judge) make a decision in favor of the defendant city not withstanding the verdict of the jury. The judge agreed with the motion and entered judgment for the city. Rowland appealed. The appellate court then had to determine the status of Rowland, whether he was an invitee, permittee, or trespasser. He had not paid a fee, thus eliminating the invitee status, nor did he have any business relationship with the city to qualify him as a permittee. In view of his status as a trespasser, the appellate court affirmed the decision of the judge in favor of the defendant City of Corpus Christi.

No trespassing signs are commonly seen in our society. Most people do not understand the liability ramifications if the sign is ignored. Signs declaring no trespassing are not necessary but are helpful, for a plaintiff to pursue a case in trespass to land. Consider the following hypothetical in the context of trespass.

The Baptist mixed league softball team played the Methodist mixed league softball team in a city league sanctioned and organized by the City Parks and Recreation Department. Sally hit a long drive over the fence in left field, and Jimmy ran onto the private property to retrieve the ball from the owner's flower beds. The property was posted with No Trespassing signs along the entire length of the property. Because hitting an object into the field and running after the ball constituted unauthorized entry, the property owner, should he or she choose to do so, could pursue a suit of land trespass. The suit would likely name as defendants the individual who hit the ball (Sally) into his garden, the person who voluntarily entered the property (Jimmy), and the sponsors of the activity, the Methodist Church, the Baptist Church, and the City Parks and Recreation Department.

Trespass to land includes the area beneath the surface as well as the air above the land. If another party owns the mineral rights, the exploitation of those minerals can be exercised with certain precautions by the owner of the mineral rights. Mining operations or oil exploration cannot take place under the land owned by another without permission and compensation to the owner with property rights. Additionally, liability might exist for a golf course where balls are hit from the course onto the property of an adjacent landowner.

The area above the land has to be considered with good common sense. If someone wants to place an electrical transmission line above your property, he must have an easement or right-of-way. If it is in the public interest to have a public utility corridor across the land of a private owner, the public interest can be served through a condemnation[3] proceeding. Compensation must be made to the land owner if a right-of-way is obtained by condemnation.

An aircraft flying high over your property would not be considered a trespass to land. Some states do not award trespass damages for any flight occurring above minimum flight altitudes dictated by the C.A.B. See *U.S. v. Causby*, (1946).[4] A very low flying aircraft or helicopter that significantly disturbs the tranquility of the property, however, may be considered a trespass.

In *Highline School District Number 401 v. Port of Seattle* (1976),[5] the plaintiff school district maintained that the defendant Port of Seattle, who manages the SEATAC airport, interfered with their property rights. The school district was forced to build 14 new schools away from airport approaches because the level of noise from the aircraft made it impossible to hear teachers and conduct school when aircraft were overhead. The plaintiff was seeking compensation for interference with their property rights. The airport had been at the site for a number of years, but in the last three years there had been a dramatic increase of air traffic. In addition, jet engine noise became more common in air travel. The trial court decided in favor of the Port of Seattle. The Supreme Court affirmed the decision of the lower court, stating that "trespass doctrine protects a landowner's interest in exclusive possession, not his right to be free from interference in the use and enjoyment of his property."

In lieu of No Trespassing signs, there are certain categories of activities that by their nature invite entry onto private property. If the property has a sidewalk leading to the front door, it is an invitation for people to come to the door to conduct business or inquiry. A mailbox authorizes the mailman to deliver mail. Water, sewage, gas, or electrical service allows the utility company to maintain the lines and read the meters. There are a number of special categories such as tax assessment and fire protection that authorize property entry as a function of government. Legal entry onto real property can be made in connection with a criminal investigation if the situation includes hot pursuit[6] of a person who allegedly committed a felony or with a court-authorized search warrant.

The plaintiff must prove actual damages to prevail in a trespass to chattel case. Nominal damages[7] cannot be awarded. This is not true in cases of real property (land) trespass. While there is no apparent reason why there is a different standard of damages between land and personal property trespass, the variance does exist.

Land trespass by adults, receives very little compassion by the courts. However, trespassing children, particularly those who are very young, may have special privileges not afforded to adults. Most privilege cases involve trespassers who are less than 12 years of age.[8]

An adult trespasser who enters or remains upon land in the possession of another without permission to do so,[9] is subject to suit. Children may be drawn to private property because of a special feature, and must be protected from harm under the doctrine of attractive nuisance.[10] Small children may not be liable as trespassers, but rather, if an accident resulting in death or injury occurs, the property owner may be held liable. An owner of property may have attractive man-made or man-controlled attractions such as animals, ponds, swimming pools, and so forth, on his property that are appealing to children.

The courts have held that the doctrine of attractive nuisance does not apply to natural conditions such as hills, lakes, and rivers.

In order to have an attractive nuisance case, the plaintiff must show:

1. The owner of the property had knowledge or should have had knowledge of the condition of his property.

2. Children are attracted to the property, or it is foreseeable that children would be attracted to the property.

3. Features on the property would be perceived as being inherently dangerous to children by the average adult person.

4. The owner of the property failed to exercise reasonable care to protect the children.

The doctrine of attractive nuisance is not applicable to children who have been invited to the area, only to those who are trespassing. The land owner is subject to negligence actions by those who may be injured on his property after they have been invited. The doctrine of attractive nuisance has only limited applicability to open parks and recreation and sports facilities. Attractive nuisance situations applicable to parks and recreation and sports facilities usually involve closed facilities such as closed swimming pools and golf courses, buildings left unlocked, and other unattended physical facilities. An example of a typical attractive nuisance suit involves small children gaining access through an unlocked or damaged gate surrounding a swimming pool that was closed for the winter, and a subsequent drowning in the residual pool water.

In *Skaggs v. Junis* (1960),[11] a minor received serious injuries (quadriplegia) when he struck his head on a submerged tree stump in an artificial pond maintained by the defendant Junis. After the pond's construction, some people would ask permission to swim or fish at the site. Some people simply trespassed onto the land and used the area for recreation pursuits. The defendant Junis allowed those asking to use the area to do so without a fee and said nothing to the trespassers. The plaintiff alleged that the defendant was willfully and wantonly negligent in maintaining an attractive nuisance (pond) that was used by the trespasser Skaggs. The plaintiff was 16 years old at the time of the accident and heard about the pond from two friends who had been given permission by Junis to use the area. During the summer, the plaintiff had visited the pond 15 times prior to the accident and was seen by Junis approximately six times. The trial court's decision was for the defendant Junis. Skaggs appealed. The appellate court reversed and remanded the lower court's decision, determining that there was a cause of action for negligence in leaving stumps underwater and maintaining an attractive nuisance.

Trespass to land is common where lands are unfenced and unmarked. Intentional trespass by public employees or private individuals upon private lands or property can lead to serious legal problems. Uninvited use (trespass) on closed and locked sports fields or facilities is common, but certainly not appropriate. Warning (no trespass) signs should be utilized when land and property owners do not want people using or occupying their land and facilities.

SECTION 2: TRESPASS TO CHATTEL AND CONVERSION

Trespass to chattel and conversion are discussed together, because the differences between the two categories relate to the seriousness of the trespass rather than any substantive differences. Trespass to chattel[12] involves the interference with the plaintiff's right to use his or her personal property, while conversion involves the complete control of personal property by the defendant.

The elements of a cause of action for trespass to chattel are:

1. An intentional act by the defendant,

2. to interfere with the personal property of the plaintiff,

3. which act did interfere with the plaintiff's right to possession,

4. causing damages.

There are many considerations or aspects to trespass to chattel. The tort can include temporarily using, taking, destroying, or damaging goods, abusing animals, interfering with ownership, and unpermitted use. The plaintiff should have been in possession of the chattel prior to the trespass, but that is not always necessary if the plaintiff was entitled to possession, as would be the case of assets given in a will or a mortgagee after a default.

If a person owned a basketball, and another person temporarily used the ball, denying the rightful owner the use of the ball, even though the person taking the ball intended to return the ball, a trespass to chattel occurred. Interference with the rightful owner's enjoyment and use of the basketball was denied. Intent to do wrong is not the primary issue. The key fact is that the owner was denied use. Trespass to chattel is a tort of intentional interference.[13]

Conversion

Conversion is a very serious trespass to chattel. The plaintiff is completely denied access or use of his or her property. The seriousness of this tort entitles the plaintiff to claim the full value of the property, as well as damages, such as loss of income or additional costs resulting from denying the plaintiff access to his property. If tools used to provide a means of living were taken, then compensation for the lost wages would also be appropriate. As common law, the tort of conversion occurs when the defendant substantially interferes with the plaintiff's ownership of the property to the extent that it is fair to require the defendant to pay the plaintiff the full value of the property. Substantial interference may amount to an exercise of ownership resulting in the exclusion of ownership rights of the true owner. Or the interference may involve the alteration or destruction of the property. The main distinction between this tort and trespass to property is the fact that the interference is so substantial that it results in an action for the full value of the property. The following scenario serves as an illustration for this concept.

A city recreation department sold an unused gymnasium building to a manufacturing company located adjacent to the gymnasium. The manufacturing company planned to use the gymnasium as an employee health and fitness center. The city was using the building as a storage facility prior to the sale. The city did not remove its stored materials from the building after the sale. After repeated attempts to get the materials removed, the city told the company they did not have an available building to store the material and the city was in the process of building a facility. A city official said, "It will take about a year to finish the building, then and only then will they move the materials." The manufacturing company could likely institute a successful suit against the city for conversion.

In *Plymouth Fertilizer Company, Inc. v. Balmer* (1986),[14] the plaintiff owned gas and mineral rights under its 160-acre farm. Balmer had a gas well drilled and subsequently capped it, because it did not produce in commercial quantities. The Plymouth Fertilizer Company rented the farm, now in an estate, tapped the well, and used the gas for heating the house and drying crops. The defendant fertilizer company argued that the gas was part of the property rental, though not specified in the rental contract. The owners argued that it was a flagrant case of conversion. The trial court decided in favor the defendant fertilizer company. The plaintiff appealed. The appellate court determined that natural gas is property that can be converted if it was extracted and consumed without knowledge or consent of an owner.

A conversion had occurred. The court ordered the fertilizer company to pay $141,808.95 for conversion of gas, the commercial rate for an estimated 5,400 million cubic feet used by the defendants.

Society sometimes measures a person's worth by the possessions he owns. Most people place high value on their home, automobile, jewelry, and other possessions. Because of society's standards and ethical considerations, the courts have determined that unauthorized use of another's possessions can result in both criminal and civil legal action. The use of another's personal property without permission can result in serious legal problems.

Discussion Questions

1. What is attractive nuisance, and why is it important for the recreation manager to know about this concept?

2. Describe trespass and provide an example in the recreation context.

3. What is the difference between trespass, trespass to chattel, and conversion?

Notes

1. *Mantle Ranches v. United States,* 945 F.Supp. 1449 (D. Colo.1996).
2. *Rowland v. City of Corpus Christi,* 620 S.W.2d 930 (Tex. App.1981).
3. Inverse condemnation—the legal process of taking private property for the public good through the power of eminent domain.
4. *U.S. v. Causby,* 328 U.S. 256 (1946).
5. *Highline School District Number 401 v. Port of Seattle,* No.; 43804, Supreme Court of Washington, 87 Wn.2d 6; 548. P.2d 1085, 1976 Wash.
6. Hot pursuit refers to the right of an officer of the law to enter private property without a warrant if he witnessed a person he was pursuing enter onto the private property or dwelling. This principle also allows police to chase people across state lines to make an arrest if they are in close pursuit and the adjacent state has similar criminal statutes. Also see model legislation referred to as the Uniform Extraterritorial Arrest on Fresh Pursuit Act.
7. Nominal in this context means damages that are a trifling sum where there is no substantial loss to be compensated.

8. Kaiser, R. A., (1986). *Liability and law in recreation, parks, and sports,* Englewood Cliffs, NJ: Prentice Hall.

9. Restatement of Torts (2nd) §329.

10. The doctrine of attractive nuisance is that a property owner has the responsibility to determine if any man-made feature on his property would be attractive to play and dangerous to children. When identified, he would have the duty to protect the trespassing children from the danger.

11. *Skaggs v. Junis,* 190 N.E.2d 731 (III. App. 1960).

12. Chattel means an article of personal property as opposed to real property. It may refer to animate as well as inanimate property. *Black's law dictionary*, (5th ed.), St. Paul, MN: West Publishing Co., p. 215.

13. Prosser, W. L., (1971) *Law of torts* (4th ed.). St. Paul, MN: West Publishing Co., p. 77. 5.

14. *Plymouth Fertilizer Company v. Balmer,* 488 N.E.2nd 1129 (lnd. App.1986).

Chapter Eight

DEFENSES TO INTENTIONAL TORTS

When a person is accused of committing an intentional tort, it does not mean the defendant is automatically liable.[1] The defendant may avoid liability in intentional tort cases if:

1. The defendant can prove that the plaintiff failed to establish all the elements for the tort at issue; or
2. The defendant has a privilege that justifies his/her action.

There are a number of legal defenses to intentional torts. These include the following:[2]

1. Consent
2. Self-defense
3. Defense of others
4. Defense of property
5. Recapture of chattel
6. Forcible entry upon land
7. Necessity
8. Arrest
9. Discipline
10. Justification

Consent

Consent is technically not a defense, but rather a principle of law that is used as a defense. The consent of the plaintiff will usually avoid liability[3] unless consent is obtained through duress or force. If a person voluntarily agrees to participate in a boxing match and is injured, he cannot claim battery. If a plaintiff invites someone onto his or her property, she cannot claim a land trespass. Consent is subdivided into two broad categories: Express Consent and Implied Consent.

Express Consent

Express consent occurs when someone tells another, "Just try to hit me with the baseball, you have my permission." There is a willingness to consent to the conduct of the defendant. The exceptions would include an invitation to commit an intentional tort by a person with impaired judgment, such as a minor, an infant, or an adult person with a mental impairment who lacks responsible judgment. The mentally impaired would include an intoxicated person or an individual who is mentally incapable of understanding the consequences of his or her permission. Additionally, express consent might come in written form. For example, a homeowner who lives adjacent to a golf course might consent in writing when buying a house or property to having golf balls come onto her property.

Implied Consent

Implied consent does not involve direct oral or written permission, but rather it is manifested by signs, actions, or facts. It can also be implied by inaction or silence, which leads to the assumption that consent has been given.[4] For example, an adult athletic team is receiving its annual physicals. The physical includes blood tests. A team member, by offering his arm to the nurse taking the blood sample, implies consent to have his blood taken. His silence and the gesture of presenting his arm constitute implied consent. A formal or oral contract (agreement) to maintain a private lawn or garden also includes implied consent to enter private property.

In *Turpin v. Shoemaker* (1968),[5] three men were drinking alcoholic beverages and playing cards at Shoemaker's home. Toward the end of the evening, two men decided to participate in a quick draw contest. Turpin was given a pistol from the third member of the party. Turpin's weapon was thoroughly checked to ensure it had no rounds of ammunition in the chambers of the pistol. The cylinder of the pistol was then rotated again to check for live rounds. Shoemaker unloaded his own revolver, a Ruger single-action revolver, and put the ammunition in his pocket. The Ruger is designed in a manner to require each cylinder to be unloaded separately. Shoemaker could not spin the cylinder to see that all ammunition had been unloaded. The contestants stood six feet apart to see who could draw and "click" their guns first. On the second draw, Shoemaker's weapon fired, killing Turpin. Turpin's widow sued. Shoemaker argued that Turpin had consented to the contest. The trial court determined that Turpin had indeed agreed to the quick-draw contest and decided in favor of defendant Shoemaker. Turpin's widow appealed. The Missouri Supreme Court reversed the decision and remanded it back to the trial court stating that "voluntary consent to danger requires knowledge of a known and appreciated risk. The decedent (Turpin) was unaware that his opponent's revolver contained a live cartridge."

Self-Defense

The right of self-defense allows a person to use reasonable force to protect himself. Self-defense is usually a defense for assault and battery but may be used as a defense in false imprisonment, land trespass, or conversion. People are given the opportunity to protect themselves when they believe there is danger. It is not necessary for people to be physically harmed before they take defensive action. People can defend themselves when there is the threat of physical harm.

Self-defense is appropriate only when there is an imminent danger of harm, and the level of force exerted must be consistent with the danger. If a camper observes someone stealing his lunch, he cannot justify a self defense plea when the response to the incident is shooting and wounding the thief. Deadly force is allowed only when the circumstances indicate that the person is in danger of being killed or receiving serious injuries.[6] It should be noted that a defendant has no specific duty to retreat in his own home. Some courts have indicated that retreat is the most prudent method to avoid violent reaction to an intentional tort; however, the majority of court decisions have ruled that a person does not have to retreat from a threatening situation.

Defense of Others

A defendant is allowed to intervene and defend a third party. The defendant is allowed to apply as much force as the law would allow the third party to use in his or her own self defense. In most cases, if the defendant makes a mistake and goes to the aid of the aggressor, he will lose the privilege of using defense of others.

Defense of others is applicable and best applied when the party defended is well-known to the defendant, a relative, member of their immediate family, or employee.[7] The defense must be applied immediately as part of the incident. Verbal threats to another person made in the past do not justify intervention by the third party, because other legal alternatives are generally available.

Defense of Property and Chattel

If the plaintiff is attempting to steal, damage, or destroy property, the owner of that property (defendant) can use appropriate and reasonable force to protect his or her land or personal property. The reasonableness of the force will be determined by the judge or the jury. There are certain limitations as to the amount and type of force used, much like the limits set in cases of self defense. The law has always set the value of human safety above that of real property, and to greater extent, the value of real property above that of chattel.

The privilege to defend property is not dependent upon the real necessity of the situation, but rather that of the reasonable man doctrine, or that which would have been done under the same circumstances.[8] Force can be used to expel or force a plaintiff to abandon the defendant's personal property as well as leave the premises. Deadly force cannot be used in defense of property or chattel. The applicable law of your jurisdiction should always be consulted before determining the proper method of protecting life and property.

Prior to using any force in defending property, the defendant must first request that the plaintiff leave or return the defendant's property. Caution must be exercised to ensure that the plaintiff does not have legal right to the property. If the plaintiff has a right to ownership, then the doctrine of defense of property as a defense does not apply.

Personal property that has been taken from the defendant can be recaptured, providing the defendant acts promptly upon receiving information that the property has been taken or observing his or her property in the possession of the plaintiff.

In some cases, under extenuating circumstances, the defendant may not have a privilege to expel a plaintiff. Tossing a stowaway off a truck or train when it is moving or a trespasser out of a building when the weather conditions would likely result in death would not be a privilege.

Watch dogs present a particular problem to the owners. Dogs cannot judge the nature of the intrusion. If a dog is used to protect property, yet the owner maintains walkways, or easily accessible fences and gates, a sign must warn of the presence of the watch dog. If those entering the property, even for illegal purposes, are attacked by an unknown dog, the trauma of the attack by a dog and the possible physical damage done may exceed the limits set by the court as to what would be an acceptable level of response for petty theft or property trespass. If the dog attacks small children or those entering the property for legitimate purposes, the property owner could be subject to both civil and criminal action.

In *State v. Lumpkin* (1993),[9] an undercover police officer purchased $20 worth of crack cocaine from a house in Kansas City, Missouri. He returned a couple of hours later with a search warrant, backed up by a dozen officers from the tactical response squad. He knocked on the door to present the search warrant. Lumpkin answered with a gun in his hand. When the plainclothes undercover police officer tried to present the search warrant, another man came to the door and struck the officer with his fist. Lumpkin then shot the officer, shattering his shoulder bone, and slammed the door shut. Lumpkin was arrested, tried, and convicted by a jury for assault and armed criminal action. He was sentenced as a prior and persistent offender to consecutive terms of 20 and 10 years imprisonment, respectively. He appealed on the grounds that he was defending his property and chattel. The State Supreme Court affirmed the trial courts conviction stating that *defense of premises* can only be used as a defense when the entry is illegal and unlawful.

Forcible Entry Upon Land

Certain situations exist that require a rightful owner of the land to eject a possessor or occupier of the land by force. This force, however, may technically constitute assault and battery. This defense is an historic defense from English common law that is seldom used today. One of the situations that may activate this defense is when a landlord defendant forcibly removes a tenant from a room or house because of lack of payment. Some force would be justified in such cases, when proper legal notices have been given to the tenant. Some states, however, significantly limit this privilege and therefore a determination of what is allowed in a particular jurisdiction must be first ascertained.

The rightful owner of the property must first try to gain possession of his land peaceably or use law enforcement personnel to accomplish the repossession of the land. It should be noted however, that an owner generally cannot enter his leased or rented property without the consent of the possessor, when no violation of the rental or lease agreement has occurred. The lease or rental contract should specifically detail when the property owner has the right to inspect or enter the land and premises.

In *Berg v. Wiley* (1978),[10] a tenant restaurant owner sued the landlord on a claim of wrongful eviction, contract violation, and negligence. The landlord counterclaimed for damages to the premises. Three years prior to the disagreement, the landlord, Wiley, executed a five-year lease of the property to Berg for use as a restaurant. The lease specified that no changes in the building would be made without specific approval of the landlord. Wiley also reserved the right to take possession of the property should the lessee fail to meet the conditions of the lease. Wiley objected to modifications that Berg was required to make as a result of an inspection by the Minnesota Department of Health. While the restaurant was closed for remodeling to meet the state's department of health standards, Wiley entered the premises accompanied by a policeman and a locksmith and changed the locks without Berg's knowledge. Berg was locked out with more than two years remaining on her lease. Berg sued Wiley for damages for lost property, damage to chattels, intentional infliction of emotional distress, and other damages based upon wrongful eviction and contract violation. Wiley claimed that Berg damaged his property, and he was forced to enter the leased property to protect his interest. The trial court decided in favor of the restaurant owner Berg, stating that the tenant did not surrender or abandon the premises so as to justify the landlord's conduct. The Supreme Court of Minnesota affirmed the decision of the lower court.

Necessity

A defendant may have the privilege to injure an innocent plaintiff when there is a chance for an imminent and serious injury to his person, others, his property, or property of others. There are two types of necessity defenses recognized by the law—Public and Private. Acts done on behalf of the general public are privileged. Private necessity is also privileged, but the defendant may be liable to compensate the plaintiff for injuries.

The necessity defense is closely related to self defense, but differs from it because the plaintiff is not the aggressor or a wrongdoer.[11] The defendant is, in fact, injuring an innocent person to save himself or his property. For example:

- A boat is sinking and goods need to be thrown overboard to save the ship and its passengers. The defendant is destroying an innocent person's property.

- To stop the spread of a forest fire, a defendant may have to cut down the trees and destroy houses in the fire's path in order to stop the fire from destroying additional land and property.

When no public interest is evident and a defendant injures another to protect his own interests, the application of this defense is limited. When the defendant's life or property is at stake, the defendant may trespass on another's property. This privilege is limited and partial, and does not allow the defendant to cause significant damage to the plaintiff's property.[12]

In *State v. Esslinger* (1984),[13] the defendant was convicted of two counts of first-degree murder and receiving stolen property. He received two life sentences and one five-year sentence, to run concurrently. Esslinger appealed the trial court verdict, claiming he attacked the two men to prevent them from committing a murder and that his motives were noble. He said he acted out of necessity to prevent a felony. The appellate court's review of the facts of the case disclosed the following:

Esslinger escaped from jail and stole a car and three pairs of jeans. The next evening he was seen with the two murder victims, all three were drinking alcoholic beverages. One pair of the stolen jeans was found on a fence line near where the victims' bodies were found, the defendant was wearing one of the pairs of stolen jeans when arrested, and the defendant had bragged about hitting two men with a tire iron in a fight.

The Supreme Court of North Dakota affirmed the judgment of the lower court based upon the facts of the case. It further stated that the noble intention was lost in the real facts of the case.

Discipline

In an era where child and spouse abuse are part of the daily headlines in newspapers, discipline takes on a significantly different meaning than it did in the past. In the distant past, husbands were privileged to discipline their wives and children. Now, every state has laws specifically designed to protect spouses and children from excessive use of force.

Parents are allowed to confine, chastise, and use corporal punishment to enforce family discipline within specific limits set by the law. School teachers and coaches, in the absence of parents, are privileged to temporarily confine or restrict the freedom of movement of children who have misbehaved. The fact that the parents send children to school gives teachers and coaches the same privilege as parents to maintain order, decorum, and morale.[14] It is when corporal punishment is administered in the school or sports setting that problems arise. Excessive physical force is difficult to define; however, the courts will determine if the force used matches the offense. When bruises, abrasions, or worse occur, the courts have determined that the corporal punishment exceeded that privilege. Children generally cannot sue their parents for civil tort when they believe excessive force was used. Actual child abuse cases are generally handled by the legal authorities as a criminal act.

Categories of privileged discipline include parents, guardians, teachers, coaches, military officers, jailers, penal institutions, situations at sea (maritime), or any classification when *in loco parentis*[15] applies. The following case illustrates a situation t hat arose when a coach disciplined a student-athlete.

In *Adams v. Hazelwood* (1999),[15] a high school football player sued his coach for an injury he received while carrying out a punishment imposed by his coach. The player had damaged part of the football field as part of a senior prank. The coach found out about it and disciplined the student by having him cut weeds beneath the stadium bleachers with a pair of scissors. While cutting the weeds, the plaintiff claimed to have injured his wrist. He then sued the coach. The coach claimed he was immune from suit under Georgia law that grants immunity to coaches unless they act with actual malice or ill will toward their athletes. After several appeals, the case went before the Georgia Supreme Court. The court could find no evidence that the coach had acted with a deliberate intent to commit a wrongful act or to harm the plaintiff. Therefore, summary judgment was entered in favor of the coach.

A thorough understanding of the defenses to intentional torts provides the recreation and sports professional with an understanding of how to avoid intentional tort suits. While people do not have the right to lie, steal, destroy, assault, batter, or defame, there are circumstances provided by law that allow us to protect others and our property.

Discussion Question

1. Describe, for each of the listed defenses, the type of intentional tort for which the defense can be raised and how the defense might act as a protection from liability.

Notes

1. Rae, N., Landau, N., & Hartmann, C.(1980), *Private law: An introduction to the law of torts.* Center for Legal Studies, Antioch Law School.
2. The defenses listed are those indicated in Chapter 4 of Prosser, William L., *Law of torts* (5th ed.), p. 98.
3. Prosser, W. T. (1971). *Law of torts* (4th ed.). St. Paul, MN: West Publishing Co., p. 101.
4. *Black's law dictionary,* (5th ed.), St. Paul, MN: West Publishing Co., p. 276.
5. *Turpin v. Shoemaker,* 427 S.W.2d 485 (Mo.1968).
6. Rae, N., St. Landau, N., & Hartman, C.(1980). *Private law: An introduction to the law of torts.* Center for Legal Studies.
7. *Black's law dictionary* (5th ed.), St. Paul, MN: West Publishing Co., p. 1077.
8. Reasonable man doctrine—The standard of a reasonable man under the same circumstances, including foreseeability considerations—*Black's law dictionary* (5th ed.), St. Paul, MN: West Publishing Co., p. 1138.
9. *State v. Lumpkin,* 850 S.W.2d 388 (Mo.App.1993).
10. *Berg v. Wiley,* 264 N.W.2d 145 (Minn. 1978).
11. Prosser, W. T. (1971). *Law of torts* (4th ed.). St. Paul, MN: West Publishing Co., p. 125.
12. Prosser, W. T. (1971). *Law of torts* (4th ed.). St. Paul, MN: West Publishing Co., p. 127.
13. *State v. Esslinger,* 357 N.W.2d 525 (S.D.1984).
14. Prosser, W. T. (1971). *Law of torts* (4th ed.). St. Paul, MN: West Publishing Co., p.136.
15. *Adams v. Hazelwood,* 520 S.E.2d 896 (Ga. 1999).

Part Four

———————————

CONSTITUTIONAL RIGHTS

Chapter Nine

HUMAN RIGHTS LIABILITY

What does the Constitution of the United States[1] have to do with recreation, swimming pools, playgrounds, sports, and tourism? The answer is everything. Recreation, sports, and tourism flourish in a free society where people can utilize their leisure in the manner that is best suited to their lifestyles. In our democratic society, the Constitution seeks to provide the citizens with a means to establish justice … insure domestic tranquility … promote general welfare, and secure the blessings of liberty … (words from the Preamble of the Constitution of the United States). It is by understanding the words found in the Preamble that we start to understand the purpose of recreation and sports in a democratic society. It should also be remembered that many of the early 1950s and 1960s civil rights issues related to racial discrimination in public recreation facilities, such as swimming pools and parks.

There are a number of broad rights that all citizens enjoy, all related to recreation, sports, and tourism. They include:

- THE RIGHT OF PERSONAL FREEDOM—This right includes:
  - Freedom of Movement—We may go camping, travel with a group, be a tourist, and so forth, all without governmental permission.
  - Freedom of Speech—We may disagree with decisions, petition for change, and express our displeasure.
  - Freedom of Association—We may join teams, and enjoy friendships and associations.
  - Freedom of Religious Belief—We may practice our own belief system, worshiping as we please.

- CIVIL RIGHTS[2]—We may be free in recreation pursuits from discrimination of race, color, creed, religion, national origin, gender, and age.

- RIGHT OF DUE PROCESS[3]—People cannot interfere and intrude in our lives without first proceeding in a legal and equitable manner.

- RIGHT TO PERSONAL SAFETY—This right includes: The right to personal safety and protection of ourselves and our property. We may bear arms, protect ourselves from attack by others, and protect our property and families. Personal safety is a primary right.

- RIGHT TO ENJOY A GOOD REPUTATION—This right includes:

  - Right of Privacy—others cannot intrude into our lives by divulging private information in a public manner.
  - Right to Defend Yourself—you have access to a court of law to defend yourself from false and damaging accusations and be tried before a jury of your peers.
  - Right to be Secure in our Own Property (Fifth Amendment)—This right includes:
    - Right to contract with others for goods and services.
    - Right to own property.
    - Right of due process for government to enter property, conduct searches, and proceed in administrative matters.
    - Right to be fairly compensated when the government creates easements or takes property for public purposes or good.

The following cases illustrate what happens when one's property right is challenged.

In *Loveladies Harbor, Inc v. United States* 1994,[4] a developer sought a fill permit from the U.S. Army Corps of Engineers under Section 404 of the Clean Water Act.[5] After many years of negotiations and delays, the Corps of Engineers denied the developer's permit claiming that they were protecting a wetland. The developer then sued, claiming that the federal government violated his constitutional rights by denying him a permit to build on his own land and the Corp's action in denying the permit was in fact a taking of land, protected under the Fifth Amendment to the U.S. Constitution. The trial court (District Court) determined there had been a taking and decided in favor of the developer. The plaintiff developer was awarded $2,658 million, the fair market value of the land and $13,500 for the value of the permit denial. The government appealed. The appeals court affirmed the lower court's decision in favor of the plaintiff, stating that the "plaintiff had shown that their private interest in developing and utilizing their property outweighs the public value in preserving these wetlands."

A parallel case, *Lucus v. South Carolina Coastal Council* (1992),[6] was decided by the U.S. Supreme Court two years before the decision in Loveladies. Plaintiff Lucus had purchased two lots on the ocean with the intent of building two homes, one for him and one to sell. Between the time he purchased the property and the time he was to build, the state of South Carolina enacted legislation protecting the fragile ecology of the state's beach and dune areas. The state denied Lucus a building permit. Lucus claimed that the economic value of his original investment had been destroyed by the new state statutes. After being denied compensation for the alleged violation of his property rights by the South Carolina court system, he appealed to the U.S. Supreme Court. The U.S. Supreme Court decided in favor of the plaintiff Lucus, and stated that based upon the facts of the case, a taking occurred when the government denied the building permit. Therefore, the state was required to provide compensation to the landowner.

Should a recreation, sports, or tourism professional violate the basic constitutional rights of others, he or she may be sued. If someone violates the constitutional rights of recreation and sports professionals, they may sue. The courts consider the violation of constitutionally guaranteed rights a very serious matter.

The Constitution of the United States provides the framework that guarantees all citizens the lifestyle of free choice and movement. When federal constitutional questions and issues arise, the lower courts deal with the question and render judgment as to its constitutionality. If an appeal of the lower court's decision is made to the Supreme Court, the Supreme Court will issue a *writ of certiorari*,[7] which is a discretionary device to choose the cases it wishes to hear. The Supreme Court cases set national legal precedent, and its decisions reflect upon the political, social, economic, and religious sentiment of the era in which the decision was rendered. Some Supreme Court decisions have set legal precedent and effective case law that have remained unchanged and effective case law for over 200 years.

Each of the 50 states has its own state constitution. State constitutional questions are treated essentially in the same manner as the federal courts handle U.S. constitutional questions, except they are tried in the state court systems.

An example of a State Constitutional case is *Semore v. Pool* (1990).[8] In this case, the plaintiff Semore brought suit against his former employer, KerrMcGee Chemical Corporation, for violating his constitutional rights of privacy as provided in the California Constitution.[9] The company conducted random pupillary reaction eye tests to test employees for drug use. All employees were given the drug test, but the plaintiff refused to consent to the test and was immediately dismissed for insubordination. He sued Pool, chief executive officer of the KerrMcGee Chemical Corporation, for violating his constitutional rights of privacy.

The defendant chemical corporation argued that Semore had no constitutionally protected right to refuse to undergo a nonintrusive and simple eye reaction test requested by his employer. The defendant claimed the tests were necessary to protect company interests in safety, environmental protection, and quality control. The trial court decided in favor of the defendant chemical company. The appeals court reversed the lower court's decision in favor of the plaintiff Semore, stating that while protecting company interests is a legitimate reason for drug testing, the tests themselves threaten an individual's security and must be part of the basic employee contract and disclosed in pre-employment interviews. It further stated that constitutional rights to privacy apply to private employers as well as governmental agencies.

Speaking of the importance of the Bill of Rights[10] in the lives of U.S. citizens, U.S. Supreme Court Justice Hugo Black wrote:

> In my judgment, the people of no nation can lose their liberty so long as a Bill of Rights like ours survives and its basic purposes are conscientiously interpreted, enforced, and respected so as to afford continuous protection against old as well as new devices and practices which might thwart those purposes.[11]

Conservative judges will render conservative decisions, and liberal judges will render liberal decisions within the framework and context of the Constitution and the common law. While the Constitution is changed only when it is formally amended, the interpretation of the language of the document varies from time to time.

Many Supreme Court decisions are not particularly popular with the general public. The Constitution was never intended as a great protective force for the majority population in a democracy; but rather, a protection for those disenfranchised or in a minority status, to ensure that their rights are not infringed upon by the majority. The majority has the power to enact laws, regulations, and ordinances that benefit the majority. These laws, however, may infringe upon the rights of the minority. The Constitution allows those being subjected to what they believe to be oppressive laws or policies to have redress in the courts.[12]

All citizens will at some time in their lives be classified in a minority status. A person's minority status may be the result of age, religion, economics, race, creed, or gender. The Constitution of the United States applies directly to the field of recreation and sports in that it provides for justice and rights to all participants.

Constitutional questions arise continuously from recreation and sports-associated activities. As an example, the question of drug tests for high school athletes was taken before the Supreme Court in 1995 in the case of *Vernonia School District Acton v. Acton* (1995).[13] The suit began when seventh grader James Action was barred from his junior high football team for refusing to undergo drug urinalysis. The Vernonia School Board required student athletes to undergo random drug testing throughout the season of their sport.

Teachers and some parents blamed student drug use, particularly among student athletes, for an increase in unruly behavior in school. Arrest statistics in the community appeared to validate their concern. Teachers and parents noted that student athletes were setting a poor example for the rest of the students because of alleged heavy drug use among them. Plaintiff James Acton's parents, Wayne and Judy Acton, sued the school district on behalf of their son. The Actons claimed their son was an honor student who had never been in any trouble, and the drug-testing amounted to an unconstitutional search and invasion of privacy. The trial court decided in favor of the plaintiff Acton. The defendant school district appealed. The appellate court reversed the decision in favor of the school district. The plaintiff Acton appealed the decision to the U.S. Supreme Court.

On June 26, 1995, the United States Supreme Court, in a six-to-three decision, decided for the defendant school district. Associate Justice Scalia wrote for the court,[14] that:

> (D)eterring drug use by our nation's school children is at least as important as enhancing enforcement of the nation's laws against the importation of drugs. It seems to us (the Supreme Court) self-evident that a drug problem largely fueled by the role model effect of athletes' drug use ... is effectively addressed by making sure that athletes do not use drugs.

The Court determined that public schools can require drug tests for athletes, whether or not they are suspected users. It reasoned that the right to privacy is sometimes overshadowed by the fight against illegal drugs and the harmful implications of youthful drug users. The ruling involved mandatory drug tests for athletes in an Oregon school district; however, because it was a U.S. Supreme Court decision, drug testing laws will likely be changed, and the principles of the Acton case can be applied nationwide.

It is a direct responsibility of all recreation, sports, and, tourism professionals to protect the human rights of all participants. Historical abuses and traditional American values of fairness and ethical behavior provide the basis of human rights. All citizens should have the right to own property and pursue legitimate activities free from excessive governmental limitations and restrictions. The Constitution of the United States guarantees the rights related to citizens' personal freedoms.

Discussion Questions

1. Provide two examples of how constitutional issues arise in the recreation, sport and tourism context.

2. List the broad rights that all U.S. citizens enjoy.

3. Explain in the context of recreation, sport, or tourism, the application of one of these rights.

Notes

1. The Constitution is the fundamental law that governs a nation or state. In this text, it refers to the United States Constitution with its seven original articles established in 1789 along with all ratified amendments. It is the charter that allows the government to function with the concurrence of the people.
2. Civil rights or civil liberties are personal rights guaranteed and protected by the U.S. Constitution. They provide the citizens with natural rights. A series of Civil Rights Acts were enacted following the Civil War and more recently in 1957, 1964, and 1990. Such acts prohibit discrimination based on race, color, age, gender, or religion.
3. Due process clauses are found in two locations in the Constitution: the Fifth Amendment (protects people from the excesses of the Federal Government) and the 14th Amendment (protects people from the excesses of the State Government).

4. *Loveladies Harbor Inc. v. United States*, 28 F.3d 1171 (U.S. App. 1994).
5. Clean Water Act, Public Law 92500 § 5, 86 Stat. 884 (Oct 18, 1972) amending the Federal Water Pollution Control Act (codified as amended at 33 U.S.C. § 1344 (1988).
6. *Lucas v. South Carolina Coastal Council*, 505 U.S. 465 (1992).
7. A discretionary document used by a superior court, the term commonly associated with the Supreme Court of the United States to choose the cases it wishes to hear.
8. *Semore v. Pool*, 266 Cal.App.3d 280 (Dist. Ct. 1990).
9. California Constitution Article 1, Section I provides that privacy is one of our inalienable rights.
10. The Bill of Rights constitutes the first nine amendments that were adopted to guarantee individual liberties.
11. Lockhart, W., Kamisar, Y., & Choper, J. (1980). *Constitutional law* (5th ed.). St. Paul, MN:West Publishing Company, page 482.
12. Redress refers to gaining satisfaction in the courts for injuries or damages sustained. Black, H. C. (1979). *Black's law dictionary* (5th ed.). St. Paul, MN: West Publishing Co., p. 1150.
13. *Vernonia School Dist. 47J v. Acton*, 515 U.S. 646 (1995).
14. "The Court and Drugs in the High School," Laurie Asseo, Associated Press, Pages A1 & A5, June 27, 1995. Bloomington, Indiana: *Bloomington Herald Times*.

Chapter Ten

DUE PROCESS, PRIVACY, SPEECH, AND RELIGION

SECTION 1: DUE PROCESS (14TH AMENDMENT)

When recreationists, athletes, or tourists are denied their rights to life, liberty, and property, the constitution guarantees them that their rights cannot be denied without a process or hearing of some type. Due process requires that a notice of a hearing be given. The complexity and timing of the notice differs considerably, depending on the subject and activity involved.

In order to understand the extent of due process, there must first be a balancing test.[1] The balancing test to determine the scope and nature of due process must weigh the following:

1. The effect of the action on private interest.

2. The risk of an error that would deny the rights of an individual if a hearing was not available.

3. The interest of government, and the burden of a hearing or procedures on the efficient function of government.

Due process must be given. A person must be given notice, written, oral, or both, on actions that may affect his constitutional rights of life, liberty, or property. If the situation warrants, based upon the balancing test, a hearing may be held to allow both sides of the issue to express their arguments and opinions.

Due process, much like all constitutional rights, limits the power of government and protects the individual from government excesses. The central due process right is found in the 14th Amendment. This was the second of three Amendments to the Constitution that followed the American Civil War that dealt with individual rights:

- 1865—Thirteenth Amendment abolished slavery.

- 1868—Fourteenth Amendment established due process.

- 1869—Fifteenth Amendment gave all citizens the right to vote regardless of race, color, and so forth.

It is important to understand that there was a distinct historical setting for the 14th Amendment. While due process limits the power of the federal government, the primary purpose of the 14th Amendment was to ensure that the individual states, specifically the southern secession states, did not enact laws that would circumvent the reasons for fighting the Civil War or pass state laws that would limit the freedom of some of their citizens. This was particularly important to Congress and the northern states after so many died in the Civil War to preserve the Union and free the slaves. Due process is one of the "umbrella" doctrines of constitutional rights. It is fundamental to many other rights, and is found broadly in the Preamble, (…"Justice … secure of Blessings of Liberty…"); in Articles III and IV ("The trial…shall be by jury" and "The Citizens in each State shall be entitled to all Privileges and Immunities of Citizens in the several States"); and specifically due process is found in the 14th Amendment adopted in 1868. Section I of the 14th Amendment states in part:

> No State shall make or enforce any law which shall abridge the privileges or immunities of citizens of the United States; nor shall any State deprive any person of life, liberty or property without due process of law; nor deny to any persons within its jurisdiction the equal protection of the laws.

Supreme Court Associate Justice Frankfurter wrote that the 14th Amendment incorporates the first eight amendments.[2] Justices Paul Douglas and Hugo Black wrote in dissent to *Adamson v. California* (1947)[3] concerning the importance of the 14th Amendment: "...I would follow what I believe was the original purpose of the 14th Amendment—to extend to all the people of the nation the complete protection of the Bill of Rights."

The court has broadly interpreted the application of due process into day-to-day proceedings related to work and leisure activities. Due process protection applies broadly to day-to-day activities. Situations where due process rights might arise include: being fired without cause by an employer or a search of personal belongings for illegal items in an automobile, work setting, or entering a locker without a search warrant.

When individual rights are infringed upon and an individual, organization, or law enforcement agency acts without decency and fairness, there may be questions related to the violation of the fundamental right of due process. There are certain limits placed upon the courts in litigating due process questions. When people simply do not get their way, they will try to use due process arguments. Alleged due process violations should not be used in petty or argumentative situations. The courts (judges) must act on due process motions within the limits of accepted standards of justice, and the judges are not free to make decisions based upon individual opinions or personal judgments.[4]

In *University of Nevada v. Tarkanian* (1994),[5] the basketball coach sued the university, his employer, the president of the university, and the university regents over an alleged due process incident. The legal action was related to a severance order barring him from associating or being involved in any matter with the university athletic program. The coach claimed his civil rights had been violated through denial of due process. The trial court awarded the coach severance damages and reasonable attorney fees. The University appealed, seeking declaratory[6] and injunctive relief[7] from paying the coach, pending a hearing before the supreme court. The supreme court held that, because this was a civil rights issue, the coach was entitled to the award of reasonable attorney fees, and the district court was correct in its award of damages.

Due process involves constitutionally protected liberty and property rights. A due process plaintiff must prove that he or she has been denied a constitutionally protected interest. One of the precedent-setting cases in sports is *Goss v. Lopez* (1975).[8] Plaintiff Goss was suspended from school for violating school conduct rules. He claimed that he was entitled to a due process hearing if the suspension lasted more than 10 days. The opportunity to present his side of the case, present evidence, and to hear his charges were his primary requests of the court. The United States Supreme Court agreed with the plaintiff Goss: that he had a right to hear the charges against him by the teacher whose charges led to his suspension. The court also said that he had the right to present his side of the story. The court noted that the due process problem in the case could have been taken care of in one short and simple meeting. The court noted that Goss could still be suspended, but the school's failure to allow him a hearing violated his right to due process. Goss is frequently noted in sports due process cases.[9]

People who believe their due process rights have been violated must prove the following:

1. The action in question was a government action and not a private action.

2. The action affected the individual personally.

3. There were life, liberty, or property interests.

Simply stated, due process is a doctrine of fairness. Due process rights guarantee that people will be given the right to intervene on their own behalf and present arguments before individuals, organizations, and the government regarding actions that effect their personal life, liberty, or property.

SECTION 2: PRIVACY

The right of privacy[10] involves the right to be left alone and to be free of unwarranted publicity. Privacy rights prevent government interference in personal, intimate relationships, associations, and activities. Individuals have the right to make fundamental choices involving themselves, their families, and their relationships with others without having their personal choices publicly exposed. Constitutional torts for invasion of privacy fall into four classes:

1. **Appropriation**—consists of another person taking the plaintiff's position, name, or likeness. As an example, a person cannot use your name or impersonate you in a degrading manner.

2. **Intrusion**—consists of intruding into the plaintiff's privacy, solitude, or seclusion, such as entering another's home, eavesdropping, constant and persistent telephone calls, and so forth. For example, it is an invasion of privacy to enter another's home without specific invitation. This issue currently arises in workplace settings with technology that allows employers to monitor e-mail and Internet usage.

3. **Public disclosure of private facts**—consists of publicity that is very private in nature and highly objectionable. The publicity may be true and used by the defendant to embarrass or for sensational purposes. An example is one cannot disclose a private psychiatric report of another.

4. **False light in the public eye**—consists of erroneous publicity that places the plaintiff with a poor public image. This category of invasion of privacy is much like defamation of character.

Recreation, sports, and tourism managers should constantly promote and maintain the rights of privacy for people engaged in sports and recreation activities. Most people have natural curiosity related to the personal lives of others. Recreation, sports, and tourism activities provide a social contact with others that is usually personal in nature. Strong curiosity and social relations aside, there still remains a basic need for privacy. The issue of privacy also arises with security issues. For example, campus recreation facilities sometimes use closed-circuit cameras to monitor for security on the premises. An issue of privacy might arise if someone is videotaped in an area where privacy is expected. Counsel should be sought when using surveillance given privacy concerns and the related legal implications.

Cameras can be a useful deterrent to crime but must not invade privacy rights.

Sports participation varies from team activities, such as softball and volleyball to individual acts, such as tennis and skiing. Recreation can vary from organizational camping to solitude in a wilderness area. Even in group participation activities, a search of private property or records cannot be done without due cause. Curiosity or prurient interest[11] does not justify intrusion into the private lives of others.

In *Roe v. North Adams Community School Corporation* (1995),[12] female participants in lifeguard training were videotaped by a hidden camera in the locker room of the high school. The camera had been concealed in the locker room by a high school student not participating in the lifeguard training. The plaintiff females brought suit against the high school, the school corporation, the organization sponsoring the lifeguard training, and the teacher who conducted the training. The plaintiffs did not sue the student who placed the camera in the locker room. The likely reason they did not sue the student was because of the deep pocket doctrine of collectability. The plaintiffs sued those they felt were responsible to see that their privacy in a dressing room was assured. The appellate court determined that the culpable individual in the privacy action was the student. He was solely to blame for the invasion of privacy. The appeals court determined that the school could not have foreseen the action by the student, and the plaintiff failed to establish the legal duty or causative connection between the incident in the locker room and the school district, the sponsoring organization, and the teacher. The appellate decision was for the defendant school district.

An exercise, sport, or high-risk recreation organization may legally require an applicant to take a physical examination in order to participate in a particular activity. The results of the physical are a private matter that cannot be published or discussed casually. The physical is only the concern of the applicant and the decision-makers who determine the physical qualifications necessary for eligibility to play the sport. Drug testing also raises privacy issues as the following case illustrates:

In *Hill v. National Collegiate Athletic Assoc.* (1994),[13] student-athletes brought suit claiming that the drug testing program imposed on athletes violated their right to privacy. Before being allowed to participate in NCAA-sponsored competition, college athletes were required to sign a consent form allowing random drug testing. The plaintiffs refused and were subsequently not allowed to compete on their college teams. They brought suit claiming that the drug testing scheme was an invasion of privacy in violation of Article I, Section I of the California Constitution. After appeals from the trial and appellate courts, the Supreme Court of California agreed to hear the case. They held that the student-athlete privacy was not violated, primarily because student-athletes have a lowered expectation of privacy given their status as college athletes. The court maintained that the NCAA has a legitimate interest in protecting the health and safety of college athletes.

In outdoor recreation activities, particularly camping, privacy becomes a difficult and somewhat complex problem in an open setting. Privacy rules for recreation managers in overnight camping situations are similar to the access granted hotel and lodging employees as they require access to guest rooms for maintenance and service.

While an outdoor campsite will likely require a fee, payment does not guarantee privacy. There is an inherent lack of privacy because of the outdoor and no walls or blinds environment. Managers and maintenance personnel may enter the camping site during daylight hours to conduct necessary business without invading the privacy of the campers. When it is dark, the need for access into the campsite must be of an emergency or critical nature. Nighttime entrance into the campsite should be announced prior to entering the site, for the sake of the campers and the safety of the employee. If tents, cars, trailers, or other items need to be searched for some legitimate reason, day or night, a search warrant must be sought. In criminal investigation when visual evidence or close pursuit indicates a crime has been committed, searches of the individual and his personal property are warranted if conducted by a law enforcement officer.

Searching lockers and other personal items of sports participants is a rather complex subject area. The courts have determined that the rights of privacy must give way to a social need to control illegal drugs and deadly weapons. If recreation, sports, or tourist officials have reason to believe that illegal drugs or weapons are stored in lockers, then working with law enforcement officers, searches of specific lockers, random locker checks, or checks of all lockers can be made with a valid search warrant or as a result of a previously announced policy. A constitutional tort may occur when lockers are checked without probable cause or without the organization establishing a policy and informing the locker users and/or their parents of its policy regarding locker searches.

In an era of concern about HIV-positive athletes, team trainers and physicians are faced with some very difficult questions related to protection of other players' health versus the right of privacy of the individual HIV positive athletes. The right of privacy and other existing state and federal laws regulate the physician's disclosure of an athlete's HIV status to coaches, team members, and opposing coaches and team members.

There is a risk to an individual if exposed to the blood and other bodily fluids of an athlete who is HIV positive. As a result of recommendations from the Center for Disease Control and Prevention, the NCAA in 1988 recommended that all sports persons (coaches, trainers, physicians), coming into contact with body fluids wear protective masks, gloves, and eyewear.[14] While there is a right to privacy, there is also the conflicting legal principle of negligent failure to warn of a known danger.[15]

Tarasoff v. Regents of the University of California (1976),[16] is often used as a precedent-setting case and a classic example of failure to warn. In Tarasoff, the court determined that when a patient confided in his psychiatrist that he planned to kill a specific woman, the psychiatrist had a duty to warn the authorities or the woman that such a threat was made. Even with the traditional and legal mandate of patient/doctor confidentiality, the life of another was deemed more important. The court had to weigh the right of privacy against the duty to warn of a serious threat. While the Tarasoff case is still debated within the legal community, the message of the decision presents a dilemma to the sports and recreation managers. The Supreme Court determined that the life of an individual was more important than that of relationship between a psychiatrist and his patient.

Coaches and others who gain the trust of their students, athletes, and participants must be able to make the difficult decisions related to what information is kept in strict confidence and what information is passed on to authorities and parents. The decision is difficult and may subject a trusted person to ridicule and possible litigation.

Right of Association

Recreation and sports associations are common in our society. These usually take the form of teams, leagues, and associations. Examples of these associations would be Pop Warner Football Incorporated, the National Collegiate Athletic Association (NCAA), the Amateur Athletic Union (AAU), and the Little League Baseball Association.

Sometimes associations are formed that are dedicated to the promotion of a sport or recreation activity by location. Examples would be the "City" Ice Hockey Association, the "State" Indiana Spelunkers Association, and the "National" Parks and Recreation Association. People have a right to form associations, thereby choosing with whom they wish to socialize. Most recreation and sports associations promote an activity and/or protect the interests of participants. The right of association is guaranteed by the Constitution as long as the association does not engage in criminal conspiracy activities[17] or violate a person's civil rights related to gender, race, age, national origin, or religion.

SECTION 3: SPEECH AND RELIGION

Two important and sometimes conflicting constitutional rights are the right to express an opinion and the right to believe and worship as we please. Certainly, these two First Amendment rights are central to the political and social structure of our nation.

The First Amendment declares "Congress shall make no law respecting an establishment of religion, or prohibiting the free exercise thereof." This rather simple and important amendment has two significant aspects:

1. The government cannot embrace or establish a specific religion. That has been further expanded to mean that there must be a separation between church and state.

2. The government cannot interfere with a person's practice of his religious beliefs. This is generally referred to as the free exercise part of the First Amendment.

The courts have determined that our freedom to say whatever we wish has some limitations. Expressing damaging and inaccurate information (defamatory statements) about another, advocating the violent overthrow of government, and shouting "fire" in a crowded theater certainly run counter to good order in our society. There must be some reasonable limits to our right to express ourselves.

Employees have broad rights to express their opinions, criticize policies and procedures, and advocate employee organizations and unions without losing their positions. An objectionable opinion by an employee expressed internally is protected under the First Amendment; however, if that opinion is false or vindictive and expressed publicly to embarrass the organization, it is not protected.

The First Amendment states in part: "Congress shall make no law ... abridging the freedom of speech or of the press ..." Freedom of speech is synonymous with freedom of expression. We may express our opinions about policy, political figures, and so forth, without breaking a federal or state law. People engaged in recreation and sports activities are also free to criticize policy, supervisors, or coaches without being punished. The question that always arises is whether the exercise of freedom of speech results in insubordination, is defamatory, or invades a person's privacy.

In *Milwaukee Mobilization for Survival v. Milwaukee County Park Commission* (1979),[18] the plaintiffs claimed that the park permit ordinances violated the exercise of free speech by denying the plaintiffs a park permit to peacefully assemble. The defendant county argued that parks must be regulated to encourage good order. The county had offered to provide a park, other than the one requested, that could be used by the plaintiffs. The county ordinance limited the circumstances upon which a permit would be granted, charged $20 to process the permit, and limited the use of offensive language. The plaintiff sued, challenging all the provisions of the ordinance as unconstitutional limits on free speech. The federal court issued a restraining order prohibiting the enforcement of the county ordinance. The court determined that the park permit ordinance unconstitutionally denied the plaintiff's request to conduct a political rally in a particular park; however the decision stated that the $20 fee required was nominal in nature and the fee itself did not violate any constitutional rights.

There is a sensitive area related to advocating a particular political party or political position as a public employee. If the exercise of free speech rights interferes with the rights of privacy or the general businesslike atmosphere needed in most work environments, then management can take actions to protect others and conduct its organization's business in a manner that is conducive to good internal and external relations. Federal law prohibits federal employees from conducting political activities of any kind on federal property. The law also prohibits civil service employees from running for political office. Exceptions are made for nonpartisan offices such as school boards.

The right to free exercise of religious belief was the primary reason the first Europeans migrated to the new world. It is important that recreation and sports administrators understand that protection of religious freedom and implementation of religious limitations are important factors in the management of recreation and sports. Religious camps, church-sponsored teams participating in league play, Easter sunrise services in parks, and employees who want to exercise their religious beliefs are all part of the recreation and sports management field.

Policies must be in place to ensure that everyone receives equal treatment in access and use of public facilities. Problems occur when administrators determine they will be the moral conscience of the community, rather than treat all people with equity.

In the case of *Invisible Empire of the Knights of the Ku Klux Klan v. City of West Haven* (1985),[18] the Ku Klux Klan was denied a permit to march in a public park. The city did not have a standard regarding public gatherings or marches. The city would simply reject those organizations they did not approve of and choose not to allow the use of the park. They would issue permits for those organizations they felt were worthy. The plaintiff Ku Klux Klan alleged that the denial of the permit constituted a violation of its First Amendment rights of free speech and "...the right of the people peaceably to assemble..."[20]

In a somewhat similar case,[21] the Chicago Park District denied a neo-Nazi group a permit to rally in a public park. The Nazis sued the city for violation of their right of free speech and were granted a rally permit by the city. In both cases, the cities were forced by the courts to allow what most people would consider repugnant groups to peacefully assemble.

Speech

The right to protest does not necessarily give protesters rights that others do not have. In *Ward v. Rock Against Racism* (1989),[22] a rock concert promoter, organizers, and musicians challenged the city's right to limit the level of sound amplification in a city park. The ordinance that limited the sound level was developed to protect the privacy and intrusion of sound into the homes of nearby residents. The residents had complained about loud music and sound prior to passing the ordinance. The plaintiff claimed that because the concert's purpose was to fight racism, the right to express that opinion through rock music was being suppressed through control of amplified sound. The plaintiff stated that rock music was always amplified and should be considered an expression of constitutionally guaranteed free speech. The U.S. Supreme Court determined that the level of sound amplification was not a protected First Amendment right under free speech and decided in favor of the city.

The exercise of free expression does not always take the form of speech or written materials. In *Tinker v. Des Moines Independent School District* (1969),[23] a group of students wore black arm bands to protest what they believed to be discriminatory practices in their high school. The school district took disciplinary action against the students, demanding that they remove the arm bands. The students sued, stating that wearing the arm bands was not a violent or disruptive act, and that their First Amendment right of free expression was violated. The school district stated that wearing arm band apparel was disruptive in an educational institution, and wearing certain types of clothing was not a guaranteed right under the First Amendment. The Supreme Court decided in favor of the students, stating that students' First Amendment rights did not stop at the school door.

Religion

Specific religious beliefs and practices, particularly the beliefs set forth in the Ten Commandments in the Judeo/Christian tradition, form the essence or core of American jurisprudence (English common law). The First Amendment of the Constitution provides individuals protection from governmental interference with religion practices. Yet, through the Establishment Clause[24] of the First Amendment, there is a requirement that public entities such as public schools and park/recreation departments separate church and state to insure that no religion or even secular belief dominates and oppresses the free religious expression of others.

As an example of the public emphasis to protect religious rights, the U.S. Congress passed specific legislation that provides protection of Native American religious beliefs. Many believed that Native Americans were not being given the right to exercise their traditional religious beliefs.[25] The legislation was widely supported by the public and has particularly impacted the management of public lands, particularly federally managed resource lands in the western United States.

In the controversial court decision of *Jagar and Jagar v. Douglas County School District and Douglas County School Board* (1989),[26] the federal courts determined it was unconstitutional to offer public prayer prior to the beginning of Douglas County High School District (Georgia) football games. The prayers were specifically Christian in nature. The suit claimed that the prayers conflicted with the Jagar's Native American beliefs. The Eleventh Circuit Court of Appeals agreed with the lower court and the Supreme Court refused to hear the appeal, thus confirming the decision by the Eleventh Circuit Court of Appeals.

Many communities have ignored or by consensus determined to avoid this decision to no avail. The Jagar case applies to public schools only and does not affect the policies of privately owned schools. The Jagar decision has also affected prayers by coaches, clergy, and administrative officials before and after athletic events. Optional (non-mandatory) team prayers organized by the players themselves appear not to be affected by the Jagar case.

Supreme Court decisions have curtailed seasonal religious displays such as manger scenes on park (public) property. Some exceptions do exist when the religious display is part of a historical context of other displays or where other religious groups are given the opportunity to display their beliefs in a parallel manner. Religious groups have been permitted access to public facilities such as outdoor amphitheaters and auditoriums to conduct religious services, as long as access to the facilities is allowed to other groups. Singing Christmas carols in public school classrooms has been restricted by the courts, while singing Christmas music on public park property has yet to come under the critical scrutiny of the court. Depending upon the social and political context of the various state and federal courts, the decisions regarding separation of church and governmental institution have varied considerably over the last 20 years.

A public recreation or sports organization may allow religious groups to use public property for religious purposes. Public and private agencies serving public needs must ensure that:

1. Specific religious groups do not have an exclusive relationship with government to use public property for religious purposes.

2. Management does not favor one religion over another.

When both of the above criteria are met, use of public property for religious purposes may be appropriate, based upon written agency policy.

For example, if a specific religious organization wanted to utilize a public park for an Easter sunrise worship service, the park administrators could allow the use as long as it did not interfere with the park's primary purpose. Other religious groups must also have an equal opportunity to utilize the same facility.

If an employee wanted to express his or her beliefs (including both religious and speech rights), that expression of belief could take a number of forms—some allowed, some discouraged, and some not allowed. For example, a public employee may wear a symbol of her belief such as a crucifix, crescent, or Star of David. The wearing of the symbol in public shows individual preference and not organizational support.

When the religious symbol becomes more obvious and takes on the dimension of a large desk or wall display—something that is dominant in the view of others, the questions of separation of church and state, propriety, intrusion into the feelings of others, and purpose must be considered. If a public employee is distributing unsolicited religious literature to other employees and business visitors, action must be taken by management to protect the rights of customers and employees to be left alone. When religious pressure is placed upon employees by supervisory personnel, it becomes particularly serious. It is simply good business practice to minimize the amount of non-business activities in an organization. The offices of religious organizations are an exception to the intrusion rules.

A recreation manager, playground supervisor, coach, or teacher whose position or status may influence others, particularly youth, may be restrained from wearing or displaying religious symbols or from discussing religion with his or her peers, students, or subordinates. As an example, a public sector recreation supervisor leading his or her employees in prayer every morning would be counter to the separation of church and state. While there is an element of free exercise of religion, the act of leading the prayer under the circumstances shown above, demonstrates a conflict between free exercise and separation.

In the case of *Moody v. Cronin* (1979),[28] Debbie Moody, a minor and member of the United Pentecostal Church, filed a First Amendment freedom of religion action on behalf of herself and others seeking redress because she was required by the school district to attend coeducational physical education classes, dressed in what her church beliefs considered "immodest apparel." She was not only concerned about wearing immodest attire, but also the fact she had to participate with and observe other students whom she also considered to be dressed immodestly. She stated that "immodest apparel" exposed her to "worldly influences," and violated the church teachings against "being a party to lust."

The church described immodest apparel as "attire that exposes and reveals parts of the body that are associated with sexual provocation; and that attire would include gym shorts, miniskirts, sleeveless blouses, and any clothing that would expose parts of the bosom or the chest." A religious historian and expert witness for the plaintiff testified that the church's objections to immodest apparel were not a matter of personal preference, but rather a deep religious conviction shared by all members of their church.

The school district had sent the plaintiff a letter stating that "there would be no exception to the coeducational physical education attendance and dress code requirements for religious beliefs." The school policy stated that all students must attend physical education, with the exception of those students with a physician-documented health problem. The school policy further stated that if students did not attend physical education classes they would not receive physical education credit, which was required for graduation.

The school district did not challenge the sincerity of the plaintiff's beliefs, but rather argued that coeducational gym classes with students dressed in shorts and blouses/shirts for purposes of physical exercise are normal and healthy. The school further stated that dressing with long sleeves and long pants would not be appropriate, recognizing a need to dress to facilitate health, and address exertion and perspiration concerns. The court issued a declaratory judgment in favor of the plaintiffs. The declaratory judgment did not direct the school district to do anything specific about the problem, but rather told the school district what it could not do. The court issued a permanent injunction informing the school district that it could not deny graduation or take any disciplinary action against the plaintiffs because of their religious beliefs in exercise of their guaranteed rights in the First Amendment of the constitution.

Religious protection and religious tolerance laws do not reach out to U.S. citizens traveling in foreign countries. Tourists must conform to local laws and customs when traveling in a foreign country.

Some religious beliefs require certain dress standards and symbols that some sport and recreation administrators may consider awkward or even inappropriate dress for some sports and recreation activities. Hair is sometimes worn very long, and the tenets of some religions require that hair not be cut. Some religions require specific attire, such as yarmulkes[30] that may be deemed unsafe in some sporting activities such as basketball.

In *Menora v. Illinois High School Association* (1982),[31] the association had a rule that no hats or headgear, except a sweatband, could be worn while playing basketball. The rule was challenged by a Jewish student/athlete who stated that the rule was unconstitutional as it was applied to athletes who were Jewish, because they could not wear their yarmulkes, a requirement of their religious faith. While the court sympathized with the plaintiff, the appellate court agreed with the lower court in deciding in favor of the defendant high school association. The appellate court determined that the student/athlete must make the final determination if in fact the religious requirements precluded his participation in the voluntary sport of basketball. Hats or headgear are simply inappropriate for basketball. Constitutional requirements in voluntary or discretionary sports activities are not as stringent as in mandatory or required activities. Also see *Keller v. Garden Community Consolidated Grade School District* (1982).[32]

A student's refusal to submit to a physical examination on religious grounds is seldom successful. The religious rights of the individual student/athlete are outweighed by the need to protect the school from litigation; the teammates from possible harm of being infected by a serious disease; and the individual student from unnecessary harm and danger from his own medical condition.

Discussion Questions

1. Explain what is meant by the term "due process."

2. What must a plaintiff prove in a due process case?

3. Which constitutional invasion of privacy tort is most like defamation? How do they differ?

4. What are some things we still cannot do even though we have the right to free speech?

Notes

1. The balancing test doctrine for due process stems from the results of *Mathews v. Eldridge,* 424 U.S. 319, 335 (1976).
2. *Adamson v. California,* 332 U.S. 46 (1947).
3. Ibid.
4. Lockhart, W. B., Kamisar, Y., & Choper, J. H. (1980). *Constitutional law* (5th ed.). St. Paul MN: West Publishing Co., p. 484.
5. *University of Nevada v. Tarkanian,* 879 P.2d 1180 (Nev. 1994).
6. Declaratory judgment is a noncoercing decision by the court indicating the duties of various parties to the litigation.
7. Injunctive relief is the court ordered redress of a wrong to command the person or organization to perform some act or refrain from performing some act.
8. *Goss v. Lopez,* 419 U.S. 565 (1975).
9. Buss, W. G. (1982). *Law and amateur sports.* Bloomington, IN: Indiana University Press, p. 482.
10. Black, H. C. (1979). *Black's law dictionary* (5th ed.). St. Paul, MN: West Publishing Co., p. 1075.
11. Prurient interest refers to shameful or morbid interest in nudity, sex, and excretion in an obsessive and immoral manner. Black, H. C. (1979). *Black's law dictionary* (5th ed.). St. Paul, MN: West Publishing Co.
12. *Roe V. North Adams Community Sch. Corp.,* 647 N.E. 2d 655 (lnd. App. 1995).
13. *Hill v. National Collegiate Athletic Assoc.,* 26 Cal.Rptr.2d 834 (Cal. 1994).
14. *NCAA Sports Medicine Handbook* (1988).
15. Claussen, HIV-positive athletes and the disclosure dilemma for athletic trainers. (1993). *Journal of Legal Aspects of Sport 3*(2), p. 2534.
16. *Tarasoff v. Regents of the University of California,* 551 P.2d 334 (Cal. 1976).
17. Conspiracy is an act between two or more individuals for the purpose of committing illegal act(s). Conspiracy requires a concerted effort of the conspirators.
18. *Milwaukee Mobilization for Survival v. Milwaukee County Park Commission,* 477 F.Supp. 1210 (E.D.Wisc. 1979).
19. *Invisible Empire of the Knights of the Ku Klux Klan v. City of West Haven,* 600 F. Supp 1427 (1985).
20. The right to peaceably assemble is found in the First Amendment to the constitution adopted in 1791.
21. *Collins v. Chicago Park District,* 460 F.2d 746 (7th Cir.1972).

22. *Ward v. Rock Against Racism*, 491 U.S. 781, 105 L.Ed.2d 661, 109 S.Ct. 2746 (1989).
23. *Tinker v. Des Moines Independent School District*, 393 U.S.503 (1969).
24. First Amendment of the United States Constitution. (1791). A Congress shall make no law respecting an establishment of religion, or prohibiting the free exercise thereof, …
25. American Indian Religious Freedom Act of 1978, 92 Statute1393; Native American Graves Protection and Repatriation Act of 1990, 104 Statute 3048.
26. *Jagar and Jagar v. Douglas County School District and Douglas County School Board*, N. 86-2037A (D.Ga. Feb 27,1987; *Jagar v. Douglas County School District*, 862 F.2d 824, (11th Cir 1989); and *Douglas County School District v. Doug Jager*, 109 S.Ct. 2431 (1989).
27. Sawyer, Thomas H. (1997). A separation of church and state: Are invocations and team prayers legal? *Journal of the Legal Aspects of Sports*, 24-30.
28. *Moody v. Cronin*, 484 F.Supp. 270 (D.C. Ill. 1979).
29. Declaratory judgment is a court action that determines the rights of the litigants or answers legal questions. There is no award of damages as a result of a declaratory judgment.
30. Yarmulke: A skullcap worn by Jewish men, especially those adhering to Orthodox or Conservative tradition. *Webster's II New Riverside University Dictionary* (1984). Rolling Meadows, IL: Riverside Publishing Company, p.1334.
31. *Menora v. Illinois High School Association*, 683 F.2d 1030 (7th Cir 1982).
32. *Keller v. Garden Community Consolidated Grade School District 72C*, 552 F.Supp. 512 (N.D. Ill. 1982).

Chapter Eleven

DISCRIMINATION

Race

Recreation, sports, and tourism are three areas that lead the nation in fighting the insidious character of racial discrimination. These three areas are unique in their potential to break down barriers between people of differing backgrounds. Unfortunately, discrimination still occurs in recreation, sport, and tourism settings. It is essential that leaders and administrators seek ways to reduce the problem of racial discrimination. There is no place for any type of racial discrimination in any aspect of our society.

Since the famous case of *Brown v. Board of Education*,[1] the concept of "separate but equal" in participation, facilities, and programs was replaced with the words "integrated or desegregated." Public sports facilities and agencies serving the public for recreation, sports, and tourism purposes must be racially integrated. The courts have determined that one of the criteria for knowing whether an activity is integrated is the "snapshot" comparison. The demographic makeup of sports and recreation participants should reflect a "snapshot" (picture) of the community, state, or region it represents. This means that if the community has a 25% minority population, the activity would be considered integrated if approximately 25% of the participants represented the minority population.

The courts have stared down a number of cases involving amateur athlete organizations that were based on the predominance of one race. In *Louisiana High School Athletic Association v. St. Augustine High School*[2] and *Lee v. Macon County Board of Education*[3] the attempt to establish two "separate but equal" athletic systems were struck down by the courts. The segregated systems were determined to be in violation of the equal protection sections of the Civil Rights Act.[4]

Exempted from the nondiscrimination sections of Title VII of the Civil Rights Act of 1964 are small businesses (less than 15 employees), religious organizations, and tax-exempt private membership clubs. It should be noted that all government organizations (federal, state, and local) are not exempt from Title VII.

In *Gilmore v. City of Montgomery,*[5] the Recreation and Parks Department for Montgomery, Alabama, allowed exclusive use of park facilities by a private, segregated all-white school. The school used the sports facilities of the park to enable it to have a complete sports program for its students. The city held the position that its actions did not interfere with the rights of all citizens to use city parks, and the facilities were superfluous to the needs of the community. The plaintiff argued that the exclusive use of these public sport facilities by an all-white school promoted segregational policies. They further argued that even nonexclusive use violated the intent of civil rights and education bills. The U.S. Supreme Court agreed with the plaintiff and ordered the city to sever all exclusive uses of the facility previously enjoyed by the segregated school.

Age

It is a common public policy and business practice to provide certain economic advantages based on age. The federal government issues Golden Age Passports to citizens over 65 years of age that allow for half price on all federal recreation areas and facilities. Many airlines provide senior fares at a reduced rate. Many sport event tickets are less costly for people under 12 years of age, and there are often senior citizen discounts as well. Many restaurants provide discounts as well for their patrons over 55 years of age.

Competition by age classification is common in recreation and sports activities. The courts have generally upheld rules that restrict participation to participants over 18 years of age, in high-risk recreation activities, such as mountain climbing, sky diving, and whitewater rafting. In any situation where physical maturity, physical strength, and judgment are primary concerns, age restrictions are appropriate and legal; however, providers must be careful about excessive restrictions. Some older people may be in much better physical condition than younger participants. It is wiser for providers to require physical exams with specific standards rather than use an arbitrary age limit.

In *Blue v. University Interscholastic League*,[6] the court upheld a high school age rule that prohibited students over the age of 19 from participating in high school athletic programs. The court weighed the purpose of the rule against the rights of equal protection. In this case, the court determined that the rule was intended to provide fair competition among athletes with less experience and equal physical maturity.

There are a number of ways to use age to indirectly ensure that participants are on an equal basis. The National Collegiate Athletic Association (NCAA) restricts athletes to four years of participation eligibility in intercollegiate athletics. In some cases, athletes have challenged the four-year eligibility rule. In *Smith v. Crim*,[7] a student athlete lost a year of eligibility when he dropped out of school for a year to care for his invalid mother. The school told Smith that he had lost a full year of eligibility. The court ruled that the four-year limitation was related to fair competition and decided in favor of the defendant Crim. More often, when the circumstances indicate a valid reason for absence, such as family needs, sickness, religious missions, significant employment opportunities, or military service, the courts have ruled in favor of the student-athlete. In the above special cases, the student-athlete does not gain a year of eligibility, he simply does not lose any. For example, in *Lee v. Florida High School Activities Association*,[8] a student had to drop out of school to support his family for a year. The court determined that if the reason for the absence was unrelated to sports or gaining more physical maturity to compete at a higher level, then the age restriction violated equal protection rights.

Gender

Three decades ago, it would have been very difficult to find a female firefighter. It was accepted practice and fact that all firefighter applicants were male. This practice of hiring only male firefighters was challenged in the courts by female applicants. The firefighters' unions stated that females were not capable of carrying a large male down a ladder to save fellow firefighters or fire victims and that women did not have the physical strength for firefighting. The plaintiff females challenged the rule by asking the court for permission to randomly test male firefighters for the same physical abilities that prohibited women from becoming firefighters. A significant part of the test was to carry a 250 lb. load, the equivalent weight of a large fireman or fire victim, down a ladder. Of the acting firefighters tested, approximately 50% were unable to pass the test. The courts determined that the firefighters either had to lower their criteria or dismiss the 50% who could not pass the test. The firefighters' unions opted to change their testing criteria. Today, a number of firefighters are women. The qualified women meet all the strength standards required of the males.

The courts have struggled for years to determine the best way to deal with gender participation questions related to sports and recreation. The decisions have not been consistent.[9] Society has made major changes over the past few decades breaking down gender barriers and negative attitudes, yet bias still exists. When a large male knocks down and injures a female when playing touch football, there may be a cause of action for battery. If the same large male knocks down and injures another male, the chances for a battery cause of action would be less likely. In general, society considers the female injury, a result of willful and wanton negligence on behalf of the larger and more aggressive male; while the male who was injured assumed the risk because of the type of game he chose to participate in.

As much as possible, recreation and competitive sports should not be gender-specific. When recreation and sports managers determine the make-up of teams, they should try to facilitate as many mixed-gender teams as possible. When managers and administrators plan and program team and league play, there are a number of alternatives that may satisfy constitutional questions of equal protection, civil rights acts, and Title IX of the Education Act.[10] Managers can:

1. Designate gender-specific teams and leagues in contact sports. Courts have determined that society's standards dictate a separation of the sexes when contact is expected in the sports. Examples may be football, basketball, boxing, ice hockey, wrestling, judo, and so forth. Some exceptions continue to exist in limited contact positions in what would normally be considered a contact sport. An example of these positions may be field goal kickers in football, because the game's rules limit the amount of contact. A few organizations, such as high school and youth leagues, have made the decision to allow female field-goal kickers.

2. Create teams and leagues based on age. This is particularly applicable to youth teams prior to puberty. Physical characteristics are less pronounced, and mixed teams appear to be more appropriate. Some care must be taken in selecting adult team participation based upon age. Age discrimination takes place in recreation and team activities. Some people believe that older citizens need a more sedentary lifestyle, and while some older citizens are not interested in vigorous activities, some are

very interested and skilled. For example, the criteria for participating in a river float trip should not be based on age (i.e., less than 60), but rather, if a certain physical condition is needed for safety, a physical fitness test or a medical exam could be an appropriate requirement.

3. Establish teams and leagues based on physical characteristics such as weight and height (basketball). This criterion is generally applicable to non-contact sports. The Special Olympics provide sports activities for a select segment of the population. Those individuals who are not part of the Special Olympics population cannot compete.

4. Establish single-gender teams and leagues based on the fact that both genders have the same activity available to them. In order to be in compliance with Title IX of the Educational Act of 1972,[11] the teams should have generally the same opportunity to compete in a common geographical area. For example, a school or organization should have both male and female teams and leagues so both genders can compete. A city softball league is not required to have mixed leagues, as long as there are men and women's leagues with parallel and equitable facilities and schedules.

5. There may be a requirement to have a specific number or percentage of females/males on each team to avoid a claim of "tokenism." Some mixed softball or volleyball teams require a percentage of players to be a specific gender. Accompanying this percentage is normally a minimum playing time percentage for the targeted group. As an example, a mixed volleyball league could have a specification that at least 40% of the players on the floor at all times must be female.

Title IX regulations permit separate gender teams in two circumstances:

1. When the sport is a contact sport.

2. When the selection of team members is based upon competitive skills and the results of the competition create a single-gender team (applies to both contact and non-contact sports).

The following factors[12] are used to see if an institution is meeting the intent of Title IX for equal opportunities for both genders:

1. Whether the selection of activities accommodate the interests and abilities of both sexes.

2. There are equal equipment and supplies.

3. Scheduling allows equal game scheduling and practice time.

4. Teams have travel and per diem allowances.

5. Athletes receive coaching and academic tutoring.

6. Coaches are compensated for their coaching labor.

7. Access is available to locker rooms, practice, and facilities.

8. Access is available to medical and training facilities and services.

9. Provision for housing and dining facilities.

10. Publicity opportunities.

In *Cook v. Colgate University*,[13] several women's ice hockey players sued the university for failing to make ice hockey a varsity sport. Women's ice hockey was a club sport that received less funding and status than varsity sports. The men's team had varsity status. The suit was brought claiming in part a violation of Title IX. The university claimed that due to funding constraints, they were not able to elevate the women's ice hockey team to varsity status. Reasons given for their decision were 1) women's ice hockey is rarely played on the secondary level; 2) a women's championship is not sponsored by the NCAA at any intercollegiate level; 3) the game is only played at approximately 15 colleges in the East; 4) there is a lack of student interest; 5) the players lack ability; and 6) hockey is expensive to fund. The court disagreed with the defendant's arguments, stating that the law demands equal athletic opportunities between men's and women's sports. This decision was reversed on appeal.

In cases where males have attempted to gain access to female teams, the courts have been very reluctant to allow males on female teams. In *Clark v. Arizona Interscholastic Association*,[14] a male high school student sued the Arizona Interscholastic Association (AIA), because Arizona schools, under the rules of the AIA, specified that competition for all athletic teams were gender-specific except where specifically allowed under their rules. They denied the male plaintiff's request to try out for a female public school volleyball team. The plaintiff Clark sued the school district for gender discrimination. The court determined that allowing males on the team would, over time, change the team from a female team to a male team. The court reasoned that, in general, the physical characteristics of male high school athletes would permit them to dominate the sport of volleyball. Since male volleyball teams were available in the school, the plaintiff's rights were not violated because of gender. The court decided in favor of the defendant Arizona Interscholastic Association.

Title VII of the Civil Rights Act of 1964[15] protects citizens from sexual harassment. While most actions are filed by women, there have recently been some suits instituted by men. While some may mistakenly consider that sexual overtures are part of the dynamics of human existence, sexual harassment problems become particularly serious when they involve physical touching and repeated offenses over the protests of the one being harassed.

In *Priest v. Rotary*,[16] a waitress (Priest) brought action against her former employer (Rotary) following termination. Priest claimed she was harassed and fired from her job on the basis of her gender, claiming her employer created a hostile, offensive, and intimidating work environment. In court, the plaintiff proved that her employer gave his consensual sexual partner preferential job assignments, and that other female employees who tolerated sexual advances were given better job assignments. These facts were sufficient evidence to establish a violation of the Civil Rights Act of 1964.

The evidence further showed that Rotary removed Priest from her full-time job as a cocktail waitress because she refused to wear suggestive clothing. Priest had witnesses who could verify that in two incidents she was trapped by her employer so she could not retreat and was constantly fondled and touched in an inappropriate manner in the work environment. She constantly told Rotary that his actions were distressful and upsetting and told him numerous times to "keep your hands off" and asked him to "please stop this." Rotary wore obscene T-shirts and circulated obscene photographs among the employees. Priest claimed damages for severe physical pain, intentional infliction of emotional distress, assault and battery, false imprisonment, and a violation of her civil rights.

Rotary denied the sexual harassment charges and claimed that Priest was fired because she failed to complete her assignments, was a poor waitress, used "bad language," did not get along with other waitresses, and violated restaurant policy which forbade socializing in the lounge. The decision of the court found that Rotary humiliated, harassed, inflicted extreme mental distress, physically touched in an outrageous manner, and abused his employer-employee relationship. Under the California tort laws related to severe infliction of mental distress, the court determined that the defendant met all the elements of the tort because his conduct was outrageous and resulted in severe emotional distress. The court awarded Priest back pay and projected wages, tips, attorney fees, and punitive damages.

The Priest case illustrates some important considerations for recreation, sports, and tourism professionals:

1.   A person cannot be forced to wear sexually suggestive attire.

2.   Job or team opportunities must be based upon merit only.

3.   Preferential treatment cannot be based upon an employee's good-natured endurance of sexual misconduct.

Managers must understand that females belong to a protected group under the Civil Rights Act, and unwelcome sexual advances violate the law. Recent cases indicate males under similar circumstances can also be a protected group in regard to unwelcome sexual advances.

Discussion Questions

1.   What factors are used to see if an institution is meeting the Title IX requirements?

2.   What law protects citizens from sexual harassment?

3.   What law protects citizens from racial discrimination?

4.   Give your own example of age discrimination in sport, recreation or tourism?

5.   Can a "women-only" gym exclude men who want to be members? Explain.

Notes

1. *Brown v. Board of Education*, 347 U. S. 483 (1954).
2. *Louisiana High School Athletic Association v. St. Augustine High School,* 396 F.2d 224 (5th Cir. 1968).
3. *Lee v. Macon County Board of Education*, 283 F.Supp. 194 (M.D. Ala. 1968).
4. Civil Rights Act of 1870 (42 U.S. C.A. §1981) provided that all citizens, regardless of race, be given the same rights; the Civil Rights Act of 1871 (42 U.S.C.A.§ 1985) made conspiracies against race illegal; and Title VII of the Civil Rights Act of 1964 as amended by the Equal Opportunity Act of 1972 protected civil rights in employment and narrowed the differences between public and private clubs.
5. *Gilmore v. City of Montgomery,* 417 U.S. 556 (1974).
6. *Blue v. University Interscholastic League,* 503 F. Supp. 1030 (N.D. Tex. 1980).
7. *Smith v. Grim,* 240 S.E.2d 884 (Ga.1977).
8. *Lee v. Florida High School Activities Association,* 291 So.2d 636 (Fla. 1974).
9. See *Bucha v. Illinois High School Association,* 351 FSupp69 (N.D. 111.1972); Commonwealth v. Pennsylvania Interscholastic Athletic Association, 334 A.2d 839 (1975); and O'Connor v. Board of Education of School District 23, 449 U.S. 1301 (1980).
10. Title IX of the Educational Amendments of 1972, 20 U.S.C. §1681, 1682 (Supp 1973).
11. See Public Law 93551, Act of December 26, 1974, 88 Stat.1744. This amendment to the Federal Little League Baseball Charter changed the wording from "boys" to "young people." The obvious purpose for this change was to allow girls to participate on Little League Baseball teams.
12. Shubert, G., Smith, R., & Trentadue, J. (1986). *Sports law,* p. 10. St. Paul MN: West Publishing.
13. *Cook v. Colgate,* 802 F.Supp. 737 (D.C. N.Y.1992).
14. *Clark v. Arizona Interscholastic Association,* 695 F.2d 1126 (9th Cir. 1982).
15. Civil Rights Act of 1964, Title VII § 701 et seq., amended, 42 U.S.C.A. § 2000eetseq.
16. *Priest v. Rotary,* 634 F.Supp 571 (N.D. Cal 1964).
17. Shubert, G., Smith, R., & Trentadue, J. (1986). *Sports law,* p. 96. St. Paul MN: West Publishing.
18. *Kissick v. Garland Independent School District,* 330 S.W.2d 708 (Tex. App. 1959).

19. *Bell v. Lone Oak Independent School District*, 507 S.W.2d 636 (Tex. App. 1974).
20. *Indiana High School Athletic Association v. Raike*, 329 N.E.2d 66 (lnd. App.1975).

Part Five

RISK ASSESSMENT IN RECREATION, SPORTS, AND TOURISM

Chapter Twelve

THE RISK MANAGEMENT PROCESS

Risk management should never be considered a burden or cost of recreation, sports, and tourism. It should be regarded as a part of every day business, not unlike customer service, maintenance, marketing, and management. There are a number of different models of risk management. Some have two or three steps; others have as many as eight. The risk management cycle presented below is a relatively simple four-step model that is not encumbered by onerous paper work and complicated processes.

Elements of an effective risk management process include the following (see Figure 12.1):

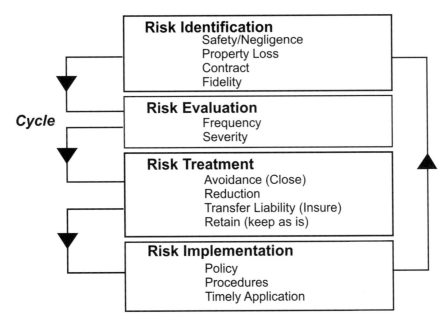

Figure 12.1. *Risk Management Cycle*

Risk Identification

Risk is identified in relation to safety/negligence, property loss, contract, or personnel (fidelity) issues. Employees must be empowered to think for themselves and through their own experiences and backgrounds and identify areas that have the potential for risk. Sometimes an agency or organization brings in an outside source to conduct facility audits that look for various types of hazards given that we sometimes need a fresh perspective when we become so familiar with our surroundings that we lose the perspective to see problems that might be "staring us in the face." Other ways to better understand and identify risks are be aware of places where accidents and/or injuries have occurred before, be knowledgeable of common hazards through reading the applicable literature, attend conferences and presentations on risk and safety, and remember lessons learned from past experiences.

Risk Evaluation

Risk is evaluated as it relates to the historical or anticipated frequency and severity of incidents. Frequency is based upon the potential for injury, or the likelihood that an injury will take place. Severity indicates the type of injury that could occur (e.g., from minor scrapes or bruises, to paralysis or death). The world is filled with various risks, some minor and some major. Evaluation allows an individual to take actions on those situations that are truly important.

Risk Treatment

Risk is treated in a manner that retains the status quo (retain), reduces the potential of an incident (reduce), shifts the risk to another person or organization through insurance, or through contracts or lease agreements (transfer), or by canceling or prohibiting an action program or project (avoid). Some large companies or governmental units deal with risks by being self-insured. Organizations that are self-insured have large sums of money held back to pay for legal settlements and claims. Obviously, small companies, organizations, or sole proprietors are often not able to deal with the risk of financial loss in this manner.

Actions taken in risk treatment are often the result of good risk evaluation process.

Risk Implementation

Risk avoidance actions should be implemented in a timely and effective manner. It does little good to know about risks and then do nothing about them. Risk implementation takes place when something is repaired, changed, or constructed. Implementation can also take the form of policy change, verbal warnings, brochures and other publications, signs, and mass media releases.

A Practical Process

It is important that each member of an organization be responsible for the safety and risk management program in their area of specialty. Employees should be empowered to take immediate action, make recommendations, and discuss with their supervisors risk and safety matters in their areas of responsibility. They should also be empowered to make recommendations in areas in which they have no direct responsibility. Personal commitment and the feeling that all opinions are important are paramount to a good risk management program.

"Everyone is the safety officer" should be standard operating procedure. A personnel system that rewards those who have identified potential risks should be in place in every organization. Litigation as a result of negligence is simply too expensive and time consuming for most organizations. The energy expended in risk management activities is returned many times over to the organization in employee productivity, pride in the organization, effective public relations, and financial stability.

The risks involved in climbing are often easily identified.

It is commonly understood, however, that there is some level of risk in all of life's activities. Actions to reduce unacceptable risk in recreation, parks, tourism, and sports should be directed at those areas with the highest potential of significant injury or loss. Risk surveys should occur first in the areas of highest recreational use.

Consider a trail starting at a parking lot, extending one-fourth mile and ending at a scenic overlook with no railing. The worn and eroded trail has some tree roots extending into the tread of the trail that has caused people to trip and fall. The overlook stands above a scenic river valley with a 200-foot vertical drop. The two identified hazards are the tree roots growing in the trail and the possibility of falling off the overlook with no railing.

The risk manager must evaluate the frequency and the severity of the risk in each of the identified conditions. In the case of the roots in the trail the frequency of accidents is relatively high, however, the severity (usually sprains or scratches caused by a fall) is low. The vertical cliff presents just the opposite situation, with a very low frequency, but a high potential for severe injury or death. The situation or condition with high severity would take priority. Four basic choices to treat risk are:

1.   Retention (do not take any action—a no-change alternative).

2.   Reduction (take action to reduce the risk).

3.   Transfer (insure or provide contractual provisions that transfer risk).

4.   Avoidance (stop the activity or close the facility).

In the example of the trail and overlook, the treatment may vary, depending upon the classification of the visitors and other factors discussed later in the book. Actions such as signing the trail dangers, rerouting the trail, providing railing, and covering the roots with fill materials may all be applicable to the trail. The risk treatment at the overlook requires immediate action because of the potential severity of the situation. If the area is frequented by adults, or children use the area only when accompanied by an adult (usually parents), a warning sign indicating the danger of standing too close to the cliff may be adequate; however, if children are present without parental supervision, a barrier fence (railing) will be necessary. If a significant portion of the users (25% or more) speak a language other than English, bilingual signs would be encouraged.

After the process of identification, evaluation, and treatment are completed, individuals must then act to change the situation. Actions must be taken to implement reasonable treatment as soon as possible.

An illustration of a problem with "implementation" is a case referred to as *Rost v. United States*.[1] The plaintiff, Randy Rost, was utilizing a backcountry road at the Stanislaus National Forest in California for recreational purposes. Mrs. Rost was driving, and Mr. Rost was riding in the back of the pickup truck in a camper with his children. The family was driving to their camping destination at night. A single steel pole gate, unseen by the driver, hit the front end of the camper. The gate pushed through the camper shell and struck Mr. Rost, forcing him out through the rear of the camper. He was severely injured in the accident.

The gate was painted dark green, and there were no warning signs, reflectors, or lights in the area. The gate had been bent a year earlier and had not been repaired. Because of the gate's bent condition, it extended into the roadway. The gate was under the jurisdiction of and maintained by the federal government. Forest Service crews had driven around the damaged gate during the daylight hours and observed the gate conditions almost daily, but no action was taken to correct the obvious hazard. Mr. Rost sued for his injury and was awarded $647,000 by the court.

The above case is an example of not taking timely action to avoid an accident. Many employees believe that actions to implement repairs or actions that may prevent accidents or property losses are the responsibility of someone else. This attitude has led to many serious accidents. A negligence-caused accident permanently affects the life of the victim, the family of the victim, and even those whose negligence or indifference caused the accident. A person living with the realization that they may be responsible for the suffering or death of others can be psychologically devastated. An effective risk management process is simple and involves all employees and visitors in the activity.

Discussion Question

1. Create a hypothetical situation involving a recreational, sport, or play facility. Analyze the facility given the four-stage risk management process described in the text.

Note

1. *Rost v. United States*, 803 F.2d 448 (1986).

Chapter Thirteen

RISK ASSESSMENT OVERVIEW

Risk assessment should be part of a recreation/sports manager's day-to-day routine. The assessment can be in a verbal format, in which a discussion takes place resulting in improved safety and risk management, or the assessment can take a more formal and documented approach that and is part of a permanent record. The simple fact exists that a professional's positive and proactive attitude toward risk management is better than a forced process that results in thoughtless, bulky, written safety plans that are found gathering dust tucked away on a shelf or at the bottom of a desk. The protection of program participants, employees, and agency/organization financial interests (avoiding a plaintiff's successful litigation resulting from negligence claims) should be a primary emphasis of risk assessment.

Chapter 13 provides tools to use in the evaluation of specific situations. Chapters 13 and 14 are helpful in identifying parameters that should be considered in a risk assessment. Recreation and sport professionals must evaluate the ever-changing nature of their activity, facilities, and environment. Sports and recreation directors must also be responsive to the skills and conduct of coaches, officials, participants, and spectators. While it is important to document and preplan risk-reducing activities, the professional who intuitively senses danger and takes immediate action to mitigate the danger is indeed a great asset to an agency or organization.

SECTION 1: CONSIDERATIONS

Critical considerations used in assessing a sports or recreation risk situation should include:

The Skill of the Participant

Evaluating the skills and experience of the participant is a key element in assessing potential problems. Sending an inexperienced whitewater canoeist or kayaker down a river with level three and four rapids is certainly an example of a dangerous situation. Matching a novice football player with an experienced player is wrought with the possibility of an injury. Lack of skills or experience does not mean that a person should not participate in an activity, it simply means that the person needs training and practice under close supervision, prior to attempting difficult activities or those with high risk. It is particularly important that inexperienced individuals become familiar with safety equipment, learn and practice skills in a controlled environment, and know what is expected of them. Participant and trainer certification programs can be very helpful in reducing risk. Risk evaluators should review the qualifications (training) and experience of both the participant and the trainer/teacher.

Supervision

The quality and the type of supervision can be extremely important in the assessment of risk in recreation and sport activities. While some activities have standards for instructor-to-participant ratios, most others do not. The reasonable man doctrine[1] would apply to situations without specific regulatory, industry, or professional standards. Claims of negligent supervision may involve:

1. The lack of supervision (no supervision).

2. The lack of adequate supervision (not enough supervisors).

3. The lack of training (supervisor not competent to do the work assigned).

4. Nonfeasance[2] (not doing an act that a supervisor should perform).

5. Misfeasance[3] (improperly doing an act that a supervisor might lawfully do).

6. Malfeasance[4] (unlawful conduct by a supervisor).

In *Williams v. United States* (1987),[5] the plaintiff brought a wrongful death claim against the United States after his 16-year-old son drowned in a swimming pool located at an Air Force base. The court found the lifeguards were not attentive to the activities in the diving area of the pool. Evidence indicated that one lifeguard was in her position but was engaged in conversation with a patron instead of giving her attention to the patrons entering the deep end of the pool. As a result, the court found that the lifeguards lost observation of Williams for an unreasonable period of time and were therefore negligent. The court concluded that had the recovery been prompt, Williams could have been resuscitated without brain damage so severe that it ultimately caused his death. The one lifeguard's failure to observe the decedent for several minutes was the proximate cause of his brain damage and resulting death. Her memory of the incident clearly indicated that she was inattentive to her duties. The court also noted that the lifeguard was clearly inexperienced and was given responsibility without supervision, adequate training, and preparation for the emergency use of cardiopulmonary resuscitation. The court also held that a signed release did not relieve the government of liability. The federal district court entered judgment for the plaintiff. Damages were awarded to cover medical and funeral expenses as well as $150,000 for mental grief.

In *Dailey v. Los Angeles Unified School District*,[6] a 16-year-old boy sued the school district because he was injured as a result of a slap fight in a physical education class. The court determined there was a lack of supervision by the physical education teacher. A failure to supervise the behavior of students could result in serious risk problems.

Weather Conditions

Weather has become an ever-increasing problem for recreation, sport, and tourism professionals to consider when evaluating risk and legal liability. Weather-related accidents and injuries have traditionally been considered Acts of God. Case law is starting to change that perception to a more situational context. A recent national survey[7] on laws, regulations, and operating procedures of public agencies and organizations indicates that few had formal warning procedures. While there are few statutory or regulatory requirements, the courts have increasingly awarded damages to plaintiffs in weather-related cases. Risk evaluators should check to see if the organization has an emergency weather plan that limits play in thunderstorms, windy conditions, and during periods of extreme temperatures including heat (with a humidity factor included) and cold. There should also be a procedure in place to warn of approaching severe storms, especially those with lightning. If a plan is in place, it is imperative that it be carried out in the event it is needed.

In *Dykema v. Gus Macker Enterprises, Inc.* (1992),[8] the plaintiff was attending a basketball tournament as a spectator. He paid no entrance or admission fee. While running toward a shelter, the plaintiff was struck and injured by a limb that was blown off a tree during a lightning storm. The plaintiff claimed that a special relationship existed, and Gus Macker Enterprises had a duty to protect its patrons. The defendant claimed that no special relationship existed, because the plaintiff was not there for business purposes. The defense claimed that the plaintiff could see that the oncoming storm was an obvious hazard, and that Gus Macker Enterprises did not have a duty to warn plaintiff of the approaching thunderstorm. The appeals court ruled in favor of defendant Gus Macker Enterprises.

A number of recent cases have resulted in out-of-court settlements. Many were related to golf courses and the lack of a lightning warning system for golfers, lack of safe shelters, unsafe (not grounded properly) shelters, and lack of notification of golfers on procedures when lightning is in the area.

Floods, extreme heat or cold, and high winds can result in property damage, injury, and death. Wind-blown trees can and do break or are uprooted as a result of high winds. Campground-managing agencies and organizations need to give instructions to the campground users on weather-related procedures. This can take the form of verbal notification, audible devices (sirens), or posted predicted weather information on campground bulletin boards and in information centers.

Much outdoor recreation, however, is dispersed (e.g., hiking and fishing) and warnings related to weather should be the individual recreationist's responsibility. Weather warning in remote areas offers a particularly difficult problem. Warning messages indicating that it is the personal responsibility of the recreationist/user to monitor weather should be printed on maps and placed on bulletin boards at trail heads. Risk evaluations should look into the impact of weather on the activities being reviewed.

Physical Condition of the Participants

Most states require a physical examination to be given to high school athletes. Being cognizant of and taking actions to facilitate the physical condition of a participant is important. Coaches and recreation specialists should try to match as much as possible weight, height, skills, and physical abilities of participants on the playing field. In a competitive sports setting, the sponsoring organization should require a physical examination that is specific to the expected exertion and impacts of the target sport or activity. A lack of a legislative or regulatory that requiring physical examination does not prevent an organization or agency from being sued by a plaintiff.[9]

Under the Rehabilitation Act[10] and Americans with Disabilities Act (ADA), many people with disabilities are challenging the rules requiring specific physical standards. Generally, when standards are established for the safety of all participants, challenges to allow those not meeting the medical or physical standards have not been allowed. Specific cases involve prohibiting participation by a hearing-impaired football player[11] and prohibiting a student who was blind in one eye from playing football.[12] Recent cases, however indicate a trend to more accommodation for disabled athletes.[13]

Risk evaluations should examine the matching of individuals and teams to assure that reasonable equality is exercised in sports and recreation activities. Risk evaluations should review the physical conditioning requirements of participants prior to allowing participation in the activity.

Serviceability of Equipment and Playing Environment

Evaluations should assure that the equipment used meets or exceeds the industry standard. The playing environment should not have unexpected hazards or conditions that could result in injury. Safety equipment, such as helmets, pads, gloves, safety harnesses, and so forth. must be available and in good condition. Playing fields should not contain hazards or conditions that are unexpected. For example, deep depressions or holes in a playing field or grass turf could catch a foot of someone running across the field, causing serious injury.

In *Leahy v. School Board of Hernando County* (1984),[14] (see Chapter 24) a football player was injured during a practice session at a Florida high school. The high school did not have enough helmets for every player at the practice session, so Leahy practiced without a helmet. The practice was supposed to be a series of non-contact drills. Leahy was injured when he and a player with a helmet collided. The trial jury determined that the failure to issue a helmet did not constitute negligence; however, the appeals court reversed the decision of the lower court, stating that the lack of equipment did in fact constitute negligence. The case was remanded back for a new trial.

In *Dawson v. Rhode Island Auditorium, Inc.* (1968),[15] the roof of an auditorium leaked during a rainstorm, causing a slick area on the basketball court. This condition had existed in the past, and Rhode Island Auditorium, Inc. was familiar with the problem. A player was injured when he unknowingly stepped onto the wet area. The court awarded damages to the injured player.

Lack of Timeliness in Implementing Risk Measures

When there is a failure or excessive delay in implementing a safety plan or risk assessment, the consequences can be severe. Litigation is a time-consuming and expensive process. If an accident occurs in a location where the organization or agency knows there is a high-risk situation, identifies a solution to the problem, and does not take timely action to alleviate the situation, there is a strong possibility of a successful plaintiff lawsuit. When risk problems are identified, managers should establish an action strategy and timetable whereby the problem will be mitigated.

In the case of *Faber v. United States of America* (1995),[16] a man was seriously injured when he dived from the Tanque Verde Falls at the Coronado National Forest, east of Tucson, Arizona. Five years prior to Faber's accident, the U.S. Forest Service developed a site management plan for the Tanque Verde Falls area. The plan recognized the falls area as a dangerous area. They had determined that 11% of all accidents on the Coronado National Forest were Tanque Verde Falls related. Most of the accident victims were young adults. The management plan gave the following directions: "Intensify the management for the area by constructing parking lots, trails, and heli-spots. Develop a sign plan, formulate an ongoing media program to inform the public and provide a presence at the Falls to verbally warn the public, enforce the laws, and record use patterns."

No actions were taken prior to the accident to implement the site management plan, to erect warning signs, warn orally, or have a media program that would of potential dangers to the users of the area.

The U.S. Forest Service won the lower court decision, arguing that the government was immune from liability for negligence under the discretionary function exception of the Federal Tort Claims Act discretionary function exception. However, the appellate court found that the discretionary function exception was not applicable, because of the identified safety issues, the government's failure to mitigate the problems on the site, and the fact that failure in these areas did not involve a public policy decision. The Federal Appeals Court stated: "If it is a choice to be exercised within established objective safety standards, and the plaintiff's claim of negligence is a failure to follow such standards, the discretionary function exception does not apply."

The case of *Faber v. United States of America* emphasizes the need to take action to:

1. Close the site when excessive risk is identified.

2. Warn users of known dangers.

3. Mitigate or reduce the potential of dangerous natural conditions.

Risk evaluators should check on implementation procedures once a risk is identified.

Terrorism

Terrorism can be differentiated from bullying essentially by the number of people affected by the act and the methods by which it is controlled. Acts of terrorism are normally intended to affect large numbers of people and usually result in injury or death to a significant number of people and most often includes the destruction of property. Bullying usually involves a single individual or small groups. Both bullying and terrorism are means to dominate or subject another party or nation to fear and ultimately to submit to the bully's or terrorist's will. To subject others to fear is the primary purpose of both bullying and terrorism.

Terrorism can originate from both a domestic and international source. Terrorists are usually individuals or groups who believe they have been harmed or marginalized by organizations, governments or religions. Terrorists perpetrate their acts for a variety of reasons. They may include:

1. Strong religious beliefs usually related to the correctness of their own religion and the
    perceived evil associated with other beliefs.

2. Those who have strong beliefs related to the ecology or animal rights issues who want to take retribution on those they believe are harming their interests.

3. Anti-government groups whose political beliefs differ from those in the majority or elected positions.

4. Hate groups who form associations that denounce or vilify other races, creeds, nationalities, and religions.

5. Mentally ill individuals whose reasoning or psychological state results in anti-social behavior.

The 2011 Oslo Norway bombing and murder of young campers illustrates how a single individual can cause great stress on a nation known for their tolerance and peaceful policies. Governments cannot predict what individuals may when they work independently, not receiving instructions for a parent group.

Terrorists have been part of the human experience since history was recorded. Warring factions have utilized terror as a major strategy from before Alexander the Great to contemporary wars. Religion played a major factor in acts of terrorism during the 100 Years War, Northern Ireland conflict, and the present conflicts in the Mideast.

Within the United States, a number of individuals have been killed by arsonists who set fires in forests as an act of violence or revenge against individuals or resource agency policy. Lynching in the South and hanging in the frontier West can best be described as a perverse recreation or sport event rather than a legal proceeding.

Terrorists pick targets that provide the maximum amount of physical and psychological damage to their adversary. Terrorists target the innocent with emphasis on killing or maiming the most susceptible, such as children and young people. The attack at the Atlanta's Centennial Olympic Park during the 1996 Olympic Games targeted young people waiting in a park to enjoy a free concert. The bombing of the 1995 Murrah Federal Building in Oklahoma City targeted federal offices and a large daycare center. Hijacking tourist cruise ships and airplanes were common until strict security measures were implemented.

Forest Service ranger stations and wild horse protection facilities have been burned down by those who have issues with the policies of federal government resource agencies. Animal labs have been vandalized and valuable research studies lost as a result of raids by animal rights groups. The Earth Liberation Front (ELF) set fire to a Vail Colorado Ski Resort causing $12 million dollars of damage to buildings and ski lifts.

Bombings at resorts in the Egyptian Sinai and Bali in Indonesia indicate that international terrorists believe recreation to be a lucrative and desirable target for their attacks. The Bali attack, using a powerful car bomb, killed 150 and injured 300. Seventy-five percent of those killed or wounded were foreign tourists. Anywhere people gather provides a possible target for the malcontent in conflict with the norms of society. Tourism facilities lend themselves as ideal sites for acts of terrorism.

What can we do to protect recreationists, sport participants, fans, and tourists from terrorism acts? By the complexity and widespread nature of the problem, a single solution is not reasonable or effective. Recreation, sports, and tourism planners and managers must be wise in suggesting to others what may be likely terrorism targets. Crying "wolf" too often may diminish cooperative efforts. The utilization of and consultation with local, federal, and international law enforcement agencies is paramount to success.

Increased security may be warranted in the following situations:

1. Sports, recreation or tourist events that attracts a large concentrated audience.

2. Gatherings of people or organized groups who have a history of controversy or violence.

3   Where the activity strongly conflicts with the interest of others. This may include those who may be engaged in illegal activities such as growing or transporting illegal drugs, contraband, illegal human entry into the country or other unlawful activities.

4. Areas with or without large numbers of people that have significant "National Treasure" value, such as capitol buildings, national historical areas, parks, or monuments.

5. International tourism settings where local security is not available or untrained or where State Department travel warnings have been issued.

The major question we all have is, "What should I or my organization do to avoid potential terror attacks?" The answer is not found in a "magic" formula and answers require good judgment. Networking with other security and law enforcement agencies is paramount to success. If recreation, sports, and tourism organizations identify a high potential for terrorism agencies, then concerns should be discussed with other affected and concerned organizations. Administrators should work with others in developing an event security plan and implementing it. Security can sometimes be achieved by the simplest of efforts. The presence of a police or a security officer at the event may be enough to thwart a random act of terror. Security efforts can include the following:

1. Uniformed officers visible on-site.

2. Presence of security cameras.

3. Requiring identification of each visitor/participant.

4. Recording secondary identification sources such as automobile license plates or passports.

5. Requiring a fee to enter. (this usually discourages gang disruptions or violence).

6. Examination of backpacks, purses, baggage and other items carried or shipped to the event.

7. Use of metal and explosive detection devices at entry points.

8. Use of trained dogs that identify explosives or drugs.

9. Thoroughly training all personnel involved in security.

10. Contracting with a certified and licensed security company.

11. Requiring a performance bond (insurance), permit fee, and a security plan when event is sponsored by private interests. This is normally part of a hold harmless agreement.

The potential for terrorism has become a consideration in many of our daily activities. Taking security actions to limit terrorism's potential effects should be a routine part of recreation, sports, and tourism management.

Discussion Questions

1. Why would it be a good idea to get a risk evaluation of your facility from an outside source?

2. Why is it important to implement risk measures in a timely manner?

3. Why is it important to document risk evaluations?

Notes

1. The reasonable man doctrine is the standard that a reasonable man or women must observe to avoid liability for negligence, including the foreseeability of harm to the participant. Black, H. C. (1979). *Black's law dictionary* (5th ed.). St. Paul, MN: West Publishing Co., p. 1138.

2. Nonfeasance is the nonperformance or omission of a required duty or total neglect of duty. Black, H. C. (1979). *Black's law dictionary* (5th ed.). St. Paul, MN: West Publishing Co., p. 950.

3. Misfeasance is the improper performance of some act that a person could lawfully do. Black, H. C. (1979). *Black's law dictionary* (5th ed.). St. Paul, MN: West Publishing Co., p. 902.

4. Malfeasance is described as evildoing or conduct and commission of an act that is unlawful. It is sometimes related to an act that the person has no authority to perform or interferes with the performance of official duty. Black, H. C. (1979). *Black's law dictionary* (5th ed.). St. Paul, MN: West Publishing Co., p. 862.

5. *Williams v. United States,* 660 F.Supp. 699 (E.D. Ark. 1987).

6. *Dailey v. Los Angeles Unified School District,* 2 Cal.3d 741, 470 P.2d 360, 87 Cal.Rptr 376 (1970).

7. Eleventh Northeastern Recreation Research Symposium. (1999). Presentation entitled Weather Related Liability in Outdoor Recreation, Hronek, Bruce B.

8. *Dykema v. Gus Macker Enterprises, Inc.,* 492 N.W. 2d (1992).

9. Schubert, Smith, & Trentadue. (1986). *Sports law.* St. Paul, MN: West Publishing Company, p.180.

10. Rehabilitation Act of 1973, 219 U.S.C. 794 (1982) and the Americans with Disabilities Act of 1990 Section 511, 42 U.S.C.A.

11. *Columbo v. Sewanhaka Central High School District No.2,* 383 N.Y.S.2d 518 (1976).

12. *Spitaleri v. Nyguest,* 345 N.Y.S.2d 878 (1973).

13. Schubert, Smith, & Trentadue. (1986). *Sports law.* St. Paul, MN: West Publishing Company, p.36.

14. *Leahy v. School Board of Hernando County,* 450 So.2d 883 (Fla. App. 1984).

15. *Dawson v. Rhode Island Auditorium, Inc.,* 242 A.2d 407 (R.I.1968).

16. *Faber v. United States of America,* LLR 1995 U.S. 9th Cir. 434 (No.94.16096) United States Court of Appeals for the Ninth Circuit, June 6, 1995. Appeals of Florida, Fifth District, Decided May 10, 1984.

Chapter Fourteen

APPROACHES TO RISK ASSESSMENT

There are a number of approaches to risk assessment that recreation, sport, and tourism professionals can implement that result in successful risk management programs. Each situation needs to have a somewhat customized approach. While risk assessment programs may vary in many aspects, there are some basic elements that should be included in all assessment documents. Using the risk management process explained in Chapter 12, each assessment should:

1. Identify the type or category of the risk, such as negligence, tort, fidelity, property loss, contract, and so forth.

2. Evaluate the frequency and severity of the risk by assessing how often accidents have occurred and the result of the accidents in terms or severity or level of costs.

3. Determine the applicable risk treatment, such as do nothing, reduce risk, insure (transfer) risk, or close facility or stop activity.

4. Implement the findings of the assessment in a timely manner by setting policy, changing procedures, implementing actions, and setting a completion timetable.

Risk management in an organization or agency should be institutionalized as an integral part of everyday activities. Successful programs depend
more on individual employee attitudes and organizational culture rather
than a regulatory process.

Personal Responsibility

Each employee and manager should feel a personal responsibility to risk
management concerns and respond to protect the interests and safety of fellow employees, program participants, and visitors. When an individual is
designated as a "safety officer" or "risk manager" many employees feel no
personal responsibility to be vigilant to risk. An organization that awards
employees for identifying or reducing significant risks knows that such an
effort will improve morale and be an excellent financial investment.

A risk reduction program should constantly remind employees to:

1. Be alert to unsafe conditions.

2. Take reasonable and timely action when they become aware of hazard-
    ous conditions.

Society conditions the public to believe that dangerous situations are the
responsibility of someone else, both in the workplace and in communities.
As an example, if a person sees a tree limb across a public road as a result of
a windstorm, what will be his or her reaction? He or she may respond by:

- Driving around the limb and think that someone ought to do something
  about the dangerous situation;

- driving around the limb and when they get to their destination, report
  the fallen limb to someone responsible for road maintenance; or

- stop in a safe place and remove the limb from the road.

If the person is risk management and community oriented, he should
respond by either reporting the situation immediately or personally remov-
ing the hazard. A positive risk management attitude that reflects personal
responsibility also translates to the work environment or profession as a
positive attitude that will benefit the organization, other employees, and the
participant/customer.

Risk Evaluation from an Outside Source

It is sometimes best to have someone who is not familiar with an organization's day-to-day operations and facilities be involved with a risk assessment team. Much like the picture that hangs crooked on the wall of a person's home, it is only when a visitor to the home notes that the picture is crooked does the owner recognize the problem. Employees of an organization may not recognize a significant risk because they have become accustomed to doing something or seeing something dangerous over a period of time. As examples, the protruding bolt on the play equipment, the dangerous outfield fence, worn electrical wires, and a broken ladder may not be noticed by those who use or maintain the equipment or facilities on a daily basis. A risk evaluation conducted by someone not familiar with the facilities and operating procedures of an organization may be very useful to management.

Reciprocal agreements, whereby employees from one section or office of an organization aid in risk assessment on another unit can have very positive risk management results. The diversity (job assignment, profession, and experience) of the assessment team can also be helpful.

Documenting Risk Evaluations

In many cases, procedural policies in large organizations require employees to document risk evaluations in a formal, written form and forward the information to a unit manager or safety/risk coordinator for approval and implementation. Many large organizations also have complex lines of authority that slow or limit communications originating at the lower levels of the organization.

A wise administrator will establish a procedure where first-level managers must formally write back to the employees if he or she rejects a risk reduction idea. However, if he or she agrees with the recommendation of the subordinate, the administrator can implement the recommendation. An administrator only has to endorse the evaluation and forward it to the next level for implementation or further consideration. Saying no to a risk management recommendation is sometimes the easiest answer when the supervisor is very busy with other tasks. The realization that he or she must respond in writing, if the suggestion is rejected, provides an environment more conducive to effective risk management.

Legal considerations may also require organizations to document risk evaluations. Operating and Maintenance (O&M) plans normally contain written directions indicating that an agency or organization is meeting standards of care requirements. An agency's failure to accomplish the standards set in their own O&M plan may also provide the plaintiff evidence that the agency did not meet the standard of care required. As a general rule, planning documents should reflect industry or professional standards, but should not provide directions to exceed those standards. Agencies may experience legal problems when the internal written requirements significantly exceed the standards maintained by most others (standard of care). In many cases, reduced funding results in agencies not meeting their own planned standards. As an example, an agency should not state in a plan that they intend to maintain a campground every day, when the reality of funding is that it can only be maintained three times a week.

Standard Forms for Risk Assessment

The following forms represent a "standard" approach to risk assessment. They do not fit all situations, but provide broad guidance for the risk evaluator. A risk assessment team should modify the forms for its specific activity or facility. Use these forms to conduct a risk evaluation for a class assignment.

Name of evaluator _____

Date _____

Location or program involved _____

Describe risk _____

Actions taken to mitigate or reported to _____

Follow-up or planned action _____

Figure 14.1 *Short Form Risk Evaluation*

Name of evaluator
Weather conditions
Date of evaluation
Time of day
Location of evaluation (provide detailed information)

Identification
　　1.　Describe hazard
　　2.　Describe type of injury or property loss that could occur

Evaluation
　　1.　How severe could this potential loss be?
　　2.　How often could this loss occur?
　　3.　Give your evaluation of the risk
　　　　high
　　　　medium
　　　　low

Treatment
1.　What is your recommendation to reduce the risk associated with a hazard?

Implementation
1.　Who is responsible for the risk treatment?
2.　Have the responsible parties been notified?
3.　When will the work be completed?
4.　Are there any intermediate actions that can be implemented prior to treatment?
Describe intermediate actions?

Verification of Implementation
Date
Name & position

Figure 14.2 *Long Form Risk Evaluation*

Other Written Devices That Assess Risk

Other common forms or devices should be used to evaluate and improve risk management activities. They include and are not limited to:

Accident Report Forms

All accidents should be reported. The same form can be used to identify risks and implement measures to mitigate the causes. All accident reports should be seen by managers, and they in turn should follow-up on any actions necessary to ensure that the conditions that may have caused the accident are addressed.

Risk Management Policy Statements

Policy statements should indicate the broad support management has for on-the-job, day-to-day, institutionalized risk programs. Policy statements usually set the tone for employee participation in risk management.

Waivers, Releases, and Agreements to Participate

These should include specific areas of concern and identification of known hazards or conditions.

Special Use Agreements, Leases, and Rental Agreements

These need to describe known dangers and actions needed to reduce dangers. It is particularly important that all known risks be described and noted in agreements. Each agreement should also outline the responsibility of the permittee/lessee/renter in regards to safety considerations.

Medical Treatment Forms

These forms should indicate cause of the problem, location of accident, and other factors related to time, place, weather, and so forth. The forms should include opportunities for both the patient and medical personnel to state the cause of medical condition.

Inspection Reports

Many inspection reports involve specific areas such as floor condition, playground equipment condition, etc. Each inspection report should include action items needed to bring the facility to a standard and time of project completion.

Other Risk Considerations

Because risk management is not restricted to just the facility and the program aspects of recreation and sports, individualized and specialized procedures may need to be developed. Some of the risk areas not included in a standard format may include:

Contract Risk

Contract risk evaluation may be an integral part of the contract approval process. This evaluation may include a worse case scenario analysis as well as a determination of methods of delivery and the delivery date; security and protection for merchandise, service, or materials; the critical nature of timeliness of completion of the contract, and the penalty for failure to meet contract specifications or deadlines. There may be high risks when contracts contain mistakes, involve misrepresentation, involve minors, do not include specific performance dates, include impractical requirements, or do not have quality performance standards.

Personnel Risk

Personnel performance is critical to accomplishing the needs of an organization. Personnel risk evaluation may consider training needs, potential behavior problems based on documented incidents or medical evaluation, fatigue problems on long shifts, driver training and education, health hazards, employee honesty, and other factors that affect performance.

Property Loss

There is a financial loss risk potential related to natural disasters, such as forest fires, earthquakes, hurricanes, or tornadoes, which can result in extensive property damage.

Discussion Questions

1. Use the forms on pp. 170-171 to conduct a real or hypothetical risk assessment. Explain your rationale for the evaluation of the risk.

Chapter Fifteen

INSURANCE

Prior to opening facilities, programming activities, allowing access, leasing, operating a concession, licensing, permitting, arranging travel, facilitating events, or issuing special use permits, the obvious question should always be: "Is the activity adequately covered by liability insurance?" Liability insurance[1] is an indemnity[2] against loss borne by a third party—the insurance company. When a visitor is injured as a result of a negligent act by a property owner, the third party (insurance company) bears the loss.

In the area of tourism and event planning, consideration must be made to determine if insurance is needed to "guarantee against financial loss" resulting from event and travel cancellation. Events and travel can be canceled due to sickness, international conflicts, catastrophic events, weather situations, and other unforeseen situations. Travel and event insurance should be considered to protect the financial interests of both the organization and the individual customer. As an example, if a family is arranging for an international vacation with prepaid air travel and guaranteed hotel reservations, the person arranging the trip may want to suggest trip insurance. This is particularly important if there is a possibility of intervening personal circumstances (a risk probability) that would require the family or individual family members to cancel the trip.

In 1998, the National Recreation and Park Association (NRPA) held its annual convention (congress) in Miami Beach, Florida. As the 10,000 delegates started to arrive, the National Weather Service forecasted a hurricane to make landfall in the vicinity of the conference with a high probability of the hurricane striking the Miami Beach area. The costs of staging this conference and the individual travel and lodging costs were significant. The NRPA had obtained event insurance to protect itself in case of such an event, which greatly reduced the impact to the association; however, delegates had to bear the cost of their own travel to Miami Beach and then either immediately returning home after the storm or canceling their travel plans entirely. (As a notation; there was little impact on Miami Beach from the hurricane, but the event managers wisely canceled the event to avoid the possibility of endangering the lives of the convention delegates.)

Insurance Policy Management

The general outline of most liability insurance policies includes sections on declarations, the insuring agreement, exclusions, and conditions. Each of these broad sections must be examined carefully by the insured person(s) or organization.

The declaration contains information related to the parties involved, addresses, and the intent of the agreement. The agreement sets forth the contractual aspects of the insurance policy. The exclusions describe those situations where the policy would not be in effect. The agreements serve generally as limitation risk or liability and/or impose various conditions requiring compliance by the insured.[3]

It is generally understood that liability insurance is a necessity in our contemporary world. People have the propensity and capability to sue if injured or if they suffer a loss of property. Insurance can be very expensive, even when managed properly, and an excessively heavy burden if managed poorly. Recreation, sports, and tourism providers should shop for insurance and determine the scope of their insurance needs. They should not have an insurance agent determine their requirements without considerable personal input and price comparison. The cost of insurance for high adventure travel activities has a significant impact of whether or not a private provider's operations are profitable.

As an example, private companies that provide guide services, canoes, rafts, and other outdoor equipment for river users should examine closely the length (season) of insurance coverage. A three-month liability insurance policy may cost only a fourth of that of year-around coverage. However, many insurance providers will gladly provide year-around coverage for a seasonal operation. The insured must be watchful to avoid insurance "overkill."

An insured party should analyze the following aspects of their insurance coverage to reduce premium costs:

1. Facilities, events, or activities to be covered. Cover only those things that need to be covered. As an example, you may not want to have earthquake coverage if most of your activities are in an outdoor setting.

2. The category of persons to be covered, depending on the type of operations involved, you may not want to insure some of the categories of visitors-paying, non-paying guests, contractors, trespassers, employees, and so forth.

3. Types of losses to be covered (See list under Types of Insurance Coverage).

4. Locations or property to be covered, An organization may want to only include property visited by the public under participant accident coverage.

5. Period or time of day, day of the week, or season to be covered. If the operations occur during a specific time period or specific days of the week, the insurance should reflect the limited scope of the operations.

6. Special conditions included in the insurance (certain activities may require special coverage such as weather insurance).

7. Deductible costs the recreation provider is willing to pay (a high deductible on an insurance policy will significantly reduce the cost). A deductible is the amount of money on a claim for which the policyholder is liable.

The joining of specific interest groups or associations, such as park districts, private companies, school districts, and so forth into a cooperative entity can significantly reduce the cost of insurance. It is a simple fact that the larger the organization, the more negotiable the insurance rate. All insurance rates and conditions should be negotiated with the insurance agents or underwriters. The following case illustrates the importance of knowing the specific circumstances under which an individual is covered by a policy.

In *USAA Casualty Insurance Co. v. Schneider* (1985),[4] professional tennis player John McEnroe, was angered by the heckling of a spectator (Schneider) during a tennis match. As the game progressed, McEnroe grew more irritated at Schneider's heckling. McEnroe finally jumped into the stands to exchange heated words with Schneider. Schneider alleges that McEnroe waved his hand at him causing grains of rosin to fall onto him, causing injury. Schneider sued McEnroe for six million dollars, and McEnroe turned it over to his insurance company. McEnroe's insurance did not cover business-related suits. McEnroe argued that the incident was not part of his business. The insurance company subsequently sued both Schneider and McEnroe to get a court decision whether or not the act of confronting a fan during a game was part of the business of a professional tennis player. The case was decided in favor of the USAA Casualty Insurance Company, stating that "The business of tennis is not confined solely to the game of tennis." As an example, the court noted that tournament participants must attend final ceremonies and professional tennis rules direct players to "not verbally or physically abuse any spectator within the precincts of the tournament site."

Types of Insurance

The types of insurance needed for recreation, sports, and tourism settings may include:

1. **Accident (Casualty)**—needed for losses caused by injuries to persons or damage to property.

2. **Automobile**—needed to insure against personal injuries and property loss resulting from a broad list of categories.

3. **Inclement weather**—needed when an activity is weather dependent.

4. **Travel and event**—needed when circumstances may require organizations and individuals to protect their financial interest by canceling travel or an event.

5. **Product liability**—needed when an individual or organization develops or uses products or equipment.

6. **Professional liability**—needed in some cases when advising, treating, or guiding people. (See below for further explanation and considerations.)

7. **Theft and dishonesty (Fidelity)**—needed to protect against losses due to internal losses from employees and contractors.

8. **Contractual liability**—to insure against losses resulting from problems associated with contract performance.

9. **Crime insurance**—needed when crime is a specific problem and not covered by comprehensive insurance.

10. **Property loss (fire, tornado, earthquake, lightning, etc.)**—needed when other insurance coverage does not adequately include property risk.

There is a constant debate related to whether or not recreation professionals should obtain professional liability insurance. Those engaged in private consulting, planning, designing, and other private enterprises should seriously consider purchasing professional liability insurance. Those seeking insurance should consider what types of insurance coverage is needed. Insurance coverage should extend beyond injury and property loss to include protection from losses due to a broad category of suits, including libel, professional mistakes (engineering, architectural, etc.), slander, false arrest, and invasion of privacy.

Other situations might also dictate whether those in the public sector need to purchase professional liability insurance. In the majority of situations, a public agency will come to the aid of its employees embroiled in a lawsuit, resulting from their performance on the job. If a public sector professional has the propensity to violate job performance standards or get drunk and hit people, he or she as an individual should definitely purchase some type of insurance. In all cases, public sector professionals should consult with their legal counsel to determine their personal situation regarding professional insurance. The following case illustrates a situation where public employees would have been wise to have held professional liability insurance.

In *Bivens v. Six Unknown Named Agents of Federal Bureau of Narcotics* (1971),[6] six federal agents conducted a drug raid on the home of Mr. and Mrs. Bivens. The raid occurred at night when the Bivenses were in bed. The agents forced the unclad Bivenses to the floor, handcuffed them, and proceeded to virtually destroy their home looking for drugs. After a long and complete search of the premises, they found nothing. The agents checked the search warrant and realized they had the wrong address. The Bivenses sued the individual agents for violating their constitutional rights under the

Fourth Amendment. The six federal agents argued that they were immune from suit under the discretionary functions of government. The Bivenses argued that the six agents were outside of their protection in violating a person's constitutional rights. The Supreme Court agreed with the Bivenses. The court in its decision stated:

> It (the Constitution) guarantees to citizens of the United States the absolute right to be free from unreasonable searches and seizures carried out by virtue of federal authority ... and where federally protected rights have been invaded, it has been the rule from the beginning that courts will be alert to adjust their remedies so as to grant the necessary relief.

Insurance is also necessary in the private sector and in many smaller governmental units. Only the larger government entities, such as the federal government and state government, can afford to be self-insured. Groups of small governmental units or private recreation and sport providers can join together in an association and significantly increase their insurance bargaining position and reduce the cost of liability insurance coverage.

Discussion Questions

1. What is a deductible and what are the considerations in determining a deductible that is right for your organization?

2. What is self-insurance and what types of organizations are most likely to be self insured?

3. Decide upon a hypothetical program or organization and list the types of insurance that you would likely need, and why you would need these types.

Notes

1. Liability insurance is a contract by which one party promises on consideration to compensate or reimburse another if he shall suffer loss from a specified cause or to guaranty or indemnify or secure him against loss from that cause. This type of insurance protection which indemnifies one from liability to a third person is contrasted with insurance cover-

age or losses sustained by the insured. Black, H. C. (1979). *Black's law dictionary* (5th ed.). St. Paul, MN: West Publishing Co., p.824.

2. Indemnity is an economic compensation paid by a third party on behalf of another.

3. Black, H. C. (1979). *Black's law dictionary* (5th ed.). St. Paul, MN: West Publishing Co., p. 265.

4. *USAA Casualty Ins. Co. v. Schneider,* 620 F.Supp. 246 (E.D. N.Y. 1985).

5. As an example see: Federal Employees Liability Reform and Tort Compensation Act of 1988, Public Law 100694.

6. *Bivens v. Six Unknown Named Agents of Federal Bureau of Narcotics,* 403 U.S. 388 (1971).

Part Six

WORKPLACE RISK

Chapter Sixteen

EMPLOYEE TERMINATION

Firing an employee is one of the most difficult tasks a manager must face. Being fired from a job can strike a devastating blow to both the employee and his or her family. The manager knows that he or she has most likely placed the terminated employee in financial difficulty. The manager also knows that termination is a blow to the employee's self-esteem. Given the harmful consequences to the employee and the stress it places on a manager, it is not a pleasant experience. It is, however, a reality that every manager must eventually face. No attempt will be made here to suggest the best way of firing an employee. The purpose of this chapter is merely to inform you of some of the legal issues that arise when it comes time to fire an employee.

From a legal standpoint, it is important to first determine if a public or private entity is involved. If a public agency is involved, there are constitutional protections that a government employee is afforded that must be adhered to by the managing agency. The most important and often raised protection is the right to due process before termination. Government employees are given the right, under the Constitution, to be heard (usually at a hearing before key administrators) before they can be terminated. The principle is that they deserve the right to have their side of the story heard before the government takes away one of their constitutional rights. The property right referred to here is the right to employment. As you recall from previous chapters, the U.S. Constitution guarantees its citizens the right to life, liberty, and property. Property is generally thought of as something we can touch or see, such as land, an automobile, or some other object. The courts, however, have extended the concept of property to include the right to employment.

In some cases, courts have even recognized a college athletic scholarship as a property right afforded protection under the Constitution. The following case provides a good discussion of whether an organization is public or private and whether due process has been satisfied.

In the case of *Davenport v. Casteen* (1995),[1] Davenport worked for a private, nonprofit organization that raised money for intercollegiate athletics and athletic grants-in-aid at the University of Virginia. This organization was called the Virginia Auxiliary Services Corp. (VSAF). Davenport's salary was paid by VSAF through the University of Virginia. Problems for Davenport started when the University reported to th NCAA that VSAF had given student athletes more money than they were allowed under NCAA rules.

The university president and VSAF, the organization that Davenport worked for, began an investigation into the matter. As the investigation progressed, Davenport's conduct came into question. He therefore hired an attorney to represent him in the matter. He was asked questions to which he gave responses. Subsequently, a report was written up that included findings regarding possible NCAA rules violations. A copy of the report was given to Davenport and another copy was given to the university president.

As a result of the investigation, Davenport was found to have breached his employment contract with VSAF. A letter was then sent to his attorney saying what Davenport had done wrong and inviting him to appear at a hearing before the VSAF executive committee to tell his side of the story. Davenport decided not to attend this hearing. After the date for the hearing had passed and he had not shown up, the university president sent Davenport a letter telling him that he was suggesting that VSAF terminate his employment. Shortly after this letter was received, VSAF fired him.

On the day he was fired, Davenport brought suit against VSAF, the former athletic director of the university, and the university president. Ultimately, after some procedural matters were resolved, Davenport amended his motion to ask for four million dollars from the university president for tortuous interference and defamation. The case was brought in the U.S. District Court for the Western District of Virginia in Charlottesville.

The Constitution requires that government employees be given the opportunity to tell their side of the story (at a formal hearing) before they can be denied liberty and property rights. Since it is generally held that employment is a property right, due process requirements must be satisfied before a government employee can be fired from a job.

The court held that all of the constitutional requirements of due process had been satisfied. First, the court found that Davenport was not a government employee. Davenport argued that since the university paid his salary, he was a government employee. The court disagreed. The university paid his salary through VSAF, which the court found did not tie him closely enough to the university to make him a government employee, and thus, he was not afforded this protection.

Second, even if Davenport was considered to be an employee of the government, the court held that he was given all of the due process rights he was entitled to under the Constitution. Due process requires government agencies to follow proper procedures before terminating an employee. Before an employee can be fired, he must be given oral or written notice of the charges against him and the opportunity to attend a hearing to decide his or her fate.

The court held that all the procedural requirements of due process were offered to Davenport. He was given several opportunities to present his side of the story, once at a formal hearing of which he was notified in a letter. Additionally, before he was given the opportunity to present his case, he was notified of the possible NCAA rules he had violated.

Whether working for a public or private organization, the manager who does the firing should keep several things in mind. First, he or she must be careful not to make negative comments or allegations against the employee in the presence of a third party. For example, while standing in a crowded gym watching a basketball practice, the athletic director wouldn't want to accuse an assistant coach of stealing and give that as the reason for firing him. If the accusations are not true, and someone overhears the conversation, the employee could bring suit for defamation. You will recall that defamation includes both spoken (slander) and written (libel) communications and can subject the manager and agency to both criminal and civil lawsuits. Therefore, the manager should make certain that any initial performance allegation made against an employee be accurate. The discussion should take place in private with only the manager and employee present. In subsequent hearings, both the manager and employee may have their ombudsman or legal counsel present; however, the hearings will remain confidential.

Also, the manager must avoid discrimination at all costs when terminating employees. First, it is ethically wrong to engage in discriminatory practices. Second, the manager and the organization can be sued for discrimination. Discrimination lawsuits are brought under authority of the Civil Rights Act (1991). Direct proof of discrimination would exist when a manager, for example, fired an employee because: he or she thought the employee was too old, he or she didn't like to have women on the job, or he or she didn't like people of a certain ethnic background. A manager must have legitimate reasons to fire employees or they may be subject to a lawsuit for discrimination.

Suppose that a 45-year-old female entertainment director on a cruise ship has been fired from her job. She is replaced by a 25-year-old woman. She felt like she was doing a fine job and cannot imagine a legitimate reason the employer would have for firing her. She thinks it over and decides to sue the manager and the cruise ship line for discrimination. Are the manager and cruise ship line guilty of discrimination?

To prove that they had discriminated against her, she would have to prove the following. First, she must show that she was a member of a group protected from discrimination by law. This might include, for example, a person in her age bracket. Second, she must show that she was fired from the job. Third, she must show that someone not in that protected class, a younger woman for example, was given the job after she was fired. This makes up her *prima facie* case.[2]

Now it is the manager's turn to make his or her case. He or she needs to demonstrate with admissible evidence that the decision to fire the entertainment director was motivated by a legitimate reason. He or she doesn't need to prove the case; the burden of proof stays with the plaintiff. He or she only needs to produce the right evidence. It must be evidence, however, that can withstand a claim from the plaintiff that it is used to hide the true discriminatory reason for firing her. What type of evidence must the manager produce? There are several things that it would be wise for him or her to show.

First, he or she should offer proof of unsatisfactory job performance to show that termination was for cause. A record of frequent absences or of often being late for work would be helpful to the manager. Also, a record of complaints from customers (passengers aboard the ship) would help support a legitimate reason for firing her. Further, it would be wise, if it were true, to show that other employees in similar positions were of various ages; some in the over-40 age group. Finally, the manager should have a consistent hiring policy with employment requirements that have objective measures. For example, if the job requires physical tasks such as preparing lifeboats in the event of an emergency, the manager would need to show that women over 40 who could satisfactorily complete the tasks were hired. If the plaintiff could not perform the task when other women her age were able to, a legitimate reason for firing her might exist as shown from the evidence.

If the termination of an employee is found to be not for cause pursuant to the terms of an express contract for a period of time, then the issue arises as to what contractual terms must be honored for the duration of the contract. This issue often arises in college coaching when a coach is fired before his contract has expired. The following case provides an example.

In *Rodgers v. Georgia Tech Athletic Assoc.* (1983),[3] the head coach of the Georgia Tech football team was fired by the University Board of Trustees.

The coach brought suit claiming breach of contract and the appropriation of a property right (his employment). Rodgers had an employment contract that stated the reasons for which his employment could be terminated. The court found that he was not terminated for any of the reasons stated in the contract, and therefore his termination was not for cause. The issue then became which benefits he would be entitled to throughout the remainder of his contractual period. It was held that the coach was not entitled to the services and perks incidental to his job as a coach (e.g., secretarial services, lodging, trips to football coaches conventions), gifts, or items that were made on a year-to-year basis with no assurance that they would be continued (e.g., housing, club memberships).

The process of terminating an employee is fraught with difficulties, both emotional and legal. Knowing what to expect in the way of lawsuits and knowing how to avoid or deal with them is important for the manager. Recreation and park administrators are not immune to these problems. As changes take place in society and the law, managers need to learn how to respond to them and make the chore of firing employees as painless and risk-free as possible.

Discussion Questions

1. Can a supervisor discuss the performance of an employee with someone not meeting the "need-to-know" status? Explain.

2. What must an employee successfully prove to win a discrimination case?

3. Must all supervisors be "nice?" Explain.

Notes

1. *Davenport v. Casteen,* 878 F.Supp. 871 (W.D.Va. 1995).
2. The term "*prima facie* case" means that sufficient evidence has been presented to show that, on its face, the plaintiff should win the case.
3. *Rodgers v. Georgia Tech Athletic Assoc,* 303 S.E.2d 467 (Ga. App. 1983).

Chapter Seventeen

SEXUAL HARASSMENT IN THE WORKPLACE[1]

Suppose that you manage a municipal parks and recreation department. One day, as you are in the midst of keeping the wolves at bay and solving problems too numerous to count, a female employee comes to you with a problem. The supervisor of her maintenance crew asked her to have dinner at his home. When she refused, he became angry, began cursing, and called her some very crude names. In the past week, he has called her demeaning names and tells sexually explicit jokes in front of the crew, naming her as a fictional character in the jokes. He has bumped into her often and touched her in inappropriate ways. When she told him to stop, he said that he was just kidding around and that she should have a better sense of humor. She asks for your help.

As a manager confronted with this type of situation, the first thing that probably comes to mind is sexual harassment. To many, the word brings feelings of confusion, anger, and dread. In this hypothetical example, the maintenance supervisor has clearly overstepped the bounds of common decency; but has he engaged in sexual harassment? What should the manager do?

One thing that the manager could do is fire the supervisor immediately. This might solve the female employee's sexual harassment problems, but it could open up another can of worms. If the manager fires the supervisor right away and accuses him of doing the things the woman has claimed, the maintenance supervisor might sue for defamation or breach of contract.[2] Also, since the supervisor in this case is a government employee, if he is fired immediately without a hearing, he could sue, claiming that he had been denied his constitutional due process rights to a hearing. You will recall that employment is a property right interpreted by the courts to be protected under the Constitution.

The manager might instead take another course of action. He might ask the female employee if she would like to be moved out of maintenance to work in another position in the agency. This suggestion, however, might not be wise from a management perspective. It would merely treat the symptom and would not cure the true problem. The next female employee who worked in maintenance might face the same problems of harassment. Also, the victim of the harassment might rightly feel that the perpetrator should be disciplined. If she feels this way, it is likely that she will go ahead with a suit against the agency for sexual harassment.

A third option for the manager might be to meet with the maintenance supervisor in private and speak to him about his behavior concerning the female employee. Hopefully, the maintenance supervisor will agree to stop the conduct. Now that the manager knows of the alleged sexual harassment, he must now be extra careful that the harassing conduct stops. The important point is that once the claim has been made known, the manager must take action. To let it pass and hope the problem goes away on its own is to invite trouble.

If the conduct happens again, it must be stopped immediately. Whichever course of action the manager takes, the harm has already been done and the female employee may still choose to file a sexual harassment suit against the agency. A basic understanding of sexual harassment and ways to prevent and handle sexual harassment claims can help ease the fear and confusion that so often accompany these claims.

The legal concept of sexual harassment comes from several sources and needs to be untangled to be best understood. First, sexual harassment has been recognized by the Supreme Court as a component of gender discrimination, which is governed by Title VII of the Civil Rights Act of 1964.[3] When sexual harassment occurs, it is a violation of Title VII.

Second, the Equal Employment Opportunity Commission (EEOC) has developed guidelines for appraising sexual harassment claims. The EEOC is a federal government entity that employs experts on employment issues. They use their knowledge to develop guidelines to help the courts develop rules governing these issues. The guidelines have no binding power on the courts, but they do, however, provide guidance to judges when they are making decisions on sexual harassment cases. The Supreme Court has used these guidelines to develop legal standards for sexual harassment cases.

The EEOC guidelines give us some idea of what sexual harassment is and the liability imposed on employers when these claims arise. The remainder of this section discusses aspects of these guidelines that will help you better understand sexual harassment as a legal concept and hopefully clear up some confusion and misconceptions you may have about this concept.

The EEOC guidelines define sexual harassment as "unwelcome" sexual advances. By definition, therefore, it must involve conduct that is sexual in nature and not desired by the employee. In other words, a female employee who voluntarily consents to have sex with a co-employee or supervisor at his request generally cannot later claim sexual harassment. You should know, however, that even voluntary acceptance of sexual advances can land your organization in hot water. Under Title VII of the Civil Rights Act, the fact that sexual conduct is voluntary will not hold up a defense against sexual harassment charges. The following Supreme Court case illustrates this point.

In the case of *Meritor Savings Bank v. Vinson* (1986),[4] a young woman worked as a teller at the Meritor Savings Bank. She had just completed her time as a teller-trainee when her boss started making sexual advances. Fearing that she might lose her job, after several refusals, she finally agreed to have sex with him. Her boss became forward at work, making sexual demands even while she was on the job. He would fondle her in front of other employees and follow her into the women's restroom and expose himself to her.

This information came out in a sexual harassment lawsuit she brought against her boss and employer bank. The suit was brought in federal district court. The federal court held that since her boss did not threaten her with job termination if she refused his sexual advances and since the sexual relationship was voluntary, she could not prevail on her sexual harassment claim. She appealed her case to the U.S. Supreme Court.

The plaintiff had relied upon the EEOC guideline that defined sexual harassment as "unwelcome" sexual advances. Her supervisor had not told her that she would lose her job or not receive a raise if his sexual demands were not met. Still, his advances were not welcome, and it became difficult to work under the conditions he created. The Supreme Court sympathized with her predicament and looked for a fair solution. They decided to view the EEOC guideline in light of Title VII, which has the power of law. Under Title VII of the Civil Rights Act, the fact that sexual conduct was voluntary is not a valid defense to charges of sexual harassment.

The court, instead of just looking to see if sexual advances accompanied threats concerning her job, looked to see whether the work environment became hostile (or abusive) due to the things her supervisor was doing. If he exposed her to intimidation, ridicule, or insult, she might prevail on her claim under Title VII. The court held that if a hostile work environment existed due to sexual advances, a case for sexual harassment could be found. Her case was sent back to the federal district court for a new trial to see if a hostile work environment existed.

The EEOC guidelines make it unlawful to have a hostile or abusive work environment, as defined by the courts. Sexual harassment is found, from a legal standpoint, when there is a hostile work environment. The guidelines say that sexual conduct is unlawful when it has as its purpose, or results in unreasonable interference "with an individual's work performance or creates an intimidating, hostile, or offensive work environment."[5] The Supreme Court set a standard from these guidelines determining when a hostile environment/sexual harassment exists. It uses the term "abusive" work environment and explains how to determine whether one exists. The Supreme Court in the following case explains the standard it set.

In the case of *Harris v. Forklift Systems, Inc.* (1993),[6] Harris was a manager at an equipment rental company called Forklift Systems. Soon after she began working for the company, problems developed between her and the company president. She claimed that he insulted her often because she was a woman and would imply that she had been involved in inappropriate sexual situations. She said that he told her on several occasions that she was a dumb woman and that they needed a man in her management position. Also, he asked her to get coins from his front pants pocket, and told her they should go to a hotel to negotiate her raise.

After she had been working for Forklift for about five months, she decided to confront the company president about his actions. He acted surprised that she was offended and said that he was sorry for upsetting her. Soon after this, however, he questioned her integrity by making a crude remark containing a sexual suggestion. Harris decided to resign, and then sued the company and its president for sexual harassment. She claimed that the sexual remarks had created an abusive work environment for her because of her gender. The suit was brought in federal court because it involved a federal question, the violation of Title VII of the Civil Rights Act of 1964.[7]

The federal district court decided against the plaintiff. The court based its decision on the following test. First, Harris had to prove that an abusive work environment had been created. To prove that there was an abusive work environment, she must prove that the alleged sexual harassment seriously affected her psychological well-being or led to some injury.

Based on this test as applied to the facts, the federal court decided that the company president's conduct was not so offensive or severe as to expect it would seriously affect the plaintiff's psychological well-being. Also, the court reasoned that the hypothetical reasonable woman manager would not have been so offended by the company president's conduct that it would have interfered with her work performance. Harris appealed her case to the U.S. Supreme Court.

The Supreme Court rejected the requirement to find a hostile or abusive work environment. The justices felt that this determination can be made only by looking at all the circumstances. What mattered, they said, were the frequency and severity of the conduct, whether one is physically threatened or humiliated, and whether it interferes with the ability to perform work. Psychological well-being is still to be considered, but as only one factor among others. The Supreme Court felt that the case should be decided on the criteria set forth in its opinion, so it sent the case back to the lower federal court to be decided on criteria other than just psychological well-being.

The EEOC guidelines also tell us that sexual harassment can be verbal or physical. Sometimes sexual harassment claims are raised when an employer uses sexual innuendo or makes sexist remarks. Whether sexual harassment has occurred as a result of statements made is a judgment call to be made by the courts. Generally, however, courts have held that raw, rude, and off-color language will not by itself constitute sexual harassment. For example, telling crude jokes around the coffee pot during a morning break will probably not amount to sexual harassment. If however, comments are made that are sexual in nature and are said with the intention of hurting or offending a member of the opposite sex, the line becomes less clear.

In addition to verbal abuse, sexual harassment can be brought when there has been physical harassment. As the next case demonstrates, some courts might view physical forms of harassment as more serious than verbal abuse. Forms of touching that are offensive and sexually oriented bring about sexual harassment claims. Remember also that harmful and offensive touching gives rise to another legal claim. When there is harmful or offensive touching that results in physical or emotional harm (e.g., physical advances made by a supervisor), there is basis for an assault and battery claim in addition to the sexual harassment claim. The following case provides an example in which physical abuse resulted in a sexual harassment claim.

In the case of *Carrero v. New York City Housing Authority* (1989)[8] Carrero had just been promoted to probationary superintendent of the New York City Housing Authority when her supervisor began to make sexual advances toward her. She had to fight him off after he would touch her knee and kiss her on the neck. He tried to kiss her on the mouth, but she was able to keep him away. She went to the Housing Authority and told them about the situation. They told her the charges could not be substantiated, and that they could do nothing.

Her supervisor went the final step when he gave her an unsatisfactory performance evaluation and demoted her. She resigned and sued for sexual harassment. The suit was brought in federal district court. The court held that she was the subject of sexual harassment by her supervisor and could have her job back but could not get back pay; money she would have been paid had she been working during the time period. The housing authority was not held liable for the supervisor's actions. She appealed the decision to the circuit court.

The circuit court held that the housing authority was strictly liable for the acts of its employees. This was the case since she was given a demotion after her claim of sexual harassment. The court said that usually the plaintiff is required to provide more proof when verbal abuse is at issue.[9] This means that it must be shown that offensive sexual remarks were made frequently and over a long period of time. The court, however, stated that sexual harassment involving physical contact is considered more serious.

Other claims that might be brought in addition to a sexual harassment claim are malicious interference with employment, intentional infliction of emotional distress, and constructive discharge. Intentional infliction of emotional distress, as you may recall from previous chapters, involves extreme or outrageous conduct. Often, money is sought in the form of compensatory and punitive damages, and the verdict amounts can be quite high. When the claim of intentional infliction of emotional distress is made, the employee alleges that the former employer did something so outrageous that a jury should compensate the plaintiff for significant emotional distress suffered as a result of the employer's outrageous acts.

Whether conduct is extreme and outrageous is the central issue in emotional distress cases. In some cases, an employee may claim that an employer's conduct was extreme and outrageous because the employer fired or demoted the employee. Courts generally do not see the act of firing an employee as extreme and outrageous conduct; it is merely a part of living in our society. When an employer engages in sexual harassment, however, might be considered extreme and outrageous. In a case of sexual harassment, a large money award might be available under a claim of intentional infliction of emotional distress, in addition to legal remedies available under federal law (e.g., back pay) under a sexual harassment claim.

A suit for constructive discharge means an employee can sue a former employer if forced to resign due to conditions of sexual harassment which make the work situation unbearable. For example, suppose that a woman goes to work for a municipal parks department. Every day for the first two months, she is ridiculed by male employees and made the brunt of sexual jokes. She cannot handle this abuse, so she resigns. In addition to sexual harassment, she might sue for constructive discharge, since the harassing conduct made her work situation unbearable.

Finally, there is a standard of care that an employer must meet for its employees. The standard, however, varies according to the status of the individual accused of sexual harassment. There are three situations where employer standard of care is an issue. First, it is generally held that employers are strictly liable for sexual harassment by supervisors in an organization. This places a very high standard on the employer since, as you recall, strict liability means that the plaintiff will win easily if sufficient proof is presented. Employers are also strictly liable for any type of discriminatory practices conducted by their supervisors.

The previous case has an important caveat created by another case (*Natale v. Mount Sinai Medical Center*) wherein the New York Supreme Court determined a plaintiff could not apply the Civil Rights Act of 1991 retroactively to an incident that occurred prior to the enactment of the Civil Rights Act (*ex post facto*). Only exceptional circumstances justify an interlocutory (temporary or interim) appellate review.

The following case demonstrates the degree of responsibility that an employer has over the actions of its supervisors.

In the case of *Faragher v. City of Boca Raton* (1998),[10] a young woman working as a lifeguard at a public beach brought a claim for sexual harassment against her supervisor and the employer city. The woman claimed that she was subjected to a sexually hostile work environment through uninvited and offensive touching by the supervisor and lewd and offensive remarks made to her while on the job. The city had revised its sexual harassment policy, but failed to communicate it to the lifeguards and their supervisors. Faragher's claim was made under Title VII of the Civil Rights Act of 1964. Her case was appealed to the United States Supreme Court where she prevailed on her claim. The court held that the work environment was hostile, and the city was liable for failing to disseminate its policy against sexual harassment to the beach employees and for failing to keep track of the conduct of its employees.

Second, employers are liable for sexually harassing conduct by coworkers when the employer knows of the conduct. As soon as the employer has an idea that something inappropriate is happening, immediate action must be taken to end the questionable behavior by a coworker. Third, employers are responsible for harassing conduct by non-employees against employees when the employer knows or should know of the conduct and does not take immediate action to stop it. Non-employees could include such people as business clients.

It is vitally important for managers to understand sexual harassment. If a suit arises, a basic understanding of the legal principles behind the claim of sexual harassment will help to avoid the confusion and fear that often accompany it. The better path, however, is to have a plan in place to deal with sexual harassment in the workplace.

A well-conceived and implemented plan will help you develop consistent standards so that everyone is treated fairly and knows what to expect.[11] You will recall the importance of initiating policies and procedures in the process of managing risk. Think of policies or procedures you might implement to protect your organization from sexual harassment claims. A policy on sexual harassment could be given to employees in the form of an educational program. Additionally, a policy should be distributed to all employees. This policy should be clear and specify the rights and responsibilities of all employees. You might want to require signatures to verify that it has been read and understood. If everyone knows where the company stands on the issue, the problem of sexual harassment is less likely to occur. Procedures should also be in place for making complaints about harassment. For example, a recreational sports division could have a procedure where the alleged victim is required to speak first with a superior who is not involved in the conflict and can give unbiased advice.

Once an allegation of sexual harassment has been made, an investigation into the circumstances of the case must be undertaken in a timely manner (24-48 hours). What methods of investigation can you think of that would help you best determine what actually took place? One idea is to have two investigators interview both the alleged victim and the alleged perpetrator. Each person should be interviewed separately and asked non-leading, open-ended questions. Their individual responses to each investigator could then be examined to look for answers that matched and those that did not. The statements should be documented. Additionally, you would want to keep the information surrounding the allegation as private as possible to avoid the rumors from getting started. To accomplish this goal, you would want to hold the investigations in private rooms and keep all notes and records confidential.

In addition to interviewing the alleged victim and perpetrator, any witnesses to the incident must be interviewed. It would be wise to have the witness tell you who the victim and perpetrators were. This would add credibility to the information they give you. Be sure that you know whether the information you receive from the witness is coming firsthand or whether the witness is telling you something he or she heard from someone else.

When all the information has been gathered, review your organization's policy and procedures on sexual harassment. Then draft a fair and thorough report containing details of interviews with the victim, the perpetrator, and the witnesses. Additionally, the report should state whether sexual harassment occurred with specific reasons for the conclusion. Finally, the report should be submitted to the proper decision-making official for any additional followup that is necessary. The decision and its consequences could then be discussed with both parties to the dispute.

The mere thought of a sexual harassment lawsuit is something that can make even the most seasoned administrator cringe. It is often quite damaging, regardless of the outcome, to the reputations of everyone involved. Careful thought should be given to developing a plan to prevent sexual harassment lawsuits or at least make the best effort possible to fairly and equitably resolve a sexual harassment claim should one occur. Getting sound advice from experts is always a good idea when determining how to deal with the often complex issues and emotions surrounding sexual harassment.

Discussion Questions

1. In this "he said, she said" world, what methods of investigation would help determine what actually took place?

2. Can an organization be held liable for sexual harassment committed by non-employees? Explain.

3. Is voluntary conduct by both parties a valid defense against a sexual harassment charge filed by an employee against his/her supervisor and his/her employee? Why or why not?

Notes

1. This chapter draws heavily upon an excellent legal discussion of the topic of sexual harassment in Gomez, *Sexual Harassment After Harris v. Forklift Systems, Inc.—Is it Really any Easier to Prove?*, 18 Nova L. R. 1989, 1994; and Petersen, D. J., & Massengill, D. P., *Sexual Harassment Cases Five Years after Meritor Saving Bank v. Vinson*, 18 Employee Relations LJ. 489, No. 3, 1992; and Abrams, Kathryn, *Gender Discrimination and the Transformation of Workplace Norms*, 42 Vanderbilt L.R. 1183, No. 3, (winter 1992).

2. Defamation and breach of contract are both causes of action for a legal claim. Breach of contract refers to the act of violating an agreement between two parties. It is a suit in contract whereas defamation is a suit in tort.

3. 42 U.S.C. sec. 20002(a) (1988).

4. *Meritor Savings Bank v. Finson*, 477 U.S. 57 (1986).

5. See note #1 supra.

6. *Harris v. Forklift Systems, Inc.*, 510 U.S. 17 (1993).

7. Cases must be brought in federal court, as opposed to state courts, when a federal question is at issue. Generally, a federal question is involved when a federal law governs the outcome of a case.

8. *Carrero v. New York City Housing Authority*, 890 F.2d 569 June 23,1991, superseded by Statute. See *Natale v. Mount Sinai Medical Center*, 1993 Lexis 8470, 62 *Employee Practices* June 23, 1993.

9. Invasion of privacy might exist where someone intrudes on the privacy of another, causing one to be humiliated or emotionally hurt.

10. *Faragher v. City of Boca Raton*, 524 U.S. 775 (1998)

11. The information contained in the following five paragraphs are based upon a presentation on the subject in an *Employee Relations Law Journal* article by James H. Oh, Vol. 18, No. 2, Autumn 1992.

Chapter Eighteen

EMPLOYEE SAFETY AND HEALTH

A good risk management program is dependent upon the attitude of the employees, in addition to a well-implemented written plan. Employees also need to understand that their personal health and safety are just as important as the needs of the public.

Management theorists[1] maintain that once the food, clothing, and shelter needs of humans are met, there are five other needs that motivate people. Those needs in hierarchical order are:

1. Physiological needs—These are the basic physical needs which continue throughout one's lifespan.

2. Safety needs—Safety is the next highest level and reflects human needs for security and protection against danger and threats.

3. Social needs—When humans are no longer fearful about their safety, they can give and receive friendship and service.

4. Ego needs—These needs relate to an employee's self-esteem and self-confidence.

5. Self-fulfillment needs—The highest attainment in a human is self-fulfillment. This is reached when an employee reaches his or her own potential.

It is obvious that an employee's safety needs are very important to productivity and creativity. The employees of any organization must know that the administration cares about their health and safety.

Recreation and sports managers and administrators have a special challenge to keep their employees and volunteers safe and healthy. Some of the methods that may be applicable include periodic physical examinations for those positions requiring exertion and exposure to the outdoor environment. Some work is sedentary in nature, but most positions within the recreation and sports field include:

1. Stress on the cardiovascular system—running related to sports, climbing steep mountains, hiking.

2. Stress on muscular and skeletal body systems—heavy lifting, carrying heavy packs and equipment, falls on an uneven surface.

3. Constant exposure to the natural environment—excessive sun, cold, heat, humidity, insects, contact with others who have communicable diseases.

4. Psychological stress—caused by criticism of sports participants, parents of participants, friends of participants, and general criticism of public organizations. The very nature of competitive sports and the fact that 50% of the recreational sports participants lose results in tensions that are usually expressed in a negative manner to officials and managers of events. Public recreation managers are also subject to angry criticism that has become part of our culture.

While working in the recreation and sports field is considered to be a very healthy occupation, it is also an occupation that exposes people to a number of risks. Short periods of exercise that result in cardiovascular stress are important for good health; however, cardiovascular exercise may not be good for those who have heart disease or vascular restriction problems. Periodic physical examinations will screen those with heart or vascular problems and provide exertion guidelines for those employees needing to use special precautions.

The nature of sports and recreation activities exposes those who manage and participate in them to a degree of physical harm and danger. Injuries related to lifting heavy loads or excessive exertion, such as sprains and strains, are frequently experienced in the sports and recreation field. Broken bones occur as the result of many activities related to sports and outdoor recreation. Stress fractures[2] are common in young adults when excessive lifting and compression occur.

A high percentage of recreation sports and outdoor recreation activities are in outdoor settings, which subject participants to natural events such as rain, snow, sun, humidity, cold, insects, and other natural elements.

Given the hazards to both employees and recreation participants that are a part of sports and outdoor recreation experiences, special attention should be given to health and safety concerns. If the basic physical and safety needs of employees are met, the stage will be set to allow productivity and creativity in the organization to flourish. A sound risk management plan will help to reduce the risks that come with job in recreation and make the work environment more enjoyable for everyone.

Discussion Questions

1. Are employees required to keep themselves and those they work around them safe? Explain.

2. Are employers required to provide a safe environment for their employees? Explain.

3. Does an organization (management and employees) have a requirement to keep customers safe? Explain.

Notes

1. American Management Association. (1957 Nov.) *Management Review* 46 (11), 2228, 8889.
2. Stress factures are bone fractures that do not break the bone into two segments. They are sometimes referred to as hairline or green stick fractures.

Chapter Nineteen

THE AMERICANS WITH DISABILITIES ACT

Title I of the Americans with Disabilities Act (ADA)[1] was created by Congress in an effort, in part, to end discrimination by employers based solely on the disability of an employee.[2] In other words, the law was designed to keep an employer from firing or refusing to hire an employee simply because he or she was, for example, using a wheelchair or had a mental impairment. In general, the law said that unless the employer had another (legitimate) reason for firing or not hiring a person with a disability and could not or would not accommodate that person's specific needs, the employer would be legally liable to that person for firing or not hiring an otherwise qualified disabled person for a particular position.

For example, suppose that a municipal parks and recreation department refused to hire an individual with an extreme visual impairment for the position of driving a shuttle to transport children to and from various activities. The department feels that the safety of the children would be in jeopardy under these circumstances. This reason is probably legitimate. Also, it would likely be very difficult to make it possible (make an accommodation) for this person to perform any driving functions. Therefore, the practice of not hiring severely visually impaired persons to drive department vehicles would not be discriminatory, because it is based solely on safety concerns. Other positions within the recreation department, however, might be suitable for a person with this type of disability.

It is important to note that determining whether or not a person is disabled should not be made entirely by the involved organization; but rather, competent medical opinion need to be consulted.

This hypothetical scenario is easy to understand given the common-sense safety considerations. Other cases, however, are less clear. As a recreation or sport administrator, it is likely you will be faced with some difficult decisions in your attempt to balance fairness to the disabled job applicant with the realities of seeing that the tasks necessary in a given job can be performed in a safe and adequate manner. The following case illustrates some of the issues that arise in an ADA case.

In the case of *U.S. EEOC v. AIC Security Investigations, Ltd.* (1993),[3] the executive director of a security-guard company brought suit after he was fired from his job. Four months prior to being fired, he was told that he had incurable brain cancer. During those four months, the director had missed work approximately 20 times. He did, however, work extra long hours on the days he was in the office and was able to do a lot of his work at home by telephone. He could always be reached when needed and had never received any warnings from the company for being absent.

Regardless of these facts, the director was fired. He felt that it was wrong for him to be fired from a job he was performing well, so he sued the company. He claimed he was unlawfully fired because he had a disability; a disability, however, that did not render him incapable of performing the essential functions of the position he held or pose a safety threat to himself or others.

The employer, therefore, tried to show that the director was fired not just because he had a disability, but because the disability made him unable to do his job and/or created a direct threat of harm to himself and others. The employer lost on both counts. The employer could not show that the director was incapable of doing his job, since they could offer no conclusive medical proof that the cancer impaired his ability to work effectively. Also, it was found that while profits for the company as a whole went down during the last year he worked for them, the division he supervised showed an increase in profits.

The employer also claimed that the director's medical condition posed a direct threat of harm to himself and others. It was discovered that the cancer created the threat of seizures. Therefore, it would be unreasonably dangerous for him to drive; an essential function of the director's job. This argument didn't work, however, because the company itself, it was discovered, had offered to supply the director with a driver to accommodate him for his disability. The jury awarded a large verdict for the director, which included punitive damages; money awarded to the plaintiff as punishment to the company for abruptly firing, without good reason, a devoted employee with a good work record.

Obviously, to come under the protection of the ADA, an individual must have a disability. The disability may be either physical or mental. At first glance, this seems easy enough to envision, since most of us think we already know what constitutes a disability. As you will see, however, it is sometimes not so clear whether a person has a disability that affords special protection under the law. The ADA seeks to clear up the confusion by defining a disability as an impairment that "substantially limits one or more major life activities." The disability must also be permanent.[4]

Examples of physical disabilities range from impairment of muscles, bones, and joints, to infectious disease, to an impairment of the senses (e.g., blindness, deafness, etc.). The following cases illustrate some situations where people have claimed they were discriminated against because of their physical disability. These cases, although decided prior to the enactment of the ADA, have been used as precedent for more recent cases that seek to define physical disabilities under the ADA.

The case of *U.S. EEOC v. AIC Security Investigations, Ltd.* has been reversed in part and remanded in part by *Shiring v. Runyon* 90 F.3d, 827. While the Shiring decision does not modify the EEOC case substantially, it does indicate that discrimination case records cannot be vague and must show that defeat of a medical discrimination suit must be based on substantive information. The plaintiff must show that there were essential duties that he/she could perform with or without reasonable accommodations.

In the case of *Nicely v. Rice* (1993),[5] the plaintiff claimed discrimination for not being allowed to work due to a partially fused right wrist and a fused right elbow. This was found to be a disability protected by the law, since it resulted in a substantial limitation of a major life activity (namely, performing daily hygienic functions).

In the case of *Southeastern Community College v. Davis* (1979),[6] a deaf nurse was refused admittance to a nursing program. The school said that it would not let her in the program since her disability prevented her from safely performing in the nursing program and in the nursing profession. The court viewed a hearing impairment as a disability that would protect one from discrimination under the law.

In the case of *School Board of Nassau County v. Arline* (1987),[7] an elementary school teacher sued the school board after she was fired from her job. She had tuberculosis, a serious contagious disease. The court found the law in that year (1987), included contagious diseases within the definition of disability and therefore, the teacher was offered protection from discrimination for her condition.

The other category of disabilities consists of mental disabilities. The courts have struggled with cases that hung on the basic issue of what constitutes a mental disability; previously referred to as a handicap.[8] Disabilities have been claimed that stretch the limits of one's imagination. As an administrator, be ready to expect the unexpected. The following cases illustrate just how far some people will go to claim a mental disability and gain protection under the law.

In the case of *Blanton v. AT&T Communications* (1990),[9] the plaintiff had been working for AT&T for about 15 years when he was fired from his job. The reason given for firing him was that he had sexually harassed several female employees. He sued the company claiming that he had been fired because of his handicap. What was the handicap he claimed? He claimed if he had been engaging in sexual harassment, then his conduct could be considered different from his normal behavior. Therefore, this mental disorder could be considered a handicap. The court easily concluded that a person who sexually harasses other persons is not handicapped as defined under the law.

In the case of *Winston v. Maine Technical College* (1993),[10] a tenured English instructor at a technical college was fired when he violated the school's sexual harassment policy. He violated the policy after he kissed and had a sexually suggestive conversation with one of his 18-year-old female students. It was also discovered that he had four prior instances of unnacceptable sexual behavior with students.

Upon being fired, the teacher brought suit claiming that he was discriminated against because of his disability. He claimed that he was "sexually obsessive" and was diagnosed as being subject to compulsive sexual behavior, a condition that rendered him mentally disabled for purposes of anti-discrimination provisions in the state law. He did not win, since the federal law provisions of the ADA do not view sexual behavior disorders as a mental disability.

In the case of *Adams v. Alderson* (1989),[11] a computer programmer analyst for the government was fired from his job. He was fired after he violently attacked a female supervisor and rampaged through the office, breaking and destroying office equipment. He felt that he was discriminated against since he was fired based on his disability.

His disability, he asserted, was described as a condition known as a "maladaptive reaction to a psychosocial stressor." In other words, he was not capable of dealing with his supervisor (the psychosocial stressor). The court held that even if this were a mental disability afforded protection by law, the government agency was "not obliged to indulge a propensity for violence" and make accommodation for him by moving him or his supervisor to another location within the agency.

As you can see from these cases, the boundaries of what constitutes a mental disability have been pushed. In general, however, under the ADA, in order to be found to have a mental disorder, the claimant must be diagnosed as having a mental disorder by a qualified mental health professional. The facts of the following case, although prior to enactment of the ADA, demonstrate the importance of health professionals in diagnosing and giving testimony about a mental disability.

In the case of *Doe v. New York University* (1981),[12] the plaintiff applied for admission to medical school at a prestigious university. Despite the fact that she had suffered from serious psychiatric and mental disorders for a long time, she indicated on her application that she had no permanent or recurrent emotional problems. Since she had the grades and the school was misinformed about her past, they let her in. What the school didn't know was that Doe had some serious problems. The court record indicated that she had experienced severe emotional problems since the third grade.

Some of the more serious manifestations of her illness included: an attempt at suicide by drinking cyanide; self-injection of a cancer treatment drug that makes human cells susceptible to infection; carving a hole in her own stomach using a kitchen knife and deadening the pain by using local anesthetic stolen from the hospital; severing an artery in her elbow with a razor blade; scratching her wrists with a broken light bulb; biting a hospital staff member on the arm; cutting herself and writing on the wall with her own blood; and attacking her psychiatrist with a pair of scissors.

Not long after she entered the program, the medical school found out about her prior psychiatric problems. The dean of the medical school met with her and decided that she could stay in medical school if she would undergo psychiatric therapy. She agreed and proceeded with the therapy. The therapy was unsuccessful and did not last long.

Things came to a head several months later when, in a meeting with the associate dean of the medical school, she interrupted the meeting and retreated to the bathroom where she proceeded to bleed herself with a catheter. She claimed that this was the only way she could cope with her stress.

Soon thereafter, she was given a leave of absence. After some difficulty, she agreed to enter a psychiatric clinic where her condition was diagnosed by a certified professional psychiatrist. He diagnosed her as having a "borderline personality disorder." The record indicated the disorder was likely to be permanent and subject to modification only through effective treatment and a low-stress lifestyle.

Some time later, she reapplied for admission to the same medical school. She had moved away and been seeing new psychiatrists. The school reviewed her application, considering the opinion of her new psychiatrists as to her degree of improvement. It decided not to readmit her to medical school. She then hired a lawyer and threatened to sue. The school reconsidered her application on the condition that she be interviewed by a psychiatrist at the university medical school. She agreed, but only after getting opinions from several other psychiatrists, one of whom said she did not have a "borderline personality disorder" but instead had a treatable condition.

The university psychiatrist interviewed her and recommended that she not be readmitted. The school followed this recommendation and decided not to readmit her. She therefore decided to follow through on her earlier threat to sue the medical school, naming the dean of the medical school along with others who were involved in the matter. She claimed that she was fully qualified to study medicine at New York University (NYU), and that NYU refused to admit her solely because of her past mental disability (handicap). Both sides submitted extensive testimony from medical experts in psychiatry. The district court determined that the plaintiff should be re-admitted to the university; however, upon appeal by the university, the appellate court determined that there was enough material facts and expert testimony to deny the plaintiff re-entry into the medical school. She was denied re-entry to the medical school.

This interesting case illustrates the important role of medical experts in cases where a mental disability is at issue. Testimony from psychiatrists on both sides was used extensively in this trial. This brings up another important point. Even when a diagnosis has been made by a competent professional, it might be contested by a health professional brought in by the other party. These experts might differ in their diagnosis of the nature and extent of the mental disability. Therefore, the selection of a health professional to make the diagnosis is important, as well as proper documentation of this diagnosis concerning the nature and extent of the disability.

It is important for the administrator to know the nature and extent of an employee's disability. It is important to know this, because as mentioned, if the disability substantially interferes with an employee's ability to do a particular job or creates a serious safety concern, the employer has a legitimate reason not to allow this person to work for the organization. If, however, the disabled employee could adequately and safely perform a particular job if only the employer made some changes to accommodate the disability, the employer must do so. This requirement, in legal terms, is called reasonable accommodation. The following case provides an example of when reasonable accommodation was required by an employer.

In the case of *Kent v. Derwinski* (1991),[13] a mentally retarded employee became seriously disturbed by comments and jokes made by fellow employees. His inability to handle the stress resulted in a lawsuit against his employer. The court held that the employer could not fire him based on his extreme sensitivity, but instead must make reasonable accommodation for his disability. Specifically, the employer was required to ensure that fellow employees were trained in the proper way to speak and behave around this individual and that the supervisor was trained to avoid direct criticism and not cause undue stress to him.

In sports, a recent case tested a professional golfer's right to use a motorized cart so that he could compete and earn a living playing golf.

In *PGA Tour Inc. v. Martin* (2001),[14] a professional golfer, Casey Martin, sought to require the PGA tour to allow him to use a motorized golf cart. The PGA had a rule that professional golfers were required to walk the course. Martin had a mobility impairment that prevented him from being able to walk a golf course under four-day tournament conditions. Martin brought suit under Title III of the ADA claiming that the PGA Tour was a "public accommodation" and that riding a cart instead of walking the course was a reasonable accommodation. The court agreed with Martin on both counts and ruled that he would be allowed to ride a cart in golf tournaments.

In an earlier sports-related case, *Knapp v. Northwestern University* (1996),[15] a student-athlete brought suit claiming that the university violated the Rehabilitation Act by refusing to let him play intercollegiate basketball. The reason for not allowing Knapp to play was based on the fact that he had a heart condition. The university was concerned about his health and safety. The appellate court decided in favor of the defendant. The court based its decision upon its determination that his heart condition was not a disability.

In addition to protecting disabled individuals from discrimination in employment, the ADA also provides legal protection from discrimination where public access and services are involved. Recreation personnel should be aware that people with disabilities have the legal right to enjoy and have access to most of the same places and services that others enjoy. The ADA applies to both public and private organizations.

Private organizations that provide recreational opportunities and services to tourists often run what the law (the ADA) describes as "public accommodations." Public accommodations include such places as hotels, taverns, parks, restaurants, museums, and theaters. The law basically says that those who run these facilities cannot discriminate on the basis of disability. Discrimination, as you can probably guess, would exist when people with disabilities are denied physical access to the facilities or services offered to the public.

The first question that often comes to mind is to what extent is a business owner expected to go to make the facilities accessible. Suppose, for example, that you operate a century-old theater that is accessible only by climbing a flight of 50 marble stairs. To accommodate those who use wheelchairs, are you expected to build a ramp or install an elevator in the old building? The law states that physical barriers must be removed if removal is readily achievable. The main factors are cost and difficulty. The theater operator would have to consider how much it would cost to install a ramp or an elevator and the damage that construction would do to the building. If, after careful thought and consultation with experts, these ideas were not feasible, alternative methods of providing the services to disabled theatergoers must be offered. Again, the expense of any alternative measure must be considered.

What if you decided to build a new theater, or you have some alterations in the works? This would change the situation somewhat. In keeping with our example, let us say you have decided to build a new theater. The law requires that your theater be accessible to people with disabilities. Therefore, you must design the facility with the needs of the disabled in mind.

If you are making alterations to the building, the alterations must be accessible. Suppose that you are adding an outdoor area for concerts and theatrical performances. If the added costs of making the facility accessible are not disproportionate to the overall cost of the new facility (the alterations), it must be made accessible. In addition, the bathrooms, drinking fountains, and telephones serving the area must be made accessible.

Making facilities accessible is not only a legal requirement, but is also important to help persons with disabilities enjoy recreational activities that are beneficial to their personal development. Meeting the requirements of the ADA, therefore, is both a way to stay out of legal trouble and a means of serving a group of people with special needs who desire the opportunity to enjoy recreation as an integral part of their lives.

Discussion Questions

1. An employee states he has the flu and is unable to come to work. Can an employer require a doctor's certificate? Explain.

2. A individual with a hearing deficit insists that a movie theater include subtitles for movies. Does she have a valid legal argument? Why or why not?

Notes

1. Americans with Disabilities Act of 1990, sec. 511(b)(l), 42 U.S.C.A. sec, 12211 (b)(l). The Act, which became effective on July 26, 1992, also seeks to end discrimination and give equal opportunity to disabled persons in public accommodations, transportation, state and local government services, and telecommunications.
2. The ADA applies to employers with 15 or more employees. When discrimination occurs, complaints may be filed with the Equal Employment Opportunity Commission (EEOC). If the person suing has a valid claim, he may be entitled to back pay and court orders to stop the discrimination.
3. *U.S. EEOC v. AIC Security Investigations, LTD.* 823 F. Supp. 571 (ND. Ill 1993 reversed in part remanded in part (N.D. Ill 1993 *Shiring v. Runyon* 90 F.3d 827, 1996 U.S. App. Lexis 18384; 5 Am. Disabilities Cas. (BNS) 1216 1996.
4. This discussion draws heavily on a presentation of the subject in McDonald, J., Kulick, F., & Creighton, M. K. (1995), Mental disabilities under the ADA: A management rights approach, *Employees Relations Law Journal,* 20, 4.
5. *Nicely v. Rice,* 1 F.3d 1249 (10th Cir. 1993).
6. *Southeastern Community College v. Davis,* 442 U.S. 397 (1979).
7. *School Board of Nassau County v. Arline,* 480 U.S. 273 (1987).
8. Prior to the enactment of the Americans with Disabilities Act of 1990, the Rehabilitation Act of 1973 was the body of law that protected persons with disabilities from employment discrimination. Individual states enacted similar statutes offering similar protection.
9. *Blanton v. AT&T Communications,* 1 AD Cases 1552 (D. Mass. 1990).
10. *Winston v. Maine Technical College,* 631 A.2d 70 (Me. 1993).
11. *Adams v. Alderson,* 723 F. Supp. 1531 (D.D.C. 1989).
12. *Doe v. New York University,* 666 F.2d 761 (2d Cir. 1981).
13. *Kent v. Derwinski,* 790 F. Supp. 1032 (E.D. Wash. 1991).
14. *PGA Tour Inc. v. Martin,* 20 NDLR 188 (U.S. 2001).
15. *Doe v. New York University* 666 F.2d 761 (2nd Cir 1981). Disapproved and superseded by *Zervos v. Verizon N.Y. Inc*; 2001 252 F.3d 163; 2001 U.S. App. Lexis 11732 26 Employee Benefits Cas.(BNA) 1326 and 252 F, 3d (2001).

Chapter Twenty

EMPLOYEE EVALUATIONS

You should now have a general understanding of the issues that arise when discrimination based on a physical or mental disability is claimed. As an administrator, what do you do to properly manage persons with disabilities in a fair manner that also protects you and your organization from lawsuits? Additionally, the importance of treating those employees who have disabilities with fairness and equality cannot be overemphasized. This is probably the best way to eliminate or reduce the risk of lawsuits based on discrimination claims. When a manager has acted with a high degree of responsibility and yet is still faced with a discrimination lawsuit, however, what can he or she do to protect themselves and their organization from its potentially damaging consequences? Making evaluations of employees both before and after they have been hired is a good place to start.[1]

The Hiring Process: Pre-Employment Evaluations

When deciding which employees to hire among a group of qualified applicants, the administrator needs to know the important facts that will aid the decision-making process. Some information, such as a person's past treatment of mental health problems, cannot be sought. The law prohibits the employer from asking certain questions. This is done to protect the privacy of an individual when sensitive or potentially damaging information is at stake.

An employer can, however, find out whether a person is fit for employment by asking the right types of legally acceptable questions. These questions might first be posed to a potential employee on an employment application.

This document should have a certification that all the information provided by the applicant is complete and correct. It must also meet the applicable EEOC guidelines. These are the guidelines outlining which questions are legal.[2]

The application form should be designed to see whether an applicant is qualified for the position sought. In other words, can the applicant do the job? This information might answer the question: If the applicant has a disability, is he or she otherwise qualified for the position despite the disability? On this form, the employer might ask the applicant to give his or her entire employment history. Also, the application might ask about criminal convictions, current use of illegal drugs, or if the applicant has ever been fired before and why.

In addition to the application, the employer should also conduct a personal interview to see how the applicant performed on previous jobs. A lot can be learned from a personal interview about an applicant's job motivation and his or her ability to get along with others. Questions can be asked, such as: "Is he on time for work?; Does he get along with his supervisors and coworkers?"; and even informal questions about hobbies and interests. These questions and the answers to them should be documented. In addition to the interview, personal and professional references should be asked for and checked. These references should come from persons who know the applicant well.

Suppose that you, as a park administrator, are seeking to hire someone to meet and direct visitors at the main gate of your park. In the peak season, it is an extremely stressful job. Tired visitors often unleash their frustrations on the person in this position. A prospective employee has filled out an application for employment and has been interviewed and seems to have his act together.

You are familiar with some of the legal cases, however, where people have been hired and then not been able to handle the stress. After being fired, they sued, claiming they had some type of stress disorder they claimed was a disability protected by law. You wonder if there is anything you can do to prevent having this type of trouble down the road. Well, there might be something you could do. You could possibly do some pre-employment drug testing or psychological testing.

The psychological testing might, in this circumstance, be the most beneficial. A pre-employment psychological test, however, is illegal under the ADA if classified as a "medical examination." The EEOC provides guidelines to determine whether a test is a medical test. In general, a test is considered medical if it is used to determine whether the applicant has a mental disorder. If a test is administered, it must be performance based; measuring, for example, an applicant's ability to work under pressure or handle job-related stressors specific to the particular job. In this scenario, a test might be appropriate. In real life, however, a psychological test should only be conducted after professional advice has been given and you know the test is legally acceptable.

Evaluations During Employment

The evaluation process does not end when an employee has been hired. In situations where an employee has become dangerously violent or has developed a mental condition that interferes with the performance of necessary job functions, the employer can require the employee to undergo a mental examination performed by a psychiatrist or clinical psychologist. The ADA permits testing of this type under these limited conditions. The test is called a "fitness for duty" mental examination. It is the employer's duty to provide the examiner with the necessary background information about the employee and the important facts and circumstances under which the employee works.

These criteria are necessary if an employee is singled out to be evaluated. It is a different matter when an entire group of employees is evaluated. When all employees who perform a particular job, for example, are evaluated, the rules are different. They can be given medical examinations, or physical evaluations, or performance tests if the testing criteria are job related, and everyone is treated equally. In other words, the test must be objective and free of bias. Also, the evaluation must be objective and test a necessary task the job requires.

The point to remember is that tests that evaluate the abilities or performance of an individual cannot have a discriminatory purpose. The ADA protects persons with disabilities from discrimination just as the United States Constitution and certain laws protect against racial and gender discrimination. That is why evaluations must test whether an essential function of a particular job can be performed adequately.

An evaluation of firefighting ability, for example, might test whether a person can carry a certain amount of weight a certain height up a ladder. This test of physical strength and endurance is purely objective. If someone with a disability is able to meet this objective standard, they would be given a favorable evaluation regardless of his or her disabled status. The same reasoning would hold true for ethnic minorities or other protected classes of people when objective tests are employed.[3]

Every aspect of the evaluation process should be written down and be a part of company or agency policy. A written policy allows a business or agency to have a consistent evaluation policy that ensures everyone is given equal treatment. It should contain objective, job-specific performance criteria which, if followed, offer protection to the employer from false discrimination claims.

Recreation managers have the responsibility of evaluating potential employees as they go through the application and interview process. The responsibility of evaluation, however, does not end when the successful candidate has been hired. The evaluation process extends through the employee's career with the recreation organization. Evaluations, both before and during employment, must be based on objective standards as reflected by the law. Therefore, an understanding of the legal principles behind the evaluation process will help the recreation manager reduce the legal risks involved.

Discussion Questions

1. Can you call a previous employer of a prospective new employee to check on his/her evaluation and work habits? Explain.

2. Can a supervisor give a yearly performance evaluation without a written record? Why?

3. Can a supervisor give a yearly performance evaluation without previously discussing and documenting the criteria that will be used in the evaluation? Explain.

Notes

1. This chapter draws heavily upon a presentation of the subject in Mc-Donald, J., Kulick, F. B., & Creighton, M. K. (1995). Mental disabilities under the ADA: A management rights approach, *Employee Relations Law Journal*, 20,4.
2. In general, an employer cannot base the decision to hire (and not ask questions at an interview) on matters relating to age, disability, gender, national origin, race, or religion.
3. See the chapter on constitutional principles for more information on protected classes.

Part Seven

OUTDOOR RECREATION
MANAGEMENT

INTRODUCTION

There is something about the rural countryside, streams, and lakes that draw recreationists. The vast majority of American citizens live in urban and suburban areas. The general public is sometimes naive when it comes to understanding and living in a natural environment. They go to rural parks to get away from city life but often expect the same amenities, emergency medical aid, and police protection found in cities.

Some people will not camp unless they have an air conditioner and television in their trailer. Many upscale pontoon houseboats now come equipped with water slides, air conditioning, electric generators, and satellite television receivers.

Hiking, a very traditional outdoor activity, has changed significantly, with new lightweight packs, dehydrated foods, and light, but warm clothing fabrics. Hikers find that they must share the trails with horses, mountain bikes, and sometimes motorized vehicles. Hiking, camping, and picnicking have indeed changed over the last few decades.

Contemporary social and demographic changes require managers to evaluate safety and risk-management practices. The changing demands of outdoor recreation participants, increased user expectations, increasing population, and more complex physical facility needs have created new risk and safety challenges. As an example, trails, once used only by hikers, have become multiple-use trails used by hikers, mountain bikes, modified wheel chairs, horses, and motorcycles. Segregating uses or prohibiting selective uses results in discontented users. Not even considering the environmental consequences of shared use, a joint-use trail can result in serious safety considerations. Bicycles run into people and horses; wild animals, people, bikes, and motorcycles scare horses; motorcycles force people, horses, and bikes off trails; and wheelchairs find it difficult to negotiate the right-of-way. Risk management becomes a rather complex issue.

Chapter Twenty-One

STANDARD OF CARE FOR PARK MANAGERS

The standard of care is generally defined as what a reasonable person would do under the same circumstances. A reasonable park manager need not be the most super-cautious or insightful individual, only a normally prudent individual.[1] Standard of care is also defined as the action or conduct established by most of the industry or profession locally, regionally, and/or nationally. In court, expert witnesses for the plaintiff and defendant will take opposite points of view and help the court determine the standard of care for the particular activity in question.

If an accident resulting in injury or property loss occurs on public recreation lands or facilities, the plaintiff's attorneys will usually ask for agency maintenance and operation manuals and guidelines as well as the documentation of any recent safety inspections or risk assessments. They ask for these materials in an effort to determine if the agency violated its own standard of care, in addition to checking to see if the local standards were violated. The plaintiff will attempt to determine if the organization met state (area) as well as national standards. The plaintiff's attorneys will also want to know if other accidents have occurred on the specific sites or on similar sites managed by the agency. The defense will then attempt to show they did in fact meet the standard of care or there were mitigating circumstances involved.

An agency can make the mistake of developing guidelines that greatly exceed what would normally be considered the national or local standard of care. As an example, the nationally accepted standard of care for inspection of campground or picnic area trees for rot or mechanical damage is once a year, usually in the spring or at the start of the recreation season. A zealous administrator may determine that a standard of two inspections a year would be much better. The new inspection standard is placed in the manuals and operating plan. In subsequent years, budget cuts or other priorities may reduce the tree inspection rate to once a year; yet, the new standard of twice a year remains in the manual. As a hypothetical example, an accident occurs late in the season in a campground as the result of a falling tree limb. The plaintiff would present evidence that shows the agency violated its own maintenance standard by not inspecting the trees twice during the year.

While the twice-a-year manual requirement was noble, it did indeed increase the plaintiff's likelihood for a successful suit. Periodic reviews of manuals and handbooks should be made to ensure that standards of care are met but not exceeded to a point of agency liability.

SECTION 1: NATURAL FEATURE HAZARDS

There are a number of hazards on park lands that are natural but provide a real and foreseeable risk to the park visitor. Agencies and organizations should recognize that suits involving naturally occurring features are seldom successful if adequate warnings are given and reasonable safety precautions are taken.

Managers and administrators should concentrate their safety/risk management efforts on protecting public interests rather than organizational interests. Effective risk management programs must protect the public from naturally occurring dangers as well as man-made features. There is a distinct ethical and moral question for administrators who will not warn of a known hazard for fear that the warning will "increase our liability." Natural feature safety and risk policy should err on behalf of the customer, visitor, and employee, not the protection of the agency.

Common natural hazards that can cause injury or result in death are discussed below.

Water

General

Drowning is common in an outdoor environment, particularly in regard to diving accidents. Diving accidents and subsequent lawsuits often occur where water is murky and submerged objects are not visible, or where participants misjudge water depth. Swimming is the most popular outdoor recreation pursuit, and drowning is the most common cause of death in an outdoor recreation setting.

Tidal Conditions

Rip tides and normal ocean tides result in conditions that cause drowning. On some shorelines, rip tides are common (e.g., central Oregon coast, and Florida Panhandle). Visitors are usually unaware of rip tides and should be warned if they are commonly experienced in that particular water.

Water Temperature (Hypothermia)

Exceptionally cold water, both fresh and sea water, can cause death in a very short time period unless the swimmer wears special gear specifically designed to protect against frigid water. The shock of cold water on the body can also result in immobility and death.

Currents in Oceans, Lakes, and Streams

Currents restrict the ability of a swimmer or boater to reach the safety of land. Currents carry swimmers and boaters into situations where they can be drawn over waterfalls, forced against rocks, and pulled under the water.

Floods and Water Fluctuations

Stream velocity and the depth of lakes can vary significantly based upon rain and seasonal changes. Those unaware of the changes can be injured or killed by diving into shallow water or driving vehicles across streams believed to be shallow. Buoys and depth markers should be used where water is known to fluctuate constantly.

NOAA and the USLA have developed excellent rip current awareness and safety materials.

Natural Obstacles in Waters

Boulders and logs are part of the natural environment of streams. They are normally very slick when wet or moss covered. Recreationists can be seriously injured when walking upon slick rocks. Also, people should avoid walking in fast moving streams given the risk of foot entrapment. Shoals, reefs, and rocks are difficult to see and cause boat damage and injury to recreationists. Known obstacles should be marked or buoyed.

Waterfalls and Rapids

Waterfalls and rapids create extreme hydrologic conditions, including undertows and whirlpools. While waterfalls and rapids are commonly found in nature, they are also commonly recognized for being extremely danger-ous. Recreationists engaged in white water rafting, canoeing, and kayaking often assume the risk of their activity without guides so as to increase the risk of injury to participants. Recreationists should know the dangers of the waters and take actions to insure safe travel before proceeding.

In the case of *Sartoris v. State of New York* (1987),[2] the claimant[3] sued the State of New York after her husband drowned on Jones Beach. The beach had lifeguards on duty at the time of the drowning, and Sartoris was an experienced ocean swimmer. The widow of the drowned man claimed that the state failed to warn swimmers of the "dangerous sweep" (tide conditions along the shoreline). The state argued that it did not have the legal duty to warn, and if it did, the warning would not have prevented the accident from occurring. The court decided in favor of the defendant state, stating that:

1. "The plaintiff failed to establish that negligence on the part of lifeguards contributed to apparent death by drowning of claim-ant's decedent;

2. Claimant did not establish that the park and recreation commis-sion breached its duty to warn a potential swimmer of dangerous lateral sweep conditions along shoreline; and

3. Anyone who engages in water sports assumes the reason-ably foreseeable risks inherent to the activity."

In *Clem v. United States* (1985),[4] a widow sued the United States after her husband drowned at the Indiana Dunes National Lakeshore Park which is administered by the National Park Service. Upon arriving at the park, the Clems went to the visitor's center, viewed a film, and picked up a map and brochures. Both the film and the brochure had safety messages related to swimming in Lake Michigan. They used the park without paying any fee

or admission. Signs posted along the beach area read, "Use Caution, Life-guards Not Provided." The Clems went swimming in Lake Michigan when the lake was experiencing waves between two and four feet in height. Mrs. Clem proceeded out to a sandbar and could not swim back because of the strong undertow. Mr. Clem swam out to the sand bar to help his wife and drowned attempting the rescue. The plaintiff sued, claiming that the National Park Service should have warned them of the strong undertow on the day they were swimming. The court decided in favor of the defendant United States, stating three important factors that led to its decision: "1. The defendant did not breach their duty to warn; 2. The decedent contributed to his own death, and 3. The decedent voluntarily assumed any risk incident to swimming in Lake Michigan."

Geology (Topography)

Cliffs

Cliffs and overlooks are popular viewing platforms for outdoor recreation visitors seeking to see a broad expanse of area. Slick rocks, snow cover, crumbling unstable edges, and acrophobia[5] resulting in visitor vertigo result in serious and deadly accidents. Areas that are commonly visited, or featured as destination areas should have warning signs and/or physical barriers. Rock climbing is particularly dangerous to the untrained. Most reasonable people recognize the dangers inherent in naturally occurring cliffs. Because cliffs are so common in nature, only those known to have frequent visitors, known dangers, or are especially unique with hidden dangers can be reasonably signed or have barriers installed. General warnings on maps and brochures may be appropriate in some areas. Also, assumption of risk may come into play where participants voluntarily assume the risk of dangers inherent to climbing. See *Roettgen v. Regents of University of California,* 48 Cal.Rptr.2d 922 (Cal. App. 1996).

In *Walter v. State* (1992),[6] a visitor to a heavily used New York State Park was injured when she fell from a cliff. She sued the state, claiming that the signs and fence erected by the state were inadequate to warn of and protect against the hazardous cliff area. The facts indicate that the plaintiff had been drinking at the time of the accident, but was not legally intoxicated. There was a sign on the split-rail fence near the cliff that read as follows:

DANGER, KEEP INSIDE RAIL, WATCH YOUR CHILDREN

The railing was intended to keep people from accidentally going over the cliff. The trial court decided in favor of the plaintiff Walter, stating that the state did not adequately warn in an area of known heavy use. The state appealed. The appeals court affirmed the judgment of the lower court, stating that the State had failed to exercise reasonable care in a very dangerous situation. The court apportioned only 50% of the award to the plaintiff, because she contributed significantly to the cause of her injury.

Caves

Caves are common in nature, particularly in limestone geology. They present a number of very serious risks that include hypothermia, drowning, falls, equipment failure (e.g., rope breakage and loss of light source). Some people have extreme fear of darkness (nyctophobia) and enclosed spaces (claustrophobia) and should not participate in spelunking.

Thermal Pools and Geysers

Naturally occurring hot springs are used by many recreationists for bathing, health purposes, relaxation, and viewing. Yellowstone National Park is a popular place to see hot springs. Many hot springs have very high temperatures and can cause severe burns. Mineral formations[7] surrounding geysers and other thermal phenomena are unstable and crumble easily. Visitors should be warned of unstable walking surfaces and high water temperatures when those conditions exist.

Volcanoes

People have a natural curiosity related to active volcanic activities. For example, Kilauea on the big island of Hawaii and Mount St. Helens in Washington State have hundreds of thousands of visitors a year. Extreme heat, fissures, steam vents, poisonous gases, and thin volcanic crusts present very dangerous situations that are difficult to identify by the average visitor. Agencies must warn visitors of the known hidden dangers associated with active volcanic activity.

Mountain Elevation

Air temperatures normally go down as the elevation increases. An average of minus 10-15 degrees Fahrenheit for every thousand feet increase in elevation is common. Therefore, although valley temperatures might be relatively comfortable, the temperature on a mountain may be dangerously low. People recreating in mountain environments should anticipate sudden and severe temperature changes. Also, people who normally live in or near sea level environments may find it difficult to breathe in the thinner air of high elevation, especially when physical exertion is involved in the activity. Fatigue, respiratory, and coronary problems are common for people who have not adapted to high elevation conditions.

Land and Snow Structural Failure (Avalanche, Rock Slides, Crevasses, Glacier Calving)

Gravity accounts for many dangerous situations in the natural environment. Saturated soils on top of steeply tilted bedrock can result in geological land failure with resultant land slides. Some soils, particularly with a high clay content and that lie over smooth surface bedrock may slide off a steep slope when they become saturated with moisture or when they lack vegetative cover. In some cases, land failure can occur when the surface understructure support is eliminated by road cuts or other construction activities.

Snow avalanches are common on slopes exceeding a 50% gradient. Snow will avalanche when wind deposits snow on the lee side of mountains, creating overloaded slopes that are dislodged by gravity. Snow will also slide when the snow structure physically changes under the surface and forms a weak layer lacking cohesion (sometimes referred to as depth hoar) with the ground or other snow layers. Each year, a number of people are killed in snow avalanches when they ignore warning signs and ski into avalanche-prone areas. Snow physics research has developed methods by which avalanches can be predicted with relative accuracy.

When avalanche dangers are known, the public should be warned by providing precautionary messages through the news media and posting warning signs where practical in areas with heavy public use, such as downhill ski areas.

In *Twohig v. United States* (1989),[8] a skier was killed in an avalanche while skiing in a ski area permitted by the United States Forest Service on national forest lands. The plaintiff, the widow of the decedent, sued, claiming that the United States was negligent in "failing to employ adequate procedures and adequately trained personnel for detection and warning of avalanche danger and in failing to inspect for and to warn of avalanche danger." The Forest Service requested summary judgment, arguing that they were exempt from suit based upon decision-making immunity afforded through the Federal Tort Claims Act and the Idaho Recreational Use Statute.[9] The plaintiff argued that the statutes did not apply, because the Forest Service collected fees for the use of the area. The court agreed with the plaintiff, stating that "the government was not entitled to immunity."

Dust and sand (combinations of wind, soil, and sand)—in many arid and semiarid areas, windborne dust and sand, limit visibility and sometimes cause respiratory distress. Airborne dust and sand tend to wear down mechanical devices at an accelerated rate, causing equipment failure. Airborne dust reduces the quality of overlooks, scenic views, and recreation activities. Lawsuits sometimes arise in park settings where injury or death results from human encounters with airborne materials.

Flora (Vegetation)

Toxic vegetation (i.e., poison oak, sumac, ivy) is found in most areas in some form. Some people are particularly sensitive to the skin irritation caused by specific plants. Poison plant identification is not a common area of study and knowledge for most outdoor recreationists and managers. When smoke is breathed from toxic leaves and wood, the respiratory system can be adversely affected, resulting in serious health problems. Warning signs should be posted or toxic plants removed in developed recreation areas that are known to contain toxic vegetation.

Barrier Vegetation (i.e., Cactus, Thorns, Brambles)

Thorns restrict visitor movement, cause discomfort for those who make contact with the vegetation, and reduce the variety of recreation opportunities available to the visitor. Vegetation with larger thorns is usually obvious. The exception to the obvious nature of thorns is thistle, nettle, and other small plants that combine thorns and irritating or toxic oils. Many recreation facilities utilize barrier vegetation to discourage access to protected areas.

Tree Failure (Mechanical, Shallow Rooting)

Tree failure can result in damage to property, injury, and sometimes death. Falling trees, particularly in campgrounds, picnic areas, and other heavily used outdoor recreation sites cause considerable damage each year. Mechanical tree failure is usually the result of growth form (i.e., split or two-trunk trees, insects, tree disease, high winds, genetic shallow rooting characteristics, or soil conditions.) Trees in campgrounds, picnic areas, and other selected heavily used areas should be inspected each year. If trees or limbs are found to be defective, they should be removed.

In *Autery v. United States* (1993),[10] one passenger was killed and another seriously injured when a pickup was hit by a falling tree in a national park. The tree that hit the plaintiff's pickup was a species known for its shallow roots, and therefore had a tendency to fall over in winds or moisture-saturated soil conditions. The plaintiff claimed that the United States had negligently failed to:

1. Establish an appropriate tree hazard management plan.

2. Maintain the national park area.

3. Properly inspect the trees in the area where the accident occurred.

4. Identify and remove the hazardous trees.

The National Park Service claimed that they were exempt from suit under the Federal Tort Claims Act[11] (FTCA). The trial court (district court) found in favor of the plaintiff Autery. The appellate court held that the decision to inspect trees in an area that did not have a concentration of people was discretionary under the FTCA.

The court therefore dismissed the case and vacated the judgment in favor of the National Park Service.

In another case involving tree failure, *Wright v. United States* (1994),[12] hikers were injured when a rotted tree fell on them while hiking on a national forest trail in the Joyce Kilmer Wilderness Area of North Carolina. The hikers sued the U.S. Forest Service claiming that the defendant:

1. Failed to properly inspect the trail.

2. Failed to remove the tree that fell on them.

3. Failed to warn plaintiffs of danger of falling trees.

4. Allowed plaintiffs to hike on a dangerous trail.

The Forest Service argued that the action should be dismissed because of "the discretionary function exception to the Federal Tort Claims Act."[13] The government claimed that the FTCA prohibits judicial review of United States policies and decisions regarding wilderness management. The federal district court agreed with the Forest Service's position and granted the government's motion to dismiss the case.

Fauna (Animals, Insects, Etc.)

Stinging/Poisonous Insects (i.e., Bees, Mosquitoes, Wasps, Spiders, etc.)
More people are killed from insect bites each year than are killed by snake bites. Stinging insects have two broad types of poisons; those that affect the blood and those that affect the nervous system. Multiple stings, particularly with stings that affect the nervous system (i.e., yellow jackets) can be very dangerous to small children and people with existing medical prob-

lems. Spider bites normally do not kill people but can result in very painful inflammation. Skin-embedding insects, such as deer ticks and mountain ticks, carry Lyme Disease and Rocky Mountain Spotted Fever, respectively. Recreationists in an outdoor setting should check their clothing and body daily to see that ticks are removed. Both Lyme Disease and Rocky Mountain Spotted Fever can be very difficult to diagnose. If a person is unprepared for black flies and mosquitoes, a great outdoor adventure can easily turn into an outdoor disaster. Historically, insects, particularly mosquitoes, have been carriers of many diseases, particularly yellow fever and malaria. Protective clothing, nets for sleeping, and the use of insect repellent with DEET[14] are necessary in settings that have high biting or stinging insect populations. Outdoor recreationists should be warned of known insect dangers and provided information to reduce potential danger and to increase the enjoyment of their outdoor activity. In supervised activities, there might be a legal duty to know whether a participant is allergic to certain insect bites.

Poisonous Animals (i.e., Snakes, Gila Monsters, Jellyfish, etc.)

Fear of animals (zoophobia)[15] is a universal phenomenon. Snakes probably lead the list of feared animals. While few snakes are poisonous, snakes with venom can cause bites that cause serious injuries and sometimes death. Snake bites involving people in ill health and children are the most serious. Also, many people who frequent beaches on the oceans bordering the southern half of the United States can testify to the painful results of contact with a jellyfish. Like most animal stings, some people are much more susceptible to jellyfish stings than others.

Small Biting Animals (i.e., Squirrels, Possums, Coyotes, Badgers, Medium-Sized Fish, etc.)

Most small wild animals have a great fear of humans and will run or hide when confronted. When small animals are trapped or injured, their only defense is to bite. A cute squirrel has very sharp teeth (they can crack very hard nuts), and can cause serious puncture wounds. Small children have a tendency to want to hold or pet small wild animals—an act that usually results in a bitten, frightened, and crying child. Small wild animals carry a number of diseases, such as rabies, tularemia, plague, lice, and so forth. Recreationists should be warned of the dangers of small animal bites specifically to diseases that are known to be carried by small animals in the area.

In *Olloff v. Peck* (1993),[16] the plaintiff was injured when he visited Peck's Wildwood Inc. Nature Park. It included a petting zoo and a fish pond. The fish pond contained large muskellunge[17] (muskie) fish. Olloff was bitten when he reached into the pond to pet a muskie. Olloff sued Peck, claiming that "the possessor of wildlife is held strictly liable for the physical harm caused by the animals." The defendant Peck argued that the pond was certainly not a petting zoo, and that a reasonable person would not have tried to "pet a fish." The trial court decided in favor of the defendant Peck, stating that the type of animal (fish) involved in this accident was not included under the strict liability claim made by the plaintiff. Olloff appealed. The appeals court concluded that "Wildwood was only 10% causally negligent, and Olloff was 90% causally negligent." The appeals court further determined that the trial court was correct in its analysis and affirmed the lower court's decision in favor of the defendant.

Large Carnivore[18] and Omnivore[19] Animals (i.e., Bears, Sharks, Wolves, etc.)

For most people, being attacked and eaten by a bear or shark is the theme of a spectacular personal nightmare or horror movie. Most large carnivore animals are frightened of humans, but some, like large sharks and grizzly bears, appear to be naturally aggressive. Studies of attacks by grizzly bears indicate that incidents occur most often when people fail to follow basic precautions. People are told to make noise or wear bells when traveling so as to not walk up on a bear unexpectedly, to avoid female (sow) bears with cubs, and women should avoid hiking in grizzly bear habitat during menstruation.[20] Also, food should be separated from the campsite by locking it in an automobile, storing it in a locker provided by the facility, or hanging it in a sack on a limb high in a tree.

The foreseeability of a wild animal attack is an important factor in negligence cases against land-managing agencies.

As an example, a man from Wisconsin was traveling just outside of Yellowstone National Park and stopped at a campground overnight. He had not changed his clothes for a number of days and had cooked a number of meals while camping. His clothes were saturated with the odors and juices of past meals. He placed his food in his tent for the evening to protect it from the animals and went to sleep in his clothes. During the night a grizzly bear came into the campground smelled something good and pulled the man out of his camp screaming into the nearby forest. His mostly consumed remains were found the following morning by forest rangers. The entrance to the camping area in which the man was attacked had a large sign warning visitors of grizzly bears and instructing them on how to store food and deal with personal sanitation and cleanliness to avoid contact with bears. This example did not result in a lawsuit. Case law, however, teaches us that lawsuits sometimes arise as a result of human encounters with large carnivores.

In *Claypool v. United States* (1951),[21] the plaintiff sued the United States for injuries he received when a bear attacked him while camping in Yellowstone National Park. The plaintiff paid an entrance fee to enter Yellowstone National Park and received a brochure informing him it was dangerous to feed, molest, or touch bears and that bears were potentially very dangerous. Claypool asked the park ranger if it was safe to camp outside at night in a tent. The ranger answered that they had never had anyone attacked without provocation, and bears did not come around unless the campers had food. The camper (Claypool) entered his tent at night and had no food nearby. Early in the morning, a bear tore a hole in the side of the tent and gashed the plaintiff's leg with his teeth. Park records showed that a bear had reportedly entered the campground in the early morning hours just prior to the plaintiff's visit and had attacked and injured several campers as they slept. All park rangers knew of the previous attack but did not inform anyone of the incident, because they had assumed that the bear in the previous attack had been killed. The plaintiff argued that the park employee was negligent in not informing visitors of the previous incident. The park argued that they were immune from suit under the discretionary provisions of the Federal Tort Claims Act, and informing visitors of problems that they believed had been solved was not necessary. The federal district court found in favor of the plaintiff, stating that "the plaintiff suffered injury caused by the negligent omission of employees of the government acting within the scope of their employment" (i.e., their failure to warn).

Large Herbivores[22] (i.e., Antelope, Deer, Moose, Elk, Porcupine, etc.).

Large vegetation-eating mammals use their size, sharp hoofs, antlers, or other measures to protect themselves, their young, and sometimes their territory. People are killed every week after running into large animals on the highway. Some hunters have been seriously injured after approaching their kills to suddenly find the animals were still alive. Porcupines leave their quills embedded in the skin of other animals (including humans) when they are foolishly touched or attacked (to dispel a myth, a porcupine does not throw its quills.) A skunk can ruin a perfectly good outdoor activity, and render the family dog *persona non grata*.[23] Large animals are particularly dangerous during the mating season and when they protect their young. Each year a number of tourists are injured trying to get an up-close photograph of a buffalo (American Bison) and its calves. Common sense does not appear to be an important element in human behavior when tourists see a large wild animal. Regardless of the warnings, people take dangerous chances to get close-up photographs of large animals.

In *Mann v. State* (1994),[24] a deer collided with the plaintiff's car, causing extensive damage to the vehicle while driving through a state park. The plaintiff sued the state for damages to his car, claiming that the state was negligent by failing to provide deer warning signs and maintain property guards and fenced areas along all state highways that were frequented by deer. The trial court stated that it would be an unreasonable and impossible task to erect a fence everywhere in the state of New York frequented by deer. In addition to the problem of the wide distribution of deer throughout the state, deer were well known for their agility and ability to jump considerable heights. The court decided in favor of the defendant state.

SECTION 2: WEATHER HAZARDS[25]

It is true that we cannot change the weather, but we can certainly prepare for and respond to the weather. Weather is created by a combination of atmospheric conditions, ocean temperatures, vegetative conditions, and land mass elevation. Predicting weather at a specific location can be a complex process. Over the last couple of decades, meteorologists have made great forecasting strides, however. Professionals in recreation, sports, and tourism must always keep an "eye on the weather." Leaders must respond to weather conditions that may threaten an activity and be familiar with what procedures to follow when dangerous weather strikes.

Rain and Floods

Floods are the number-one weather-related killer in the United States. Flooding along rivers is a natural and inevitable part of life. Some floods occur seasonally when winter snow melts or spring rains fill river basins with too much water too quickly. Historic floods such as the Johnstown, Pennsylvania flood in 1889 occurred when a dam broke in heavy rain and a 36-40 foot wall of water killed 2,200 people.

Coastal floods are usually the result of hurricanes or winter storms. Winds generated from tropical storms and hurricanes or intense offshore low pressure systems can drive ocean water inland and cause significant flooding. Coastal flooding can also be produced by earthquakes that create sea waves or a tsunami. A Christmas 2004 tsunami in Indonesia resulted in approximately 200,000 deaths. Many of the deaths occurred in tourist resorts along the tropical beaches surrounding the Indian Ocean.

Flooding caused by Hurricane Katrina in 2005 resulted in thousands of deaths. While the winds caused a great deal of damage and some deaths, the bulk of the deaths were caused by the breaching of dikes and flood walls and the resulting water. Billions of dollars in damage occurred in the states of Louisiana, Mississippi, Alabama, and Texas.

While rain is a normal and natural occurrence, cold rain causes hypothermia. Constant rains associated with what people anticipate should be a sunshine-related recreation experience (i.e., beach vacation) can cause depression and interpersonal conflicts. In some areas, such as the Pacific Northwest, Southeastern Alaska, and the Boundary Water canoe areas, visitors should be advised to bring rain clothes and gear to protect them from cold and illness that may result from being constantly wet. Specialized equipment, such as waterproof matches, boots, and tents should be recommended for rainy environments.

When flash flooding[26] occurs, people in automobiles are most at risk. In some areas of the country, particularly the Southwest, flash flooding can occur very suddenly without rain in the immediate vicinity of the flood. Heavy rainfall in the mountains can result in rushing water down otherwise

dry streambeds (arroyos). Vehicles trying to ford the waters are often swept away by the water. Water just two feet deep will carry away most automobiles. The power of the water at 62.4 lbs per cubic foot typically flowing downstream at six to 12 miles an hour can easily float or exert enough pressure on the side of a passenger vehicle to move it. The biggest factor is buoyancy. Each foot of water that rises up the side of a car displaces 1,500 lbs.

Snow and Ice

Snow is an important element of winter outdoor recreation. Downhill skiing, snowboarding, sledding, snowmobiling, and cross country skiing are examples of the snow-related recreation activities. There are a number of safety issues associated with recreation activities in a snow covered environment. Winter camping is becoming increasingly popular, particularly in adventure and Boy Scout activities. Winter visitors to snow country should be warned to take appropriate actions to reduce the dangers of hypothermia by wearing properly layered clothing. Winter recreationists also may be subject to snow blindness, snow cave collapse, collisions related to sledding and skiing, and avalanches. Suits against land owners have arisen when children were injured while sledding.

Ice provides another important element for winter outdoor recreation and sports. Ice hockey, skating, ice sailing, and ice fishing are just a few of the activities that take place every winter in the northern climates of the United States. Ice also can present significant dangers to recreationists. Those using ice for recreation should understand that ice thickness is a critical factor.

When ice forms on lakes and streams in the northern part of the United States or at high elevations, tragic accidents may occur. Recreationists have fallen through the ice when walking, cross-country skiing, ice-fishing, ice skating, or ice sailing. Regardless of the countless warnings, many people rationalize that the ice is thick enough to bear their weight. Mass media (press, television, radio) should be used to warn the public of dangers involved in the recreational use of ice, particularly in the early and late part of the ice season. Because of a chance of fluctuating water flow levels, warm water springs, and trapped air, thin ice can be present any time of the year. Also, where management has altered the environment (e.g., installing an underwater aerator that creates water movement and thins the ice), warnings of the increased and hidden risk (e.g., thin ice) should be provided through signage or other means.

Ice and snow can also cause significant property damage. The accumulation of ice and snow on buildings and the resultant weight can cause the building to collapse. When facilities (especially pipes and pumps) are not winterized, significant damage occurs. As the ice in rivers and lakes breaks up in the spring, ice jams can form in rivers causing bridges to break and flooding to occur.

The following are helpful suggestions for safe winter travel:[27]

- Always keep your equipment (e.g., snowmobiles) in top mechanical condition.

- Always wear insulated boots and protective clothing including a helmet, gloves, and eye protection.

- Never travel alone.

- Carry a radio and let people know where you are going.

- Avoid, when possible, crossing frozen bodies of water with vehicles.

- Never travel in a single file when crossing frozen bodies of water (automobiles and snowmobiles).

- Always be alert to avoid fences and low-strung wires.

- Never operate a snowmobile, skate, or ski on a street or highway.

- Always look for depressions in the snow.

- Keep automobile and snowmobile headlights and taillights on at all times.

- When approaching an intersection on a snowmobile, come to a complete stop, raise off the seat, and look for traffic.

- Always check the weather conditions before you depart.

The following case provides an example of a sledding injury and lawsuit: In *Noeller v. County of Erie* (1988),[28] a 12-year-old child was injured when sledding down a hill in a county park. The sledding hill was segregated into three categories of use: sledding, tobogganing, and sliding on saucers. The area was heavily used by children and was supervised by county employees when it was open. The plaintiff was using a saucer sledding device when he was hit by three boys on a large inner tube. The lower court found for the defendant county; however, the appellate court reversed the decision of the lower court, stating that:

> When the County has provided and maintained hills for sledding, has invited a large number of the public to participate in the activity that, if unsupervised, could be dangerous, and has in fact provided supervision, the municipality has a duty to exercise reasonable care, which includes a duty to furnish an adequate degree of general supervision. The testimony shows that the supervisor of the facility realized the danger to young children using the slope if several larger children were to slide down together on one large inner tube.

Hail

Hail forms as a result of atmospheric moisture, low temperatures, and updraft winds, mostly during the spring and fall seasons. It can cause damage to equipment and in rare occurrences has been known to cause injury and even death among people and animals. Warning visitors of the dangers of hail is difficult, because it is virtually impossible to forecast accurately for more than a few hours prior to its occurrence. In many instances, hail results from the passage of a strong cold front or is a natural outcome of tornadic conditions. Large hail causes over one billion dollars in damage to property and crops annually in the United States. Risk coordinators should check their insurance policies to see if hail damage is included in the coverage. If the policy does not cover hail, an evaluation of the probability of damaging hail should be made.

Heat and Sun

In most climates, heat and the sun cause numerous physical problems. Many vacations have been ruined by exposure to excessive sunshine and the resultant severe sunburn. Heat exhaustion and heat stroke may result from lack of adequate water (dehydration), excessive exercise (fatigue), and high temperatures. Visitors, particularly those from areas with climates that have considerable cloud cover, need to be warned about excessive sun exposure and the need for adequate hydration. Heat and excessive sun exposure should be considered major risk factors that can cause severe injuries and death.

Winds (Tornadoes and Hurricanes)

High winds, sheer winds, tornadoes, and hurricanes can wreak havoc on camping sites, recreation areas, cruise ships, lakes, and streams. Trees can be uprooted, losing their limbs and crown. Campers may receive serious injuries, and equipment and automobiles might be damaged. When weather forecasters predict severe wind storms, recreationists should monitor news media and use good judgment when occupying wooded recreation sites.

Weather forecasters have been able to determine the presence of tropical depressions that form into hurricanes (Atlantic Ocean) or typhoons (Pacific Ocean) long before they reach a dangerous stage. Warning of hurricanes can come five to ten days before they make landfall. What cannot be predicted accurately until a few hours before the hurricane hits land is the exact path of the storm and its intensity. This makes evacuation of large populations very difficult, thus exposing great numbers of people to the wind, water, lightning, tornadoes, and flooding associated with hurricanes.

Tornadoes are nature's most violent storms with winds sometimes exceeding 200 miles per hour. Thunderstorms result in an average of 80 deaths and 1,500 injuries each year in the United States. Most fatalities occur when people do not leave mobile homes and automobiles. The exact location of tornadoes cannot be predicted accurately until a few minutes before they strike; however general forecasts of the probability of severe thunder showers can occur 24 hours prior to an outbreak of tornadoes.

Downburst winds (sometimes called straight-line or shear winds) are small areas of rapidly descending air beneath a thunderstorm. These winds are sometimes mistaken for tornados. Downburst winds are very dangerous to aircraft and can cause considerable damage to forests and facilities. They usually approach from one direction, therefore the name of "straight-line" winds. Downburst winds can reach speeds equal to a strong tornado (e.g., in excess of 100 mph) and may or may not be accompanied by rain. They are responsible for most thunderstorm damage.

Lightning and Thunderstorms

Thunderstorms, accompanied by rain, thunder, and lightning are a common occurrence. People have been seriously injured and killed as a result of being struck by lightning. Some visitors suffer from an extreme fear of lightning and thunder (astraphobia). In areas particularly subject to lightning storms, lightning warnings and safety instructions should be posted in public areas and attached to trail maps. Warnings should instruct recreationists to avoid ridges and to avoid taking shelter under large trees during thunderstorms. Shelter should be taken in lower terrain and elevation areas, and under trees shorter in height than the general forest stand. People who are outdoors, especially under or near tall trees, on open waters, or in open fields are most at risk from lightning.

Lightning is caused by rising and descending air within a thunderstorm that separates positive and negative charges. Water and ice particles also affect the intensity of the electrical charge. Lightning results from the buildup and discharge of electrical energy between positively and negatively charged areas. Most lightning occurs within the cloud (sometimes called sheet lightning) and between the cloud and ground. The chances of being stuck by lightning are estimated to be 1 in 600,000 during a person's lifetime. However, frequent participants of outdoor recreational pursuits and/or those in lightning-prone areas are at greater risk.

You are most likely to be struck by lightning while:

1. Boating

2. Swimming

3. Golfing

4. Bike riding

5. Playing sports

6. Fishing in a boat

7. Standing under a tree

8. Talking on a cell phone

9. Mountain climbing

10. Riding a lawn mower

In *Bier v. City of New Philadelphia* (1984),[29] the widow of a man killed by lightning sued the city for negligently constructing a public picnic facility. The plaintiff's husband was killed and others were injured when lightning struck a metal-roofed picnic shelter in a city park. The plaintiff's expert wit-nesses said that the metal building should have had lightning detectors, and been grounded to avoid lightning being conducted into the occupants of the shelter. The defendant city denied any liability, stating that the cause of the death, lightning, was an "act of God." The trial court agreed with the act of God defense and issued a summary judgment in favor of the defendant city. The plaintiff appealed. The appellate court reversed the decision and remanded the case back to the lower court to consider whether the lack of lightning protectors on the building did in fact contribute significantly to the accident. See *Schieler v. United States* (1986),[30] for a successful "act of God" defense to a lightning-caused death.

The National Weather Service provides a number of specialized forecasts that are important to recreation and sports activities. Most of the forecasts are available through public media[31] sources. The weather warnings that are available to the public include:

1. General weather forecasts
2. Hurricane warning (typhoon in the pacific ocean)
3. Tornado warning
4. Severe thunderstorm warning
5. Heat advisory
6. Cold temperature advisory
7. Maritime weather
8. Drought predictions
9. fog advisory
10. Flood watch
11. Flash flood warning

There is a broad understanding that the nature of outdoor recreation encompasses some unpredictable or unknown risks. The natural world that provides the backdrop for most outdoor recreation activities simply has too many variables to ensure absolute safety. A sudden windstorm on a lake or lightning from a thunderstorm often cannot be predicted with complete accuracy (although prediction has improved with new technologies) on a local basis. However, it is important for outdoor recreation managers to in-form visitors of foreseeable weather risks that are not obvious. Additionally, where there is a supervisory responsibility (especially to children) there is often an increased responsibility, one that involves planning and protection. Lightning safety plans are available from a variety of sources. The National Athletic Trainers Association (NATA) has a position statement that lists the elements of a plan for recreation providers.[32]

SECTION 3: CLASSIFICATION OF USERS

The standard of care (legal duty) owed to a visitor of a public park or recreation site is determined by the status of the visitor, applicable laws, regulations, written internal standards (manuals, handbooks, letters of direction, etc.), and common practices. The status established for the visitor requires managers to conform to a certain standard of conduct, determined by that status, to ensure against unreasonable risks.[33]

Visitor status is normally separated into three categories: the invitee, the licensee, and the trespasser. Each category is described below.

Invitee

An invitee is someone who is specifically invited and usually pays a fee for the park services or use of the facilities. An invitee is either a public invitee or a business invitee. The following defines the two categories of invitee:[34]

Public Invitee

A public invitee is a person who is invited, usually paying a fee, to enter or remain on land as a member of the public for specific recreation purposes. For example, people who pay fees to camp, boat, use a group area, and so forth, would be considered invitees.

Business Invitee

A business invitee is a person who is invited to enter or remain on land for a purpose directly or indirectly connected with the business dealing with the possessor of the land.[35] Examples of business invitees would be an engineering company constructing a new water system for a campground, a scientist conducting studies on behalf of the agency, and a service representative maintaining agency-owned equipment.[36]

An organization or agency has a duty to assure reasonable care has been used to prepare the premises and make them safe for the invitee. This includes protection from injury related to conditions of the land, facilities, equipment, or by injury from third parties. In the case of invitees, the owner, operator, or manager must inspect the premises and remove or warn of potential hazards, and as a general rule exercise reasonable care to protect the invitee.

The following describes the duties that recreation providers or landowners owe the invitee:[37]

1. Keep the premises in safe repair.

2. Inspect the premises to discover hidden hazards.

3. Remove the known hazards or warn of their presence.

4. Anticipate foreseeable uses and activities by an invitee and take reasonable precautions to protect an invitee from foreseeable dangers.

5. Conduct operations with reasonable care for the safety of the invitee.

The prudent park or recreation manager who complies with these five duties and keeps a written record of periodic inspections and repairs will be able to provide an excellent defense against potential legal actions.

To illustrate, in the case of *Thompson v. Louisiana Department of Transportation* (1994),[38] a plaintiff was injured at a camping area at the defendant's lake recreation area. The plaintiff Thompson fell into an underground trash can while walking with her daughter between two camper/trailers. She sued the Louisiana Department of Transportation, claiming that the receptacle was defective in design and negligently located. The defendant argued that Thompson had poor eyesight and was considered legally blind. The defense further claimed that Thompson was an unforeseeable visitor, because the garbage receptacle was obvious to sighted visitors. Thompson had paid a fee to occupy the camping site and was considered an invitee. The trial court granted summary judgment in favor of the Department of Transportation, stating that "it was impossible for Thompson to have been injured in the manner she described." Thompson appealed. The appeals court reversed the judgment of the trial court stating that Thompson was an invitee and was therefore owed the highest level of care. It further stated that Thompson's injuries were clearly caused by the defective underground trash receptacle located near her leased campsite.

Licensee/Permittee

The licensee classification of a user is owed a duty of care by the recreation provider that falls in the moderate category. There is not a distinct dividing line among the three categories, and a great deal of gray area exists among the various classifications. The licensee is basically someone who has permission or consent, expressed or implied, to go on the land for his or her own purpose.[39] In most jurisdictions, the recreation provider owes the licensee the duty of reasonable or due care.[40]

An example may be a mail carrier, a visitor to a park and/or interpretive center who was not charged a fee to enter the property, or a social guest. A licensee has implied consent to enter upon the property without specific permission. Though a social guest is usually an invited guest, don't confuse this with the invitee status. They are not an invitee within the legal meaning of the term, for they have not paid a fee. A social guest is no more than a licensee who is expected to accept the property or the facilities just as the owner uses them.[41]

Trespasser

A trespasser (nonpaying user) is defined as someone who intentionally or without consent or privilege enters another's property.[42] The word trespasser commonly used for anyone falling under that definition and does not necessarily imply any illegal act. A person who goes upon public or open private land to enjoy a hike or wander the land is technically an innocent trespasser, but most likely has not committed a criminal act of trespass.

Owners, operators, and managers owe adult trespassers a duty of care less than that of a licensee or invitee. They have no duty to make their property or facilities reasonably safe or to warn of dangerous conditions. They only have a duty to avoid injury by gross conduct, intentional recklessness, or wanton misconduct.

In *Steinke v. City of Andover* (1994),[43] the plaintiff was seriously injured when his snowmobile struck a drainage ditch owned and maintained by the defendant city. The plaintiff was trespassing on property adjacent to a city park, and driving his snowmobile in excess of 45 mph. He tried to jump the ditch with his snowmobile but struck the far side of the ditch. Steinke was seriously injured in the accident. Steinke sued the City of Andover, claiming that the city failed to warn him of the presence of the ditch, which he argued constituted a hidden, artificial condition. The city claimed immunity under the Minnesota Municipal Tort Liability Act.[44] The trial court and the appeals court ruled that the city was immune from liability because of the Municipal Tort Liability Act. The plaintiff appealed to the Minnesota Supreme Court. The Supreme Court found that the plaintiff was a trespasser by user classification, and the ditch was not a hidden danger and artificial condition that would entitle the injured trespasser to damages. The decision was in favor of the defendant city.

Special Visitors

There may be a question as to the status of the special category of visitor who enters a public park to view the flowers, play ball, have a picnic, or use the recreation area in a number of ways that are compatible with its intent. This situation occurs when a visitor was invited, enticed, or attracted to the facility or activity, but did not pay a fee. Where the person is a "technical trespasser," the courts will view these individuals in an in-between status and consider other standards as they relate to the care owed a visitor. They are sometimes defined as a public invitee, or simply nonpaying visitors who are on the premises at the implied invitation of the owner.

Consider the following hypothetical situation:

A few years ago in a state park, 13-year-old Joey Cannondale and his friends Sara Huffy and Billy Schwinn went for a bike ride on a warm summer day through a state park. "The mischievous three," as they were affectionately referred to by the local authorities, rode around a barricade across a portion of the road which read "Area Closed, Do Not Enter." They followed the road a short distance and then cut through the woods to a trail they had ridden often in the past. Unbeknownst to them, park managers had recently closed a portion of this trail that was in need of repair. A heavy metal chain roped off the closed section of trail, and a bright, orange ribbon was tied to the chain to help make it more obvious. The previous night's storm apparently blew the ribbon off the chain, because there was no ribbon the next day when Joey Cannondale pedaled right into the heavy chain he didn't notice. The collision caused Joey to catapult over his handlebars and he landed on his head, rendering him unconscious. Billy Schwinn ran to the visitor's center to get help, while Sara Huffy remained with Joey. Joey sustained serious injuries as a result of the incident. Joey's family then sued all parties deemed responsible for his injuries.

What is the status of the three? What duty of care do you think the park owed them? Do you believe that the park was negligent? What defenses would you raise if you were representing the side of the park? What would be your argument if you were taking the side of the Joey? Do you believe the status of the three would make a difference in the outcome of the case?

Children and the Attractive Nuisance Doctrine

Children fit into a separate and special category when it comes to the trespass categories for visitors. Children are by nature curious and have very little sense of potential dangers in their activities or in their environment.

Small children sometimes innocently trespass upon property because interesting or unusual attractions exist. The attractive nuisance doctrine provides for the protection of the curious child seeking out a place to hide or play. Warning signs have no impact on the non-reading child, and fences are meant to be climbed in the eyes of children. In the case of trespassing children, the attractive nuisance doctrine applies. Essentially, owners who have created artificial conditions where common sense indicates that children may trespass, or who possess land containing man-made features that may be expected to attract children, are under a duty to provide such care as a reasonable, prudent person would take to prevent injury. The requirement of land owners to prevent injury to children does not apply to naturally occurring conditions such as lakes, streams, and mountains. Attractive nuisance liability is created only by artificial conditions such as reservoirs, ditches, man-made ponds, buildings, facilities, or man-kept animals.

The courts can also hold parents responsible for property damage and injury to others caused by their children under civil law. Parents can also be held criminally liable for negligently allowing their children to encounter dangerous conditions or to use inherently dangerous objects such as knives, firearms, and fireworks. A child's inclination toward dangerous conduct usually has to be proven in regards to parental liability.[45] Parents can be held liable for not properly supervising their children. In a number of states, statutes have been enacted making parents liable for the negligent acts of their children when there is gross negligence or willful or wanton intent.[46]

In *Jacobsen v. City of Rathdrum* (1988),[47] a two-year-old boy suffered irreparable and irreversible brain damage as a result of nearly drowning in a ditch that ran through the defendant's city park. The ditch was normally dry, but regularly filled with water during the spring season. The plaintiff claimed that the city maintained an attractive nuisance. The trial court granted the city summary judgment based upon the Idaho State Recreational Land Use Statute.[48] The Idaho State Supreme Court remanded the case back to the trial court for further consideration, stating that the recreational land use statute did not prevent liability under the attractive nuisance doctrine.

Park Standards

The managing agency must meet its own standards or have a very good excuse for not meeting them. Managers should review their agency's written instructions to make certain they are meeting those standards. If those standards are not being met, the instructions should be changed or documentation filed as to why they chose to violate their own standards. Failure to meet the standards or failure to justify the reasons the standards were not met can jeopardize the defense during litigation.

A wise manager will determine if it is more prudent from a liability standpoint to charge for a recreation activity or make the activity free from charge. The increased legal liability may not be worth the small amount of user fees collected. The classification of the visitor is an important consideration in every outdoor recreation negligence suit.

SECTION 4: CONCESSIONAIRES, LEASES, AND CONTRACTS

There is much discussion in the contemporary field of public park management concerning privatization and contracting out. In addition to the cost saving involved in privatization, the use of concessionaires, leases, and contracts can transfer all or part of the legal liability for specific aspects of a park operation. There are limitations on the extent of the transferred liability, but nevertheless, contracts, leases, and concessions are important tools in shielding or reducing organization or agency exposure to litigation.

In many large park areas, food service provides a necessary and significant service for park visitors. The park manager has the choice of hiring his own personnel and providing the service; providing the service through a concessionaire agreement; leasing park property to enable the service to utilize the physical facilities of the park; or issuing a prospectus and/or contract to construct and operate a food facility.

All concessionaires, lessees, and contractors must sign an exculpatory agreement, holding harmless the park, park employees, the sponsoring agency or political subdivision, and so forth from liability. They must show proof of adequate liability insurance. In most situations, the amount and scope of the insurance coverage should be substantial, covering the anticipated full amount of a serious liability suit.

A lease is both a rental agreement and a right to occupy a specific area or premises. In essence, a lease gives a person temporary ownership of the property. A lease may be made orally. For example, an agreement could be made for a three-week group site rental over the telephone. An oral agreement must be less than one year in duration. It is a good business practice to have all lease agreements in writing. A short-term lease is a lease with an occupancy time of less than ten years, while a long-term lease exceeds ten years. In most jurisdictions, lease agreements cannot exceed 99 years.

The lessee normally receives exclusive possession for the period of the lease and is responsible for all maintenance and repair after the lease is signed. Lessees also assume the liability responsibility for the property during the period of the lease. When park facilities are leased in a faulty condition, do not meet construction code standards, or are unsafe, the lessee is not legally responsible for any accident that may occur unless the lease specifically included the lessee's responsibility in the matter in the lease agreement. The fault will remain with the leasing agency or organization.

There are exceptions to the general rules related to lessee responsibility. The owner (not the lessee) may be responsible for visitor accidents and property loss when:

1.   Hazards known to the lessor[49] caused the accident.

2.   The premises are leased for the purpose of admission of the public.

3.   The lessor retained control over the premises.

4.   There was an agreement for the lessor to repair the premises.

The following cases illustrate the importance of leases and contracts in managing risk for recreational facilities:

In *Stramka v. Salt River Recreation, Inc.* (1994),[50] the plaintiff recreationist rented a rubber tube for $6 from Salt River Recreation, Inc. (SRR), a concessionaire on the Tonto National Forest. The plaintiff Stramka was a recent immigrant who claimed that all he knew about tubing was what he had learned from SRR television commercials on the Phoenix stations. He claimed that he did not know about or was not informed about sharp objects in the water. After entering the water on his rented tube he fell out of the tube, cutting his hand on a sharp object under the water. The injury resulted in serious and permanent injuries to his hand. He sued SRR for negligence. SRR asked the court for summary judgment based on the fact that "it was exempt under the Arizona Recreation Land Use Statute"[51] because the accident occurred on national forest lands and claimed its lease and responsibility only included a three-acre parcel where it conducted its business. The trial court issued summary judgment on behalf of the defendant SRR. Stramka appealed. The appeals court reversed the judgment of the trial court in favor of the plaintiff, stating that the defendant charged Stramka for the tube. Therefore, the defendant did not qualify for immunity under the Arizona Recreation Land Use Statutes. The case was remanded back to the trial court with instructions to consider the plaintiff's negligence claims.

In *Gimpel v. Host Enterprises, Inc.* (1986),[52] the plaintiff was injured in a bicycle accident at a resort. The plaintiff had rented the bicycle under a contract that contained an exculpatory clause that stated: "User agrees to indemnify and hold Host free and harmless from all injuries to person or persons, including death, damages to property, loss of time, and/or any and all other loss or damages whether caused or occasioned by the negligence of Host, its employees or servants, or any other person whatsoever, arising for flowing from the use, operation or rental of the said item user."

The plaintiff claimed he was injured when the brakes failed because of the lack of maintenance and inspection by the defendant. The defendant argued that the contract for rental included an enforceable exculpatory clause. The trial court determined that the contract clause was valid and issued a summary judgment in favor of the defense. The court stated that the plaintiff's signature on the rental contract indicated his consent to be bound by the contract.

Concessions, leases, and contracts are a vital part of most successful outdoor recreation activities. These management tools will be increasingly used as government agencies attempt to be more productive and efficient. One pitfall for managers is to "lease and forget." Failure to enforce needed safety and sanitation standards contained in the agreement could result in suits against the organization or agency issuing the lease, permit, or contract.

Discussion Questions

1. How will a plaintiff's attorney establish the standard of care expected when an accident occurs?

2. How important is it when agencies or organizations have written standards of care that exceed the "industry's" normal standards? What happens when an accident occurs?

3. When a tree falls down and damages a car or causes injury can an agency claim an "act of God"? Does it make any difference if the tree that caused the damages was in a park or the middle of a forest? Explain.

4. What severe weather condition causes the most weather-related deaths in the U.S.?

Notes

1. See the historic case of *Heaven v. Pender*, 11QBD 503 at 507 (England 1883).
2. *Sartoris v. State*, 519 N.Y.S.2d 728 (A.D. 2 Dept. 1987).

3. Claimant: A person(s) who asserts a right. In the referenced case, the widow of the man who was drowned claimed that the state was negligent and asked for compensation for the loss of her husband.
4. *Clem v. United States*, 601 F.Supp. 835 (N.D. lnd. 1985).
5. Acrophobia—the fear of heights or high places.
6. *Walter v. State*, 586 N.Y.S.2d 391 (3d Dept. 1992).
7. The mineral formations formed in hot pools normally constitute calcite or sulfite compounds. Some people are very sensitive to the chemical compounds found in hot springs.
8. *Twohig v. United States*, 711 F.Supp. 560 (D.C. Mont. 1989).
9. Idaho Recreational Use Statute -Idaho Code § 361604.
10. *Autery v. United States*, 992 F.2d 1523 (11th Cir.1993).
11. Federal Tort Claims Act 28 U.S.C. §§ 1346(b., 2674.
12. *Wright v. United States*, 868 F.Supp. 930 (E.D. Tenn. 1994).
13. Federal Tort Claims Act 28 U.S.C. §§ 1346(b., 2674.
14. DEET is acronym for chemical N,N-Diethyl-m-Toluamide.
15. Zoophobia: The fear of animals, usually a specific animal.
16. *Ollhoff v. Peck*, 503 N.W.2d 323 (Wis. App.1993).
17. Muskellunge: Large freshwater game fish in the pike family of fishes of North America.
18. Carnivores are flesh-eating animals.
19. Omnivores eat both plants and animals. As an example, bears eat flesh, insects, grass, and berries.
20. Data from the Canadian Rockies and Glacier National Park (U.S.) indicates an inordinately high percent of grizzly bear attacks occur to women during their menstruation period. *Grizzly Bear Study Report*, U.S. Fish and Wildlife Service, 1983.
21. *Claypool v. United States*, 98 F.Supp. 702 (S.D. Cal. 1951).
22. Herbivores are animals that feed exclusively on plants.
23. *Persona non gratis*: Unwelcomed or unwanted.
24. *Mann v. State*, 47 N.Y.S.2d 553 (Court of Claims 1944).
25. Most of the weather data was taken from publications of the Weather Service, National Atmospheric and Oceanographic Administration, U.S. Department of Commerce, Washington. D.C.
26. Flash flooding refers to a sudden and somewhat unexpected surge of water, usually associated with normally dry arroyos and washes, or in areas where streams normally flow a low volume of water.
27. Michigan Department of Natural Resources, Safety Website, 2006.
28. *Noeller v. County of Erie*, 535 N.YS.2d 854 (4th Dept. 1988).

29. *Bier v. City of New Philadelphia,* 464 N.E.2d 147 (Ohio 1984).
30. *Schieler v. United States,* 642 F.Supp. 1310 (E.D. Cal. 1986).
31. Public media sources include newspapers, television, radio, and special weather bureau AM, FM, and short wave broadcasts.
32. See Spengler, J., Connaughton, D., & Pittman, A. (2006). *Risk management in sports and recreation.* Champaign, IL: Human Kinetics.
33. See Second Restatement of Torts, and Mudrich Standard Oil Company, 31 N.E 859 (Ohio 1950).
34. Second Restatement of Torts, Section 332, 1982.
35. Second Restatement of Torts, Section 332, 1982.
36. Today, there is little difference between a business invitee and public invitee. For sport and recreation providers, the importance is the higher standard of care usually required for those who pay a fee to use the facilities or services.
37. Kaiser, R. A. (1986). *Liability and law in recreation, parks and sports,* Englewood Cliffs, NJ: Prentice Hall.
38. *Thompson v. Louisiana Department of Transportation,* 639 So.2d 864 (La. App. 1994).
39. Black, H. C. *Black's law dictionary* (8th ed.). St. Paul, MN: West Publishing Co., p. 939.
40. Texas Tort Claims Act, Texas Civil Practice and Rem Code Ann., Section 101.056.
41. Second Restatement of Torts, Section 330
42. Black, H. C. (1979). *Black's law dictionary* (5th ed.). St. Paul, MN: West Publishing Co., p. 1543.
43. *Steinke v. City of Andover* 525 N.W.2d 173 (Minn. 1994).
44. Minnesota Municipality Tort Claims Act, Minnesota Statutes § 466.03.
45. See *Patterson v. Weatherspoon,* 225 So.2d 634 (N.C. App. 1976).
46. Frakt, A., & Rankin, J. (1982). *The law of parks recreation resources and leisure services,* p. 116. Salt Lake City, UT: Brighton.
47. *Jacobsen v. City of Rathdrum,* 766 P.2d 736 (Idaho 1988)
48. Idaho State Code, Recreation Land Use Statute.
49. Lessor: The person or organization that coveys property, real or personal, by leasing. Black, H. C. *Black's law dictionary* (8th ed.). St. Paul, MN: West Publishing Co., p. 922.
50. *Stramka v. Salt River Recreation, Inc.,* 877 P.2d 1339 (Az. App.1994).
51. Arizona Recreation Land Use Statute, A.R.S. Section 331551.
52. *Gimpel v. Host Enterprises, Inc.,* 640 F.Supp. 972 (E.D. Pa.1986).

Chapter Twenty-Two

ADVENTURE/CHALLENGE RECREATION

SECTION 1: HIGH-RISK RECREATION

One of the areas of increasing interest and growth in outdoor recreation is participation in high-risk adventure activities. Adventure recreation includes a number of activities that are known to be dangerous and have resulted in injury or death to the participant. Understanding the risks of the individual activities and taking actions to limit the risk is important in high-risk activities. Learning to be "woods wise" will result in enjoyable and safe experiences. The following section lists some of the adventure and challenge recreation activities people enjoy and some of the inherent dangers of participating in high-risk activities.

Whitewater Canoeing, Kayaking, and Rafting

Whitewater recreation activities can result in turbulent water injuries (e.g., foot entrapment, drowning, and hypothermia).

Whitewater outfitters and river guides must meet the legal standard of care when leading groups or individuals on the water. It is very important to stress safety and inform participants of potential dangers, especially where novices are involved. Oftentimes, people participating in weekend whitewater rafting adventures have never been on a river before. To strengthen a possible assumption of risk defense, verbal and written safety precautions and warnings of potential dangers should be given. Additionally, supervision is very important.

Consider the following hypothetical scenario:

Last year, 50-year-old Billy, the plaintiff, was participating in a rafting trip down section two of the Big Boulder River. Billy was in a raft with his law partner and their two sons. Prior to the river trip, Billy listened to the instructions given by one of the river guides. He then paid his fee and hastily signed a waiver of liability before heading out to the bus that would take them to the put-in point on the river. The first part of the trip was uneventful. At the midpoint of the river trip, the guides stopped for a shore lunch of cold cuts and peanut butter and jelly sandwiches. After lunch, it is customary for the guides to allow the rafters to swim the Little Boulder rapids, a stretch of Class II rapids that runs for a short distance and ends in a deep pool.

There had never been a serious injury resulting from swimming these rapids. After eating his lunch, Billy summoned his courage, put on his life jacket, and waded out to the middle of the stream where the water was about waist deep. He leaned back with his feet forward and began floating down stream. As he reached a point where the water began to pick up speed, he put his feet down to stop himself so that he could look back to see if his older son had followed him. When he attempted to put his feet down, his right foot became trapped in a hole between several rocks. The current pushed him forward, snapping his leg and driving him underwater. His son was close behind and was able to pull his leg from the hole but not without inflicting further damage. Plaintiff's leg was severely injured. Billy brings suit against all parties he believes to be responsible for his misfortune.

Backcountry Adventure Activities

Hypothermia, limited communications, dehydration, lack of medical aid when accidents occur, animal attacks, getting lost, equipment failure, falling, threat of avalanche, and falling rocks are all dangers associated with backcountry adventure activities.

In the past decade, backcountry activities, such as mountaineering and climbing have continued to grow in popularity. Additionally, there has been an increase in the number of backcountry or "out-of-bounds" skiers and snowboarders. Some of those who venture into the backcountry encounter unanticipated difficulties and require the assistance of a search and rescue team. Search and rescue, though possibly the only option for a stranded climber or skier, is influenced by both the cost to the managing agency and the risk to those involved in the rescue operation. Often these search and rescue efforts are expensive. For example, in the State of New Hampshire, it costs as much as $4,000 to outfit a single member of a rescue team. Additionally, there is often substantial risk to both parties involved in the rescue.

For example, on January 11, 1998, at Little Cottonwood Canyon, Utah, a medical helicopter rescued a backcountry skier injured in an avalanche. The backcountry skier was skiing in an area that was not designated as developed ski area. Unfortunately, the chopper crashed in a snowstorm enroute to the hospital, killing all four people (captain, nurse, paramedic, and the rescued skier) on board. The potential risks for life-threatening are evident, and accidents and fatalities do occur.

The majority of fatalities have been the result of backcountry users getting caught in avalanches. Between 1985-1999, there were 272 fatalities among backcountry users (snowmobilers, skiers, snowboarders, hikers, climbers, etc.) in the U.S. In the Province of British Columbia, Canada, 110 fatalities were reported to be related to skiers/snowboarders. In the United States, Colorado has had the highest number of fatalities in the last 14 years at 85, which includes all backcountry users. With the emerging trend and growing popularity of backcountry use, managers of parks and public lands clearly face difficult decisions when a park visitor needs rescue assistance. In addition to considerations of cost and risk to the rescuer, the park manager's judgment is also influenced by the person in need of rescue. There are considerations of moral obligations to conduct a rescue, and now the threat of litigation if a rescue is either not attempted, or attempted in an alleged negligent manner.

Consider the following hypothetical situation:

Bradley Highwalker and four of his friends decided to climb the north slope of Badger Mountain in Yosemite National Park. Bradley was a novice climber but was in decent physical condition and felt he could keep up with his middle-aged friends. The climb up the north slope was a non-technical route. Bradley and his friends began their climb at 8 a.m. after signing in at the ranger station. They had paid a fee to enter the park and for a backcountry permit. The climb began as a gradual slope but increased in difficulty as they made their ascent. They reached the summit between 11:00 and noon. The view from the summit was breathtaking, and all agreed that the climb had been well worth the effort. When the time came to leave the summit, Bradley decided to accompany his friend John back down the west slope, which was believed to be a less technical route. The other two friends wanted a greater challenge, so they opted to descend via the east slope, which was more difficult. Bradley's legs felt like lead, and he inwardly dreaded the return trip. Bradley and John began their descent from the summit with careful slow steps.

As they descended, they began to notice that the west slope was not as easy as they had been led to believe. Large boulders and loose gravel slowed their progress and made the going difficult. About halfway down, Bradley slipped on the loose gravel, tumbled forward, and crashed into a boulder. He had cracked his kneecap in the fall and badly bruised several ribs. John tried to help Bradley continue on, but his pain was too great. John left Bradley and met the rest of the party at the ranger station. They informed the ranger of the situation and asked for a rescue team to be summoned. The ranger suggested they wait, since it was near dark and a search at this time would be too risky. They waited until first light and sent a rescue team. They found Bradley alive but with a severe case of hypothermia. Bradley sues all parties he feels are responsible for his misfortune.

Hunting

Gunshot wounds can be caused by an individual to themselves or caused by other hunters. All other categories of risk listed under Backcountry Adventure Activities can also apply.

The Pennsylvania Game Commission reported 56 hunting-related incidents including four fatalities in 2004. Fourteen of the 56 incidents were self-inflicted. The incident statistics by species hunted were: deer 23 (including four fatalities) wild turkey (14), small game (13), waterfowl (14), and other (2).

Firearms are inherently dangerous. Gun safety programs should be mandatory for everyone licensed to carry a firearm, particularly young people and first time hunters. In a review of hunting accidents it was determined that hunters were more likely to drown or get lost than be shot by another hunter. Two-thirds of the fatalities were men between 18 and 23 years of age.

Hunting and the use of alcohol do not mix and are a major factor in hunting accidents. Alcohol hinders judgment, reduces reaction time and reduces visual awareness. Contrary to what some people think, alcohol does not warm a person, but actually serves to cool down the body and bring on hypothermia. Alcohol use and participation in any high-risk recreational activity are not compatible.

Horseback Riding

Injuries sustained during horseback riding are usually caused by a horse kicking, biting, bucking, falling off the horse, and equipment (tack) failures.

Equestrian activities involve a higher degree of risk than other recreational activities due to the number of elements that are beyond the control of the rider or instructor. There are conditions affecting the horse, such as temperature/weather, tack, insects, horns honking, or thunder. There is also the unpredictable nature of any animal and the potential for an unanticipated reaction to a command by a new rider. Other animals or noises in the environment might spook a horse that is otherwise quite docile. It would be rare indeed that a horse would remain docile when confronted with a bear on the trail.

Because of the number of risks that are outside the control of the equestrian supervisor, laws have been enacted in many states that limit the liability associated with equestrian activities. These laws (statutes) are generally referred to as sport safety statutes. The theme of these laws is to place responsibility on participants for risks that they voluntarily assume. These risks are referred to as inherent risks and are often listed in the statute. In general, horseback riding has a strong assumption of risk context. It should also be noted that when equipment is not properly used or a plaintiff can prove gross, or willful and wanton negligence, a plaintiff has a potentially stronger case in a court of law.

Caving (Cave Exploration)

Caving risks include drowning in underwater streams, equipment failure, becoming lost in caves, hypothermia, falling, and lack of immediate medical aid.

The primary safety consideration for cavers are training and good equipment. Cavers must be trained in the safe use of equipment prior to engaging in the recreation activity. Caving accidents are generally caused by poor judgment and lack of adequate lighting equipment. Falling accidents can be reduced by not jumping and sliding down cave slopes. Proper footwear and equipment is critical to reducing falling accidents. Injuries can also be caused by falling objects. Always wear a helmet and stay away from the base of vertical drops and climbs. When the human body's temperature drops more than a few degrees the body does not function properly.

When heavy rain occurs in the vicinity of a cave, water can rise rapidly in the cave. Outside weather conditions must be considered prior to entering a cave. Cavers must protect themselves from cold temperatures and carry enough light to compensate for unexpected delays in exiting the cave. The caving leader has a serious responsibility to train and manage the caving experience in such a manner as to reduce the likelihood of accidents in what could be best described as an unfamiliar environment.

Skiing/Snowboarding

Broken legs caused by torque during falls, avalanches, collisions with other skiers, trees, and so forth, losing direction in an unfamiliar environment, snow blindness, and hypothermia are all dangers associated with skiing and snowboarding.

When the public watches skiing and snowboarding competitions on television, there appears to be a reckless abandonment displayed by the competitors. The reckless abandonment context is sometimes adopted by the novice or beginner skier/snowboarders with tragic and/or painful results. Proper instruction and skiing under control provides for an enjoyable experience. There are some simple, yet important, considerations to insure individual safety. They include:

1. Wear proper ski clothing, including goggles.

2. Use well maintained equipment.

3. Never ski alone.

4. Avoid areas with potential avalanche conditions.

5. Monitor and respond to weather reports.

6. Properly adjust ski bindings to allow for release when torque pressure is applied.

7. Generous use of sunscreen can avoid painful burning, even in cold weather.

Consider the following hypothetical scenario:

Twenty-three-year-old Sally Chapstick decided to participate in the third annual "Polarbear Ski for Your Life" endurance contest. Sally was an experienced skier and a member of the Birchbark Ski Resort ski patrol. The contest involved hiking and skiing ten miles of rugged snow-covered terrain on SnowCap property. The race began in the early morning before the slope was open to the public. Sally signed a waiver prior to participating in the event and paid the $20 entry fee. The race began with a Le Mans start, whereby the skiers left their skis at the top of the mountain on the ridge of a back bowl. The bowl was a steep, open area with deep snow that was open to skiers only at specified times due to the possibility of avalanche.

The skiers were instructed to stay within the northeast half of the bowl. It had been cleared by the ski patrol as safe. The skiers would ski down the bowl, strap on a pair of cross-country skis and race back to the finish line at the lodge. Sally was injured while skiing in the back bowl segment of the race. She had reached the bowl and stated she was about five minutes behind the leader. She put on her skis and pushed herself off the steep ledge of the bowl. About halfway down, she decided to cut across the southeast portion of the bowl to make up for lost time. Her skis dug into the deep snow and she heard a deep rumbling sound. An avalanche was triggered by her skis, and she was buried several feet beneath the surface. A search party was organized and Sally was found; cold, wet, and unconscious, but alive. Sally suffered severe injuries to her extremities in the ordeal. Sally brings suit against all Birchbark Ski Resort, the Birchbark Ski Patrol, the Sponsor of the "Polarbear Ski for Your Life" and the SnowCap Property, all of whom she believes to be responsible for her misfortune.

Other Considerations

High-risk activities require extraordinary care, training, and specialized equipment. For example: skiers must have special safety bindings and protective clothing; wilderness users must anticipate, plan, and be equipped for personal emergencies; and whitewater canoeists must have canoeing skills appropriate for the conditions, wear protective lifesaving gear, and know something of the dynamics and hydraulics of fast-flowing rivers.

Failure to use approved and tested equipment during difficult mountain climbing activities would certainly be folly. Caving without adequate equipment, especially lights, would result in disaster. Skiing without proper safety bindings would be very unwise. Going into a wilderness area unprepared for changes in the weather could result in hypothermia. An inexperienced horseback rider on a horse whose characteristics (jumping, bucking, running, etc.) are unfamiliar to the rider poses a danger. Hunting with clothing colors that do not distinguish the hunter from the animal being hunted or vegetation can be fatal. Canoeing in whitewater without a life jacket, durable equipment, and training is indeed foolish.

People engaged in high-risk recreation activities generally assume risks that other recreationists do not. For example, in *Dillworth v. Gambardella*, the plaintiff was seriously injured while skiing with the defendant Gambardella. The plaintiff claimed that Gambardella was negligent when he skied into the plaintiff on the ski slope, causing him injury. The impact of the collision caused a serious and permanent back injury. The defendant argued that "under Vermont Law, a skier accepts as a matter of law the obvious and necessary dangers inherent to the sport." The lower court decision for the defendant centered on the assumption of risk doctrine found in the Vermont Sports Injury Statute, which states in part that "a person who takes part in any sport accepts as a matter of law the dangers that are inherent, therein insofar as they are obvious and necessary." The plaintiff requested a new trial, and the U.S. Federal District Court denied the motion. The final court decision was for the defendant Gambardella.

Most rural parks and outdoor recreation property contain all the conditions necessary for lawsuits. Parks have a combination of the natural environment, man-made facilities, water-oriented recreation (swimming, boating, fishing, etc.), and people, especially children.

SECTION 2: CHALLENGE ACTIVITIES

Many people constantly seek outdoor adventure and challenge in their lives, witnessed by significant increases in experiential education, ropes courses, climbing walls, outdoor adventure programs, and challenge courses. Some of the benefits of high-risk activities include increased self-confidence, commitment, acceptance of responsibility, leadership development, teamwork, empowerment, self-esteem, group participation, overcoming failure, insight, group interaction, increased peer trust, and group problem solving.

Some of the outdoor fixed-rope activities associated with a developed site may include rope courses, rope ladders, suspended ropes, swinging ropes, spider web ropes, climbing walls, and balance or inclined beams. Rope-related activities involve an element of risk with the potential for a serious injury if not properly managed. Rope activities are usually classified as low elements (relatively close to the ground) and high elements (three to four feet from the ground and above). Interestingly, more injuries have been found to occur on the low elements (lower leg injuries such as sprained ankles) than on the high elements. The reason for fewer accidents on high ropes is that a belay system is often in place on high elements, which provides for a greater degree of safety if performed properly. The potential for a more severe injury is of course greater on a high ropes course, creating the need for a belay system that is well planned with a backup system in place.

All adventure recreation activities should be guided by a risk-management plan. Risk management plans should include:

1. Risk communications

2. Hazard assessment

3. Incident investigation

4. Risk training

5. Reporting procedures

6. Hazardous materials handling

7. Unacceptable participant behavior

8. Appropriate off-duty activities for staff

The risk management plan should emphasize reducing accidents and the prevention of fatalities, injuries, and serious illness. All incidents involving fatalities, injuries, and serious illness should be investigated, and if appropriate, recommendations made to avoid future problems.

The use of waivers for adult participants in challenge activities should simply be a part of the program. The parents of minors engaged in these activities should sign "agreements to participate." In all cases, the signed document should be specific and detail the potential dangers of the activity. Some personal safety concerns will not be apparent to challenge course leaders unless the participants inform them. Participants might have, for example, allergic reactions to bee stings, or have diabetes or another medical condition that leaders should be made aware of. The risk management plan should therefore include an opportunity for participants to voluntarily share any special needs before participating, and after being given clear and thorough information concerning the potential risks they may encounter.

Depending upon the activity involved, attention should be given to group size. To ensure safety, there should be a minimum and maximum size for a group of participants. Consideration should also be given to limit group size numbers to protect the environment and to increase the enjoyment that comes from the ability to participate and engage in the activity. Some challenge programs intentionally have segments that require individuals to have solo experiences for personal growth; however, as a general rule, risk activities should not be undertaken unless there are companions to help if problems occur. The following are suggested staff/participant ratios for challenge activities based upon progressive difficulty, inherent dangers and need for supervision:

1:12   backpacking, orienteering, bicycle touring, group initiatives, and ropes courses.

1:8   canoe camping, rafting, top-roped rock climbing, rappelling, caving, snowshoeing, and cross-country skiing.

1:4   whitewater canoeing, single-pitch rock climbing, remote wilderness travel, snow and ice climbing, wind surfing, and sailing.

1:3   sea kayaking, multi-pitch rock climbing and glacier travel.

1:2   lead climbing and summit mountaineering.

In most situations related to high-risk outdoor recreation, risk should be managed but not eliminated, because physical and mental risk plays an important part in attracting individuals and organizations to high-risk activities. Companies, corporations, and associations have established adventure experience groups in camps or recreational settings, adventure-based counseling groups in camp settings, and adventure executive or staff development in camps or groups.

Adventure/challenge programs have been particularly important to organizational team building, youth crime prevention programs, criminal rehabilitation to reduce recidivism, and disabled rehabilitation. Rope courses, usually a vital part of the programs, can be conducted in either an indoor or outdoor setting.

The management of the risk in high-adventure activities should include a progressive program that provides for:

1. A period of peer acquaintance activities to ensure that the individual participants know each other (e.g., ice breakers).

2. A program that provides for the free exchange of ideas and encourages each participant to express themselves without hesitation and without concern of peer criticism.

3. Activities that establish trust among the participants (e.g., team-building activities, initiative activities).

Only after the above activities are completed to the satisfaction of the adventure leader and the participants are made aware that their participation is completely voluntary, should the challenge activities take place.

Those who participate in high-adventure ropes activities are usually considered to be public invitees, while those who pursue a high-risk outdoor activity (such as mountain climbing or whitewater canoeing) on their own using their own equipment may be considered legal trespassers or licensees. Participant classification will vary depending on payment of fees, supervision, age, or special circumstances.

It is particularly important that providers of adventure activities do not use homemade and designed equipment and facilities. Ropes, pulleys, walls, and harnesses should be designed, installed, and checked by those companies having expertise and experience in such matters. Liability for failure of equipment and design flaws are often shared with the provider, installer, seller, and manufacturer. A prudent recreation provider should check the competence of the installer, the candor of the seller, and the experience of the manufacturer. It would also be wise to personally check the quality of the product and the amount of liability insurance carried by the manufacturer. Instructors should check daily on the condition of the equipment. If any anomaly is detected, that piece of equipment should not be used.

No leader, student, or participant should be responsible for belaying those on a course or structure without first proving his or her competence. The instructor should maintain complete control of the ropes (the belay system) and other fail safe equipment. Falling periodically is inevitable in high-risk activities. Instructors should teach students the proper way to fall, even short distances, to minimize the potential for injury. Spotting, or having someone nearby to break the fall should be done on low element activities.

Some attention must be given to the mental and psychological readiness of the individual to participate in challenge activities. The combination of a relatively dangerous activity, and an irrational, unqualified, or incompetent participant may result in a devastating event. The instructor or person in charge must determine the physical (general health, cardiovascular, strength), and psychological health of an individual participant before allowing the person to participate.

Warnings should be given to the participants clearly and repeatedly. Safety equipment must be utilized by all participants, including the instructors, and is never optional. Correct "how-to" instruction is necessary before starting an activity. Adequate supervision is necessary in each aspect of the adventure. No person should be forced, coerced, or pressured into participating in any high-risk activity. Good sequential implementation of the activity plan will result in a minimum exposure to risk.

An example of where sequential implementation was at issue is the case of *Hulsey v. Elsinore Parachute Center*. In this case, the plaintiff's decedent brought a wrongful death suit against Elsinore Parachute Center, claiming the defendant was "negligent by improperly and inadequately instructing Hulsey in the type of parachute equipment he was given to use, by improperly and inadequately warning Hulsey of the hazards of jumping with the type of parachute equipment he was given, and by improperly and carelessly giving Hulsey a parachute that contained a bridle cord (rip cord) that was too long for a novice parachutist of his size, weight, and experience."

The defendant Elsinore Parachute Center argued that the decedent was experienced, based on the fact that he was 65 years old, a commissioned officer and pilot in World War II, and had participated in parachute training as part of his military training. Falkner had signed a waiver/release that was part of the training agreement. The agreement was comprehensive. It outlined the risks assumed and contained a covenant not to sue. The case was remanded back to the trial court for further review of the facts.

Discussion Questions

1. Wilderness users need to accept dangers, because their very purpose is the rush received when they face the dangers involved in the natural environment. True or false? Explain.

2. Will safety precautions ruin the very reason people go to the wilderness? Explain.

3. Rescuers should "put precaution aside" during a backcountry rescue operation because the life of the person being rescued is more important than the life of the rescuer. True or False? Explain.

Notes

1. *Dillworth v. Gambardella,* U.S. District Court of Appeals for the Second Circuit 970 F.2d 1113 (1992)
2. *Hulsey v. Elsinore Parachute Center.* (1995) 168 Cal.App.3d 333, 214 Cal. Rpt.194.

Chapter Twenty-Three

PROTECTION ISSUES

Law enforcement in the areas of recreation and parks is by the nature of the activity usually low key. Usually the rules are enforced by the person in charge, rather than uniformed police. If it is determined that active uniformed law enforcement is needed, then well-trained professional law enforcement personnel is a requirement.

An agency that managed a remote campground was embarrassed by a law enforcement incident a few years ago. The campground visitors were very frightened by what appeared to be a mentally unstable individual who was illegally discharging a firearm in a random manner in the recreation area. When a ranger appeared on the scene in a vehicle with emergency lights mounted on the top and wearing a uniform and badge, they quickly gathered around him to solicit his protection and inform him of the situation. He assessed the situation, climbed back into his vehicle and said to them as he drove away, "I will go for help."

The "ranger" was not a trained law enforcement officer. He only used the trappings of the law enforcement profession. The resultant furor caused some major policy changes in vehicle and uniform standards. While he did the right thing by going for help, since he was not trained in law enforcement in any manner, the people who stood by and watched him drive off were devastated. A short time later, designated and trained law enforcement officers arrived and took care of the situation without further incident. Organizations should not dress their employees as if they are law enforcement officers if they are not extensively trained in law enforcement matters. The same problem can arise when any recreation employee is driving vehicles with red and blue lights.

In a recreation, park, and sports settings, law enforcement has three basic enforcement purposes:

1. To protect the people from other people.

2. To protect the people from the environment.

3. To protect the environment (property or resources) from the people.

In *U.S. v. Tagbering* (1993),[1] the police had information linking Tagbering to trafficking in narcotics. A package addressed to the house where Tagbering lived was sent from Jamaica to Kansas City, Missouri. The package was intercepted and inspected by postal inspectors in Miami, Florida, and found to contain 900 grams of hashish oil and 142 grams of marijuana stuffed inside a toy. The police in Kansas City removed the illegal substances and set up an operation to search Tagbering's apartment as soon as he accepted the package in the mail. When they entered Tagbering's home with a warrant, they also found guns, a stolen telephone calling card, drug paraphernalia, and a false identification card. Tagbering was charged with theft of the stolen goods, possession of guns, and false identification. He was convicted of a number of offenses. Tagbering appealed his conviction, because he alleged that the search warrant was illegal because it only mentioned the false narcotics package. The appellate court agreed with the lower court, stating that all evidence was admissible under the good-faith exception to the exclusionary rule.[2]

The lower court trial decisions was affirmed by the United States Court of Appeals and the U.S. Supreme Courts; however, they modified the lower court decision by ruling that additional sentencing time could not be imposed when the listed offenses were essentially different descriptions of the same offenses.

Protecting the People from the People

One of the primary purposes of law enforcement is to protect people from the illegal or offensive behavior of others. While protecting people from other people, the behavior is often considered criminal in nature, and there can be a strong civil (tort) wrong committed. Should an organization fail to protect people using their facilities from the offensive behavior of other visitors,[3] participants, or guests, then the organization may be subject to litigation.

In *Montag v. YMCA of Oneida County* (1984),[4] a women was attacked in the YMCA locker room by an unidentified assailant. The locker room was not monitored by an attendant at the time of the incident. The attendant was absent from her normal station by the door of locker room. The appeals court determined that the YMCA had a responsibility to protect users of the locker room from invasion by criminal elements. Adequate security must be maintained where the circumstances and exposure to harm demand protection from possible harm. In their decision the appeals court stated: "A landlord has a duty to maintain minimal security measures, related to a specific building itself, in the fact of foreseeable criminal intrusion upon tenants."

Protecting the People from the Environment

People need to be protected from the environment they are using for their recreation and sports activities. Whether it is a no-diving regulation in a park lake, or a bear warning sign in a campground, people must be protected from potential injuries resulting from their participation in activities.

A sign warning of bears in a campground should provide campers with a message giving instructions about how to store their food and deal with bears if they enter the campground or they meet a bear on the trail. The warning signs do not eliminate the dangers from wild animals, but do provide a warning and helpful suggestions on dealing with bears. The sign certainly does not help those who ignore the warnings or act carelessly when bears are present. No sign, persuasion, protective equipment, or warning will help the foolish person. Each year a number of skiers are killed by avalanches, and their ski tracks usually go by a sign warning that the area is closed because of avalanche danger.

Protecting a visitor from the environment is not always effective. Some visitor behavior is such that they circumvent an organization's ability to protect them. In *Ewell v. United States*[5] the plaintiff, Stacy Ewell, a minor, was injured in a motorcycle accident on federal land in Utah. The land where the accident occurred was managed by the Bureau of Land Management and used as a gravel pit by Wasatch County. The plaintiff alleged that the Bureau of Land Management committed an act of willful and malicious negligence in failing to inspect, inform, erect barriers, and provide warning signs to visitors on their land. Ewell had not paid a fee to enter or use the land. The government said that the vast federal lands in the western United States are generally open to use by the public without a fee. The court issued summary judgment[6] in favor of the defendant, United States. In their decision, they established four major defenses to negligence on vast areas of land as follows:

1. The vast undeveloped lands in the west are basically in a natural state. Every natural hazard cannot be either identified or a warning provided.

2. The use of a motorcycle for off-road use is in itself inherently hazardous, and there is an assumption of risk when choosing this recreational activity.

3. No fee was paid to use the land, and therefore the provisions of the Utah Land Use Statutes[7] would not be applicable unless the plaintiff proved willful and malicious negligence.

4. The parents of the minor child have the primary responsibility to see that an area is safe for their child, particularly when the area is in an undeveloped and natural state.

Protecting the Environment from the People

Law enforcement and managers have a responsibility to protect the environment, from the people who, because of ignorance or intent, misuse facilities, land, and resources. Most of the time protection can be accomplished by visitor information programs, limiting access, limiting the number of users, hard surfacing areas with sensitive soils, culturally treating vegetation (irrigation, fertilization, aeration, etc.), and other management activities. If people continue to destroy and vandalize facilities and resources, then law enforcement measures are necessary. Vandalism, litter, water pollution, and air pollution laws are usually adequate to meet most law enforcement contingencies.

The design of facilities in areas with a history of vandalism or other destructive practices is very important. As an example, areas designed with a minimum of vertical surfaces reduce the risk and opportunity for graffiti vandalism. Many people are simply not informed about how to protect a natural environment or to care for a man-made structure. Information or rules on the ethics and behavior involving recreational activities, are needed in most situations. People usually respond positively to logical and understandable rules. Facilities that are not well-maintained increase the risk of accidents, vandalism, and therefore legal liability increases.

Additionally, hunting permits and regulations are necessary to maintain healthy wildlife populations. Illegal hunting practices on public and private land can result in fines and penalties for the perpetrators and, as the following case illustrates, litigation for the managing agency.

In the case of *United States v. Lee* (2000),[8] 22 hunters were convicted of violating the Migratory Bird Treaty Act after they were caught hunting dove over a baited field. The field was baited with pieces of corn that lured migratory birds to the site. The hunters had purchased licenses and paid a fee to hunt on leased property. The owner of the property had spread the corn over portions of the field before the hunters arrived. The hunters claimed that they did not realize the field was illegally baited, and claimed the property owner told them that everything was legal. The case was appealed to the federal court of appeals that affirmed the conviction. The court held that a hunter has the responsibility to inspect the field (hunting area) and try to see if it is legally planted and not baited. The property owner was found guilty of aiding and abetting the hunters.

Societal problems related to crowd control, vandalism, theft, and assaults are now common in many parks and recreation settings. Park professionals need to provide adequate protection for the participants, while at the same time allowing the participant the freedom to enjoy their pursuits without constant interference or monitoring by the police. Effective law enforcement requires skillful management and sensitivity.

Discussion Questions

1. Briefly explain the three basic purposes of law enforcement.

2. In the hypothetical at the beginning of the chapter, what would have been the appropriate action for the ranger to have taken after being notified of a camper discharging a firearm?

3. Provide an example of how "protecting people from other people" can have both criminal and civil (tort) implications.

Notes

1. *U.S. v. Tagbering,* 985 F.2d 946 (1993) modified by U.S. Supreme Court Case *Tagbering v. United States,* 522 U.S. 825; 18 S.Ct. 85 (1997)
2. Good Faith Exception to the Exclusionary Rule would apply when a search warrant was issued in good faith, but some guaranteed rights were violated as a result of unreasonable search.
3. *Bearman v. University of Notre Dame,* 453 NE.2d 1196 (lnd. App.1983).
4. *Montag v. YMCS of Oneida County* 482 N.Y.S.2d 613 (A.D. 4 Dept. 1984), Supreme Court, Appellate Division, Fourth Department November 7, 1984.
5. *See Ewell v. United States,* 579 F.Supp. 1291 (D. Utah 1984).
6. Summary judgment is issued by a court when the circumstances of the case indicate that there is no substantive issue in the plaintiff's allegations or no justifiable position in defense. Rule of Civil Procedure Number 56.
7. Utah Limitation of Landowner Liability—Public Recreation, Utah Code 57- 141 to 7.
8. *United States v. Lee,* 217 F.3d 284 (5th Cir. 2000).

Part Eight

MANAGING SPORTS AND RECREATIONAL ACTIVITIES

INTRODUCTION

Most of us would agree that one of the main reasons for participating in recreational sports and activities is to have fun and maintain a healthy lifestyle. Recreational facilities often exist in hotels and resorts as a value added attraction. Also, supervised recreation programs for both children and adults are often available for hotel and resort guests. From recreational activities as different as basketball to swimming, it is easy to recognize the benefits to mind and body. Amateur competitive sports played at the high school or college levels are often designed to fulfill a similar purpose. There are similarities in the determinants of the standard of care as it applies to both competitive sport and recreational activities. Though many of the examples used in the following chapters are set in the sport context, similar applications exist for providers of public recreation and hospitality. Regardless of the setting, when safety is compromised, the health and well-being of participants is put at risk. The number of legal cases involving sports and recreational activities is indeed great. The following is a sample of circumstances where sport injuries have resulted in lawsuits:

A lawsuit was brought when:

- A hotel guest drowned at an unsupervised pool.

- A 60-year-old tennis player tripped over a torn net.

- A star high school football player was paralyzed after blocking on a kick-off return.

- A high school softball player injured her leg after stepping into a hole near home plate.

- A high school swimmer was injured when his head hit the bottom of a pool after diving in to begin a race.

- A camper sustained a serious eye injury in a rugby game after colliding with a counselor.

- A basketball player collided with an unpadded wall.

- A student stepped on an uneven surface of the field and injured his leg during an intramural football game.

- A rugby player was kicked in the face by an opposing player who was improperly coached.

Reported court decisions involving sports number in the thousands. There are many more cases decided at the trial court level that are not published. Tort liability in sports has become a major issue. Therefore, it is very important to meet or exceed the standard of care that applies to the sport or activity that is supervised.

Chapter Twenty-Four

THE RESPONSIBLE LEADER

SECTION 1: SUPERVISION

One cannot overemphasize the importance of supervision in recreational activities and competitive sports. A coach or recreation supervisor stands in a unique and sometimes unenviable position. He is responsible for the safety and welfare of a group of people who often have differing skill levels and knowledge of a particular sport, and who are vulnerable to the hazards associated with it. A young child in a physical education class, or supervised activity at a resort, for example, might not understand the dangers of using gymnastics equipment, or a high school football player might not understand the dangers of heat illness. While a player or participant might not understand the risks, the supervisor must certainly understand them and take steps to manage and prevent those risks. There is often, in fact, a legal duty to do so. A coach or sport supervisor is responsible for the safety of his players. This responsibility translates into a legal duty to provide adequate supervision to the players under his or her control.

Adequate supervision of recreational and competitive sports is accomplished by establishing a reasonably safe place for practice and competitive play, and by watching over the activities of the athletes.[1] Thus, for a coach or sport supervisor to meet the legal standard of care, he or she must provide a reasonably safe environment in which to practice and play. Remember that when the standard is not met, a breach of duty has occurred—the second element to be proved in a negligence action. Also, the failure to provide proper supervision is often claimed as the proximate cause of injuries in recreational and competitive sports. Therefore, inadequate supervision can act both as a breach of duty and as a proximate cause of injury, thereby satisfying two of the key elements of negligence.

Negligence claims sometimes arise when a player is allowed to play again too soon after an injury. This often happens in contact sports such as football, or high intensity sports such as basketball. Decisions on when to resume playing after an injury often create a dilemma for both players and coaches. Players sometimes feel they will lose their scholarships, playing time, or position on the team if they stay out too long due to injury. This creates the tendency to want to return before an injury has had time to completely heal. The coach might allow a player to return because he needs him to play in a big game, or he may just not realize that an injury has not healed well enough.

The following cases might influence your perception of when a player should be allowed to return to the game. They illustrate the coach's duty to provide adequate supervision in the context of reinjury in competitive sports.

In the case of *Zalkin v. American Learning Systems, Inc.* (1994),[2] Zalkin was an 11th-grade student at American Heritage School in Florida and a defensive tackle for the school's football team. While playing in the last regular-season game, Zalkin injured his shoulder. He told his coach that he had been hurt, so he was wisely taken out of the game. The coach also told Zalkin that he should see a doctor about the shoulder. For the next 10 days, Zalkin was limited in how much he could practice and was made to cut back on his weightlifting routine. He followed his coach's instructions, but after ten days, his shoulder still hurt. On the 10th day, the team held a practice game; the coach put Zalkin in the game, and he soon reinjured his shoulder. The boy's family sued the coach and school for negligent supervision.

Zalkin claimed that the coach was negligent in putting him in the game when he knew or should have known that he could reinjure his shoulder. He lost at trial, but the decision was appealed. The appellate court sent the case back for another jury trial. The coach and school argued that Zalkin knew it was dangerous for him to play in the practice game but that he voluntarily chose to play anyway. Legally, this means Zalkin assumed the risk of participating in the game. The court didn't buy this argument and said that although players might assume the risk of dangers inherent in the sport itself, they do not assume the risk of negligent supervision.

This case should make a coach or sport supervisor think twice before allowing an injured player to resume playing in a contact sport. It is often a good idea to get the go ahead from a competent medical doctor before allowing a player to practice or play in games. Also, as the following case illustrates, it is a bad idea to allow an injured player to play against a doctor's orders.

In the case of *Lamorie v. Warner Pacific College* (1993),[3] Lamorie was on a basketball scholarship for Warner Pacific College. While playing in a pickup football game at his church on April 19, Lamorie was smashed in the face. His nose was in such bad shape that he had surgery to repair the damage. Also, his face was very bruised and one eye was almost swollen shut. He had to wear a nose cast to protect his nose following surgery.

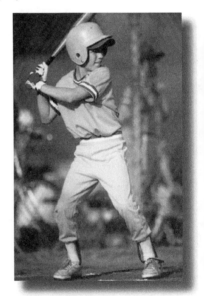

Lamorie's doctor told him not to go to classes and definitely not to participate in any athletics for a while. In the following weeks, he became well enough to attend classes, but still was advised by his doctor not to engage in strenuous physical exercise. The basketball coach repeatedly questioned Lamorie about when he could return to practice. Lamorie responded by saying it would be a while longer.

On May 11, about three weeks after the accident, the coach asked Lamorie to play in a scrimmage game. His nose was still swollen and his face was still bruised, but he agreed to play anyway, because he was beginning to feel that his scholarship would be in jeopardy if he didn't return to the court. The scrimmage became very physical, and Lamorie was hit in the face. Unfortunately, he injured his eye and reinjured his nose. Lamorie sued the coach and the school for negligent supervision.

Sport and recreation providers have a duty to provide the proper protective equipment for children.

The case was won by the coach and school in the lower court but was then appealed. Lamorie argued that the risk of injury to his eye and re-injury to his nose was foreseeable. In other words, the coach knew or should have known that he stood a good chance of being injured if he played in the scrimmage. Lamorie argued that the injury was foreseeable since the coach knew that the doctor had told him to refrain from physical activity.

Also, the coach could plainly see his swollen nose and the bruises on his face. The appellate court agreed with Lamorie on these points and also felt that it was unlikely that he voluntarily agreed to play in the scrimmage except that he feared he might lose his scholarship. This negated the assumption of risk defense for the school. The lower court's decision was therefore reversed, and the case was sent back to the trial court for a final determination.

Coaches and supervisors should be cognizant of the condition of athletes and make a reasonable determination as to when to remove them from the field of play if they appear to be suffering from pain or fatigue that might result in serious injury.

Consider the following scenario:

Buster Strongarm decided to try out for his college baseball team. Buster had pitched for a small high school in southern Georgia. Although he was an extremely talented pitcher, he had gone unnoticed by the college scouts. Buster had not discovered his own ability until his senior year. He now wanted desperately to play for a college team and improve his raw talent. At 17 years of age, the speed and accuracy of his pitches showed potential for a baseball career extending well beyond college. Before beginning tryouts, Buster was directed to sign a waiver of liability. He hastily read the agreement and signed, knowing that he must sign if he wanted to try out for the team. Buster then went through a brief orientation by the coaches who asked if any of the players were injured and when the pitchers had last thrown. Injured players could not participate in the tryouts. Buster stated that he had thrown earlier that day and felt to be sufficiently warmed up. When his turn came to throw, he stepped to the pitcher's mound and took a deep breath. His first pitch was spectacular. The fastball hummed across the center of the plate as a blur. He was instructed to pitch again. Buster threw four perfect pitches. On his fifth pitch, however, Buster felt a slight pain in his shoulder. He told the coaches of this and asked if he should stop throwing. They were so caught up in their excitement of envisioning a winning season behind the arm of this tremendous hurler that they told him not to worry about it and pitch another. Buster wound up and let loose another fastball. He immediately felt something snap and the searing pain which followed. Buster had seriously damaged his shoulder, and his baseball career was now in great jeopardy. Buster sues all parties he feels to be responsible for his injury.

Do you believe that the coaches were negligent in allowing Buster to continue pitching? Why? What would you have done if you were the coach in that situation?

Negligent supervision cases are also often litigated over the issue of sport participants who have been left unattended. A supervisor such as a camp counselor, recreation leader, or physical education teacher, should not leave the team, class, or group under his supervision unattended; especially if he or she knows that members of the team may engage in unsafe activities while he or she is away.

Also, if it is essential for a supervisor to leave, the supervisor should have an adequate replacement on site before leaving. The replacement should have similar supervisory qualifications and be adequately trained to meet any foreseeable problems. Remember that the replacement's training and qualifications will be investigated in court should a lawsuit arise from an injury occurring while the supervisor was away.

In the case of *Barretto v. City of New York* (1994),[4] a high school volleyball coach left practice temporarily, only to return to an awful sight. One of his players was lying on the floor; paralyzed from the waist down. The coach had opened the gym and told his players to set up the volleyball poles and nets while he took a minute to finish some paperwork.

While he was gone, instead of setting up the equipment for volleyball, the students set the net to a height of four feet and placed tumbling mats under it. One of the players took a running start and attempted to dive over the net headfirst. His foot, however, caught in the net as he was in midair and he landed on his head. He became a quadriplegic as a result of the injury. He sued the coach and the school for negligent supervision.

The injured student argued that the coach (and school) was negligent since they breached his duty of care to the students. The plaintiff claimed that supervision should have been provided for the entire practice and the failure to do so amounted to inadequate supervision. The court agreed and awarded the young man a large amount of money.

The facts indicated that coaches had been instructed and required to supervise all practices and to never leave the area unsupervised. Also, testimony revealed that the coach knew that the players acted up when he was not around, so it was reasonably foreseeable that something like this could happen. The coach was therefore found negligent in failing to properly supervise the activity and meeting the appropriate standard of care.

The case was appealed to the higher court where the decision was reversed in favor of the defendant. The court held that the dangers involved in diving over the net were obvious and the student voluntarily assumed this risk.

Those who supervise sports activities must position themselves in locations where they can best see and hear what is going on in the area they supervise. If this is not possible, then more supervisors might be needed for the activity. Also, just as the supervisor must be able to see and hear the participants, the participants should know that the supervisor is able to see and hear them. This can give the supervisor added control and help the activity run more smoothly.

In activities where the risk of serious harm is foreseeable, such as first-time activities or those involving children and/or dangerous equipment, closer supervision might be needed. Gymnastics, for example, often requires one-on-one supervision by someone with sufficient training and skill in the activity. Regardless of the sport activity, the minimum requirement should be to stay within sight and hearing of all participants. The following case illustrates this point.[5]

In the case of *Grant v. Lake Oswego School Dist. No. 7*(1973),[6] a 12-year-old girl was learning gymnastics in her physical education class. She was in a group of 17 seventh graders, all having their first class in gymnastics. They were supervised by their physical education teacher in the school exercise room, which had a high ceiling. A springboard was placed in the center of the room so the girls could take turns jumping off it. They would jump from the springboard onto a mat; landing on their feet. Others practiced on the balance beam or practiced tumbling.

Near the end of class, the teacher told Grant (the plaintiff) and two other girls to take the springboard back to the entrance alcove where it was usually stored. It was usually leaned against a wall and stored that way. The alcove had a low ceiling and was separated from the main exercise room by a doorway that was seven feet high. The girls took the springboard to the alcove as told, but did not lean it against the wall. Instead, they decided to jump from it through the doorway and into the exercise room.

The teacher was standing where she could not see the entrance to the alcove. She knew something was wrong when she was called to help. She came over and found Grant lying on the ground below the doorway. Grant had attempted to jump from the springboard in the alcove into the main room. In the process, she struck her head on the doorway and was injured.

Grant sued the teacher and the school for negligence in failing to properly supervise the students in the use of the gymnastics equipment. Grant's case was appealed from a lower court ruling. The appellate court decided that based on the facts, a jury might find that the injury to Grant was foreseeable. The court also held that a jury might find that proper supervision could have prevented the accident. The court noted that to meet her standard of care, the teacher could have done several things.

First, she should have specifically directed the girls to place the spring-board on its side and told them not to jump on it. It was uncertain in the case whether this was done, so the court remanded the case so a jury could decide what exactly happened. Second, she should have been in a position to see whether the girls had put the springboard away and made sure they were not jumping on it. Third, in addition to directing the girls to lean the springboard against the wall, she should have specifically warned them not to jump from it. The court left these issues to be decided once the jury had all the necessary facts.

Another aspect of supervision, which is particularly important for teach-ers and coaches, involves making sure that players are similar to one another in size and skill when going head to head in an activity—especially a contact sport. Properly matching players in an activity is important to prevent an unreasonable risk of injury. To do otherwise might result in a breach of the legal duty of care to properly supervise an activity. This is the final aspect of negligent supervision to be addressed in this section.

As with all situations where negligence is claimed, the standard of care often becomes the central issue. Also, as we have seen before, it is best to meet or exceed the standard of care where it is possible. When the standard is met or exceeded, successful lawsuits against the agency or organization are less likely. Some general guidelines are given here to help you think about when and why matching players is important and to better understand the issues surrounding the standard of care.

Contact sports are obviously the most relevant when you think about matching players properly. Some examples of contact sports are lacrosse, ice hockey, football and wrestling. It is easy to see how unreasonable it would be to put a 120 lb. high school freshman up against a 250 lb. senior with ex-perience in a first-day scrimmage. A court could easily find that the coach breached his or her duty to provide reasonable safety for his or her players under these circumstances. Proper matching, therefore, is important to pro-vide for the safety of players and to reduce the risk of lawsuits.

To meet or exceed the standard of care for this aspect of supervision, there are certain things that a coach, teacher, or supervisor can do. First, the supervisor should know each player's experience in a particular sport, his ability level, and skill. This must be known before players can be prop-erlypaired to compete or practice together. Once this background informa-tion is acquired and known, periodic tests should be conducted to learn the current skill and ability levels of the players. This information can be used to group the players and should be documented regularly and accurately records kept. Players with too much difference in skill should not be paired against one another, particularly in a contact sport.

Age, maturity, and fatigue are other important elements that must be considered when matching sport participants. Age and maturity, as most of us know, often do not go hand in hand. Therefore, it is essential that a coach, teacher, or supervisor know the players well before pairing them up to play against one another. Players should also be closely watched to determine if some are overtired or fatigued. Participants often will not admit when they are tired. This makes it important that the supervisor know the players and watch them closely so that injury resulting from a mismatch between an overly tired player and a fresh substitute does not result in injury to the tired player.

Knowing which players to match under the particular circumstances surrounding a sports activity is often a judgment call for the coach or supervisor. This judgment, made from knowing the players well, and having an understanding of the risk management considerations mentioned here, can help to reduce the risk of a negligent supervision suit from an injury caused by mismatching players.

Another duty associated with supervision is the duty to warn players of hazards that are part of a particular sport. You often think of warnings associated with products. You see warning labels on virtually every product on the market—from cleaning detergents to football helmets. Warnings, however, are not limited to products. It is often necessary to warn sport participants of the possibilities of injury associated with a sport, especially when the hazards are known to the coaches and supervisors but not known to the players. Other recreational activities also often require such a warning. The following case illustrates what can happen when dangers are known but warnings are not given.

In the case of *Pitre v. Louisiana Tech University* (1995),[7] Pitre decided to go sledding with some of his friends. It was January and there was a good hill for sledding on campus on those rare occasions when they had enough snow. They found some large trash can lids to use as sleds and started down the slippery hill. After several runs, Pitre laid down on the lid on his back and went down the hill headfirst. At the bottom of the hill was a parking lot with a row of concrete light posts. Pitre slid into the parking lot after descending the hill and ran headfirst into one of the light posts. He suffered permanent paralysis as a result of his collision with the light post. Pitre sued the university for negligence in failing to warn him of the dangers associated with sledding on the hill. Pitre lost his case in the trial court and appealed.

Pitre claimed that sledding on the hill was unreasonably dangerous for an activity that the university approved. The university allowed sledding except in one area where there was heavy traffic. Therefore, he argued the university had implied that this area was safe for sledding when it was not. He argued that a warning was necessary. The appellate court agreed with Pitre and reversed the ruling of the trial court.

The court held that the school had a duty to discover and warn of unreasonably dangerous conditions on its property. They found the facts of this case to indicate that the school knew the light posts presented a danger to students sledding down the hill and into the parking lot. Therefore, the school had a duty to warn of the danger. Placing signs at the top of the hill warning of the light posts, the court reasoned, would have eliminated or reduced the risk of a student being injured. The school, therefore, was held to be negligent and Pitre won the case.

The Pitre case was later reversed and modified by an Appeals Court decision. It was appealed again by the university with the court agreeing with the original lower court decision. The final court decision determined that the trial court was correct in finding the university owned no duty to the student, the winter storm bulletin did not create a duty for the university, and the university did not stand *in loco parentis* to the student.

The purpose of warning players about possible injuries is to ensure that players can make informed decisions about whether to play and accept the risks associated with the sport. When this is done, those who voluntarily choose to participate in a sport will bear the responsibility of participation.

As mentioned, there is a general duty to warn players of certain dangers associated with a sport activity. The duty to warn is important to consider when a player or parent of a player does not understand the inherent dangers in a particular sport. This can happen when the player is new to the sport, unfamiliar with the sport given his or her background or circumstances (e.g., a person from another country who does not understand football), or when a player participates in a sport that has been traditionally dominated by the other gender. For example, a girl who tries out for the high school football team might not understand the inherent dangers associated with the sport. If she is not warned of the possibility of serious injury, and becomes seriously injured while playing, a lawsuit might be brought claiming that the coach breached his duty of care and was therefore negligent. The following case illustrates what can happen when specific warnings are not given.

In the case of *Hammond v. Board of Education of Carroll County* (1994),[8] 16-year-old Hammond, the fastest runner at her school, decided to try out for the varsity football team. She made the team and was placed at the position of fullback. A fullback plays on offense and is one of the players who runs the ball. During her first scrimmage while on the team, she was tackled hard and severely injured. Hammond suffered a ruptured spleen and other internal injuries resulting in the removal of part of her pancreas. She had surgery and spent a long time in the hospital. Hammond sued the county school board for more than one million dollars in damages. She claimed that the school and coach were negligent in failing to warn her of the inherent risk of injury in playing football. She lost her case in the trial court and appealed.

Hammond claimed that neither she nor her mother knew about the risks involved in playing football. She testified that she had seen football games played but had never seen a serious injury occur. She thought that only a twisted ankle or a knee injury would be the worst thing to happen. She claimed that if she had been warned of the serious injuries that were possible in the game of football, she would not have played.

The appellate court held that the coach did not have a duty to warn her that serious injury was possible when she had voluntarily chosen to play on a high school varsity tackle football team. The court stated that a 16-year-old of average intelligence was held to know that football is a rough and hazardous game and that anyone playing can be injured. The court did, however, say that although not required, it would be a good idea as a matter of public policy to warn players of the possibility of serious injury resulting from playing the sport. The appellate court found for the school, and Hammond lost the case.

Exposure to infectious diseases is also an important issue in sport. And as we know, there is a duty to warn participants of the inherent dangers in a sport. Infectious conditions such as hepatitis B, herpes, and chicken pox are the most likely diseases to be passed along through sports contact. Another disease of concern is AIDS, although the likelihood of this disease being transmitted through contact in sports is thought to be very small.

If a teacher or coach knows that a player carries an infectious disease and allows him or her to play without warning the other players, the coach might be found liable for negligence in some jurisdictions if the disease is transmitted and someone becomes infected. In other jurisdictions, a court might find that the failure to warn players of an infectious condition is a willful or wanton act to which liability would attach.

The duty to warn, however, conflicts with the legal principle of medical confidentiality, which prohibits a coach or administrator from publishing (making public) personal medical information. This is one of those areas in the law where responsibilities that are required by the law are in conflict. When this happens, consultation with school officials and legal counsel might be the best way of finding a solution to the dilemma.

SECTION 2: INSTRUCTION

Adequate supervision also carries with it, especially between coaches and teachers, the duty of properly instructing players on the rules of play, skills, techniques, and strategies. The reason for proper instruction is not only to ensure the safety of your own players, but also to eliminate negligent conduct that results in injury to members of an opposing team. It is important to know that a coach can be sued when one of the players injures another player because the coach has failed to properly teach the players the necessary rules, skills, and techniques involved in the game.[9]

The following three points should be known and remembered by all who are coaching or teaching sports. First, the rules of play must be known by the coach and taught to the players. The coach should go a step further by making sure that the players know the rules and by seeing that the rules are enforced. Second, the necessary skills and techniques should be taught. This usually means that the coach should have enough skill and/or knowledge of the sport to be able to ensure the safety of the players.

Improper technique should be corrected and its importance explained as it relates to injury. Records should be kept of the skills taught and when the instruction took place. Third, a coach should guide his players to progress at a reasonable pace in skill development to make sure that they remain safe and healthy. These three points are listed and explained as follows.

Teach and Enforce the Proper Rules of Play

It is nearly impossible to think of a sport that does not have established rules of play. Often, rules are designed to reduce the risk of injury associated with an activity. They are made and enforced at many levels of government and by various governing bodies. For example, rules are made at the federal, state, and local levels, as well as by districts and conferences. The NCAA is a prime example of a rule-making body. It makes and enforces rules governing college athletics. In addition to these rules, the schools and coaches often make rules. It is interesting that when a rule is violated, it is possible that the opposing coach and school will be subject to liability rather than (or in addition to) the player who violated the rule. The following case illustrates how this can happen.

In a North Carolina case,[10] a young man was playing catcher for his high school baseball team. In a game against another high school, the opposing player rounded third base and sped toward home. When he reached home plate, he slammed into the catcher, trying to dislodge the ball. The catcher was seriously and permanently injured as a result of the collision.

There is a rule in high school baseball in North Carolina that a player shall not maliciously run into another player. It is known as the slide rule and requires that coaches teach players how to slide properly so that opposing players will not be injured. It is the coach's duty to teach the proper method of sliding. This duty is also set forth in more general terms in the High School Baseball Rules Book, which requires coaches to know the rules thoroughly and to teach them to his team.

The catcher's family subsequently brought suit, not against the opposing player, but instead, against the opposing player's coach and school. The catcher's family claimed that the opposing coach was negligent in failing to teach his players this rule and make sure they understood it. They also claimed, among other things, that the coach failed to teach his players how to slide properly.

In addition to the coach's duty, the injured player also claimed that the athletic director, principal, and school superintendent had a duty to see that the basic skills and rules were taught, practiced, and understood by team members. He claimed that this duty was breached and that negligence resulted. The case was settled, and money was paid to the catcher by the defendants.

Teach the Proper Skill Techniques and Fundamentals

Teaching the proper techniques is critical from a risk management perspective. Football, for example, is a sport where improper tackling technique can result in serious injury to a player. Spearing, a method of tackling where the helmet is used, can result in serious injury to a player's knees or head. Improper slides in baseball, undercutting a player on the soccer field, undercutting a player making a lay up on a basketball court, and high sticking in hockey, are all examples of unsafe techniques in sport that are likely to result in injury. A coach need not only be aware of what his players are doing, but he also needs to be skilled in and knowledgeable about the best and safest ways of performing techniques particular to the sport.

If a coach teaches a technique such as spearing or knows that the players are tackling in this manner but does nothing to stop it, the coach could very well be held liable on a claim of negligent instruction. This is because it is foreseeable that injury could occur from this method of tackling, which gives rise to a duty on the part of the coach to teach his players to refrain from using this technique. This is the standard of care the coach must meet. It can best be met by demonstrating the proper and improper technique (in a safe manner) and explaining to the players the injury that can occur if the improper technique is used.

Meeting the standard, however, does not mean that a coach cannot teach his players to be aggressive and play hard. Aggressive play is an essential part of many competitive sports. Teaching aggressive play differs from teaching dangerous techniques or failing to correct improper techniques that might endanger other players. There is, however, a fine line between the two, as the following case illustrates.

In the case of *Nydegger v. Don Bosco Prep. High School* (1985),[11] Nydegger was a player on the high school varsity soccer team. In mid-October, his team was playing against another high school team. The coach for the opposing team taught his players to play aggressively. During the game, an opposing player undercut Nydegger and caused him to be seriously injured. An undercut is an aggressive technique designed to take an opponent's legs out from under him, causing him to fall to the ground. Nydegger sued the opposing coach and school, claiming they were negligent in failing to properly instruct their players.

The opposing coach and high school won the case. The court found that if a coach instructs his players to commit a wrongful act or teaches moves that would increase the risk of harm to opposing players, he would be found negligent in failing to meet his duty of care. There was no evidence presented in this case that the coach instructed his players to undercut opposing players (a move likely to impose harm) or that he knew his players were apt to undercut someone. The court held that teaching players to be intense and aggressive was an attribute and not a negligent act.

Teach Skills in a Progressive Manner

We all must crawl and walk before we can run. In sports, we must learn the fundamentals of a particular athletic skill before we can compete safely and effectively. This point is particularly important for coaches of contact sports. A rugby coach, for example, would not be acting wisely to hold a full-contact scrimmage on the first day of practice. Players need to be taught the proper skills and placed in advanced drills only as their skills improve.

The idea of progression also applies to conditioning. Progressive conditioning is important for all types of athletic training. Training for endur-

Gymnastics activities require specific supervision and proper progression in instruction.

ance-type activities, such as distance running, as well as training to increase strength should be done in a progressive manner. In other words, coaches should allow their players to work up to a particular level of conditioning in a reasonable time frame. This will improve performance and improve the chances that players will remain safe and healthy.

Allowing players to progress in skill development and conditioning will help to reduce the risk of lawsuits. Players should be monitored as they improve in skill and conditioning. Detailed records should be kept of this progress. When a player's skills and conditioning are monitored, the coach can better decide how to pair up players for drills and scrimmages. This can help reduce the likelihood of injury to participants. Guiding players progressively through skill and conditioning development will better enable the teacher, coach, or supervisor to meet the necessary standard of care as it applies to the duty to provide adequate instruction.

SECTION 3: EMERGENCY MEDICAL CARE

High school and college athletics often present situations where the human body is pushed to its physical limit. Football practice in August can test the limits of a player's tolerance to heat. A female high school tennis player might be struggling alone on a far court in 100-degree heat, pushing her endurance to the limit with the only thing on her mind being to win the next point.

Pushing your body to its limits is in many cases what athletics is all about. The reward is winning or reaching a personal goal. The risk is suffering physical injury such as heat stroke or a heart attack. When a problem such as this arises, proper medical care is often needed immediately. Coaches have a legal duty to provide emergency medical care for their athletes.[12] The duty, or standard of care, recognized by the courts is illustrated in the following two cases. The first involves a high school athlete and coach, while the second involves a university athletics program.

In the case of *Mogabgab v. New Orleans Parish School Board* (1979),[13] a 16-year-old high school football player was running wind sprints at football practice. It was August in New Orleans, the second day of practice, and it was very hot. The boy had been at practice about an hour and a half when his body could take no more. He collapsed during a wind sprint and vomited as his teammates carried him to the bus. It was 5:20 p.m. He was hauled up the steps and into the bus with some difficulty. Robert was conscious but unable to walk. He vomited again while on the bus and appeared dazed.

The bus went directly to the high school where it arrived at 5:40 p.m. The boy's teammates moved him inside the school cafeteria where they laid him on a blanket and undressed him. His complexion was pale, and he looked very tired. The boy was taken to the shower, dried off, and given an ammonia capsule by the coach. His condition, however, only worsened. A first-aid book was found and looked over by the coaches. They tried to give the boy salt water, but by this time his skin was clammy, his breathing was heavy, and he could not drink anything.

By 6:40 p.m., the boy's condition had deteriorated to a dangerous level. His skin had turned a grayish-blue color, which indicated a lack of oxygen in his system. At 6:45 p.m., the boy's mother was called and told of the situation. She then called a doctor who arrived at the school 30 minutes later. The doctor, the boy's treating physician, found him in critical condition.

The boy was unconscious, with no pulse in any of the major vessels. He had severe heat stroke and was in a state of shock. He was immediately taken to a hospital where several specialists tried to revive him. The boy did not recover. His parents sued the school board, the head coach, assistant coach, the school principal, the school superintendent, the health, safety, and physical education supervisor, and the insurance company. They claimed negligence in that the duty to provide prompt treatment and safe playing conditions was not met. The parents prevailed against the school board, the head coach, and the assistant coach.

The court, upon viewing the medical evidence, noted that heat damage works over time. At some point in the continuum, the damage done to the body is irreversible. Therefore, it is necessary that proper medical care be administered early, before any irreversible damage is done. The facts indicate that the symptoms of heat stroke were apparent early on. The boy did not have access to treatment for more than two hours after the first symptoms appeared. Given these facts, the court held that the coaches were negligent in delaying proper medical care and in applying incorrect methods of first aid.

This case illustrates the standard that must be met by those coaching high school sports. From this case we learn that coaches need to be aware of symptoms of potentially severe medical conditions such as heat stroke and head, neck, or spinal injuries. When these symptoms arise, medical help must be summoned immediately. Proper first aid procedures must also be known and followed. Once medical help is summoned, first aid can be used to stabilize the patient's condition so that it does not become worse. The following case also addresses the issue of providing prompt medical care, but in this case, the context is a university athletic program.

In the case of *Kleinknecht v. Gettysburg College* (1993),[14] Kleinknecht was a lacrosse player for Gettysburg College. Lacrosse is a fast-paced contact sport in which players use netted sticks to catch and propel a small ball with the purpose of shooting it into the opponent's goal. Kleinknecht, a 20-year-old college student, was practicing with the team in the late summer. He was involved in one of the drills as a defenseman when he simply stepped away from the play and fell down. Kleinknecht had suffered a heart attack. When it was noticed that he had collapsed, his coach and teammates ran to his aid. They suspected that he had been hit and that was why he had collapsed. They also suspected he had sustained a serious injury, such as damage to his spinal cord.

The coach and several players ran for help. There were no trainers present, and no one was certified in CPR. There was no plan in case of a medical emergency (there had never been a serious emergency before) and there

were no radios on the practice field. The nearest phone was 250 yards away inside the training room at the stadium. An eight-foot fence that surrounded the stadium had to be climbed to reach the training room.

Players and staff ran in all directions. The coach ran toward the stadium. The team captain ran toward the stadium training room. Another player ran toward the student union building. The team captain found a student trainer and notified others who called the head trainer and advised him of the situation. At the student union, an ambulance was called that arrived six minutes later. The student trainer was the first trained in CPR to reach Kleinknecht. She monitored his condition but did not perform CPR. Next, nearly at the same time, the head trainer and a band member who was trained as an emergency medical technician arrived at the scene. They performed CPR on Kleinknecht until the ambulances arrived. He was then rushed to the hospital, where he later died.

The Kleinknechts sued the college. They claimed that the college breached its duty when it failed to provide prompt and adequate medical services at the time of their son's death. The court agreed that the college owed a duty to its student athletes to provide prompt and adequate emergency medical care. The court left the issue of whether the college breached this duty to the jury in another trial. Jury trials often spell bad news for the defendant in cases where there is death or injury, and emotions run high.

The court reasoned that since lacrosse is a contact sport and life-threatening injury during participation is foreseeable, the college owes student-athletes a duty to take reasonable precautions against the risk of death while engaged in the sport. The duty was further explained as the standard of care, which required the college to be ready for any life-threatening injury and to respond swiftly and adequately to a medical emergency.

These cases, though tragic, have provided information from which we can learn. What can be learned is that proper procedures can be put in place to help coaches and schools meet and exceed the standard of care they may be required to meet. The procedures are easy to learn and some are very easy to implement as well. The procedures should be a part of a written emergency action plan (EAP) that is communicated to all coaches, trainers, and staff.

Coaches and trainers should have CPR certification and be trained in basic emergency medical procedures. Those with proper training in CPR and first aid should be located at or very near the field or court where practice or games are held. Athletic trainers should be a part of an athletic program if at all possible. The importance of athletic trainers to both high school and college teams cannot be overstated. Studies have shown that having an athletic trainer in the program reduces the incidents of first-time injuries and lowers the rate of reinjury among athletes.[15]

Also, properly administered first aid in a medical emergency might work to stabilize an injury, and properly administered CPR might save the life of an athlete. Where certain types of injury are foreseeable to a coach or supervisor, however, CPR and first aid might not be enough to meet the duty of care to an injured athlete. For example, in a contact sport such as football, specific training in how to administer CPR to a player wearing a helmet would be wise. Taking off a helmet could create or worsen a head or neck injury. Therefore, the coach or supervisor would need to know the technique of administering CPR through the face mask. Additionally, of increasing importance to those who manage and supervise sports and recreational activities is a knowledge of automated external defibrillators (AEDs). AEDs are now required in certain states in fitness centers, high school athletic programs, and park and recreation organizations. In many recreation-based organizations, it is becoming a community or industry standard given the increasing adoption of these devices. An AED is a device that is simple to use and effective in reducing the number of deaths due to sudden cardiac arrest (SCA). AEDs are important for recreation-based organizations given that three of the top 10 places for SCA are sport stadiums, golf courses, and fitness centers. Managers and supervisors should be familiar with their state's AED immunity provisions, mandates for use, and requirement of use such as training, medical oversight, and having trained (AED/CPR) users present on site.

Second, coaches should have a well-planned communication system in place. As the previous cases demonstrate, time is critical when an emergency arises. In those cases, neither staff had a plan to get professional medical help to their practices quickly. Coaches and trainers would be wise to have handheld radios or cell phones on site. At the very least, the nearest phones should be identified and made easy to reach. You should not have to climb locked gates or run several hundred yards to reach a phone, and the phones should not take more than a few minutes to reach. In addition to locating phones and getting to them quickly, there are other things to consider. First, a list of emergency numbers should be on hand at all times and exact change must be available if a pay phone must be used. The emergency numbers should identify who to call, where they can be reached, and in what order.

The points discussed thus far are very important from a risk-management perspective. As such, these considerations should be thought about in the context of the particular athletic program; be it soccer, football, tennis, or any other sport, and spelled out in the form of a written emergency action plan. Everyone on the staff should be given a specific assignment in the plan. For example, the coach or recreation supervisor might be responsible for ensuring that all staff members are trained in CPR and first aid. The assistant coach and team captain might be responsible for locating phones or acquiring handheld radios and keeping a list of emergency phone numbers. Once the plan is in place, it should be rehearsed periodically, so that everyone is prepared should an actual emergency occur. With proper planning based on sound risk management considerations applied to the particulars of a program, coaches and school officials can maintain a standard of care that the judicial system would deem reasonable.

Discussion Questions

1. Who is responsible when a 13-year-old player with a history of recklessly throwing the bat after hitting the ball injures another player? The player, the coach, the parent, the league officials? Explain.

2. In youth league contact sports, is there any liability when one team is significantly larger than another? Significantly more skilled? In better physical condition? Is older than another? Are significantly more polite than the other? Explain.

3. Explain why it is important to have a comprehensive, proactive emergency action plan, and the basic components of such a plan.

4. What has the Kleinecht case taught us about preparation and planning for medical emergencies?

Notes

1. Ball, E. (1991). *Sport injury risk management and keys to safety.* North Palm Beach, FL: Coalition of Americans to Protect Sports.
2. *Zalkin v. American Learning Systems, Inc.,* 639 So.2d 1020 (Fl. App. 1994).
3. *Lamorie v. Warner Pacific College,* 850 P.2d 401 (Ore. App. 1993).
4. *Barretto v. City of New York,* 655 N.Y.S.2d 484 (1st Dept. 1994).
5. The discussion of sport supervision in this chapter draws heavily upon a presentation of the subject in Merriman, J. (1993 Feb.). Supervision in sport and physical activity, *Journal of Health, Physical Education, Recreation and Dance,* 2023; and Rushing, G. (1993, Dec.). Risk management for athletic coaches: supervision. *The Sports, Parks, and Recreation Law Reporter,* Vol. 7, No. 3., 3338.
6. *Grant v. Lake Oswego School Dist. No. 7,* 515 P.2d 947 (Ore. App.1973).
7. *Pitre v. Louisiana Tech University,* 655, So.2d 659, reversed and remanded in part by *Pitre v. Louisiana Tech University,* LA 95-1466, 673 So.2d.585 1996, (La. May 10, 1996)
8. *Hammond v. Board of Education of Carroll County,* 639 A.2d 223 (Md. App. 1994).
9. The discussion of instruction in this section draws upon various legal cases and a presentation of the subject in Adams, S.(1992). Duty to instruct: Correct and proper. *The Journal of Legal Aspects of Sport 2*(1), 79.

10. The case cited is *Cheek v. Matanzo,* et al., 90CVS883 (1990), and is explained in Hall, K.(1993). A survey of selected North Carolina high schools: liability of coaches/trainers. *Journal of Legal Aspects of Sport,* 3(2) 4449.

11. *Nydegger v. Don Bosco Prep. High School,* 495 A.2d 485 (N.J. Super. 1985).

12. The discussion of emergency medical care draws upon an article entitled Duty of Care Owed to Athletes in Light of Kleinknecht, *Journal of College and University Law,* Vol. 21, No.3, 1994, 591613.

13. *Mogabgab v. New Orleans Parish School Board,* 239 So.2d 456 (La. App. 1979).

14. *Kleinknecht v. Gettysburg College,* 989 F.2d 1360 (Pa. App. 1993).

15. Pike, L. L., & Rello, M. N. (July 1994). "Training Rules: Athletic Programs May Be Taking Risks with Athletic Injury Care." *Athletic Business,* pp. 10-13.

Chapter Twenty-Five

FACILITIES AND EQUIPMENT

SECTION 1: FACILITIES

The law recognizes the duty owed by coaches, hotel and recreation managers, and staff to provide safe facilities for both participants and spectators. Coaches and recreation supervisors are held to a high standard of care when it comes to facilities maintenance and management. For the standard to be met, coaches and supervisors must be able to recognize potential safety hazards in their gyms, on their fields and courts, and in the play areas over which they have control. Once the hazards have been recognized, measures must be taken to make the play area reasonably safe.

Cases that involve negligence for failure to meet the appropriate standard in providing safe sport and recreation facilities are numerous. Therefore, good risk management of safety conditions and elimination of hazards through proper maintenance is essential. Consider the following scenario, based on an actual case.

The doctors had done all they could, but the nerve damage was just too great. Sam would lose the use of his left arm. He remembered running for the fly ball as he neared the five-foot-high metal fence that separated the outfield from the railroad tracks that ran just beyond.

Sam had not played any sports since his high school football days, and he was now at least 20 pounds overweight. He had been encouraged to play by his buddies at the factory who had put a team together. They thought it would be fun. The game had given him something to look forward to after the long hours on the assembly line, and it was one of the few recreational activities his wife actually encouraged.

His mind told him that he would not be able to stop in time to avoid the fence, but the desire to catch the ball overpowered any sense of caution. He ran forward, and then came the inevitable crash with the fence. He didn't catch the ball. Sam also didn't anticipate the sharp post support that protruded upward at the top of the fence. His left arm was severely damaged.

The city parks department had installed the fence to serve as a boundary for the outfield. The maintenance crew was scheduled to put plastic sleeves over the sharp post supports in the fence but had failed to do so. It had been six months since the request was made, but the department was poorly organized, and no one followed up to see if the job had been done. The parks department faced a $1.5 million lawsuit for negligent failure to provide safe facilities for the softball players. Sam lost his job and was now unable to work and support his family. He also lost the one form of recreation that had given him the most happiness.

Do you feel that the injured man in this scenario should be compensated for his injuries? If you were on the jury, how much of the $1.5 million would you award him? As a manager of the facility, you would doubtlessly feel sorry for Sam's condition.

You would also face difficult questions from the plaintiff's lawyers about your competence as a manager. They would argue that you had not met the standards of facility maintenance that every manager should meet. They would also say that your failure to meet the standard was the direct cause of Sam's injury. They would build a case against you and the city for negligence. Looking back, you would realize that immediate steps should have been taken to eliminate the hazard to prevent such a tragedy.

Negligence lawsuits centering on sport and recreation facilities are common in a variety of settings. One of these settings is gymnasiums. Potential hazards are commonplace in many gyms. A window at the end of a basketball court, for example, is a safety concern. Basketball players have smashed into glass windows chasing balls out of bounds. In such instances, managers were found liable for breaching their duty to provide a safe place to play basketball. Additionally, facility managers should consider not only the manner in which a gym might be used for its intended purpose, but also any other foreseeable manner in which the facility might be used. Consider the following hypothetical scenario.

Ginny Got-game and a group of her friends broke into the gymnasium through an unlocked back door at her local high school to play a game of ultimate soccer. They would play this game often in the summer with a large group of people, where both a game of soccer and a game of ultimate frisbee would be played simultaneously. It was often chaotic trying to keep pace with both the frisbee and the soccer ball in a fast-paced game. They preferred to play outdoors on the soccer field, where they would have more room to run, but the weather this time of year was too cold. The gym was made for basketball with several courts running side by side across the gym. At one end of the gym, five to 10 feet from the basketball sideline, there was a door with a glass window about midway up. They chose the goals for the game to be an area marked by cones placed at the basketball sidelines on each end of the gymnasium. The goal on the end near the door was placed approximately five feet to the left of the door. They had played for about 45 minutes and the score was tied. On the next play, the team advancing toward the goal on the side of the gym with the glass-paneled door had possession of both the soccer ball and the frisbee. Ginny raced across the court from left to right in an attempt to catch the frisbee as it sailed near her. At that same moment, she looked back to see the soccer ball was also traveling in her direction. The confusion of the moment caused her to lose her concentration and she stumbled into the door and ran her hand and arm through the plate glass window. Ginny, an accomplished violinist, suffered severe lacerations and nerve damage to her arm. Her musical career is in serious jeopardy due to the injury. Ginny brings suit against all parties she believes to be responsible for her misfortune.

Should the facility management be liable for the injury to Ginny, even though she used the gym in a manner that was not intended? Why? What arguments might you make for or against negligence liabilty?

Softball and baseball fields are places where injuries occur frequently. Risk management is critical in preventing lawsuits resulting from injuries incurred by spectators and players in and around ball fields given the popularity of softball and baseball as a form of recreation and its growth in recent years.

Often, a substandard facility lies at the heart of the trouble. For example, holes in the turf or defective screens behind home plate are often to blame for an injury to a spectator or player. Therefore, it is essential that agencies, schools, and park department ball field providers are aware of how to manage risk at their facility. Four major ballpark features often give rise to liability. These features are turf, lighting, outfield fencing, and protective screens.

The playing surface, or turf, might be the most important feature from the perspective of risk management. It is the most important because it is the most litigated. A recent court case illustrates litigation that can result from poor turf management.

In the case of *Foley v. City of La Salle* (1993),[1] an experienced softball player was playing a game at the city-owned park. A few weeks earlier, a festival had been set up on the softball field where he was playing. Trucks had run across the area and post holes had been dug to support the tents for the festival. This activity had badly marred the playing surface. When Foley was running to catch a fly ball, his foot caught in a rut caused by the festival setup, and he injured his knee. He sued the city for negligence. Costly and time-consuming litigation resulted.

As a manager of a ballpark, what could you do to ensure that natural and artificial surfaces are maintained in a safe condition? For natural sur-

Baseball facilities and equipment should be properly maintained.

faces, routine maintenance and repair of holes, ruts, and divots in the turf is advisable. Suits sometimes arise when teeth or bones are broken from a bad hop from a hard ground ball. Therefore, sand and other additives can be mixed to reduce the hardness of the infield and the probability of injury to players. Also, a softer surface that is properly maintained will reduce the presence of ruts that develop from players running between the bases.[2]

General policies should be initiated and followed to keep a natural surface in reasonable condition. First, facility use should be monitored, and overuse should be discouraged. Also, adequate staff and equipment must be available to keep the turf in reasonable condition, and field downtime schedules should be adopted to allow the turf to regenerate.

For artificial surfaces, liability is again a major concern. Liability issues relevant to artificial turf are likely in the future to focus on the interaction between the type of playing surface and the type of shoe. Three major instances when injuries occur are where players trip on exposed seams or tears in artificial turf, slip on hard areas that have been over-painted and the turf fiber filled with paint, and where the turf lacks shock absorption.

These and other problem areas can be avoided if proper safety guidelines are followed. First, the surface should provide shock absorbency or cushioning properties similar to those encountered on the best natural surface. A simple and reliable method of testing shock absorbency is available from the American Society for Testing and Materials (ASTM). Second, a player's footing should be uniform and predictable. The determining factor here is the friction between the shoe sole and the surface. Third, the surface should not have unforeseeable hazards such as chuckholes, mud, stones, or ruts. Last, artificial surfaces should not be unreasonably abrasive. The ASTM also provides a test for the abrasiveness of a synthetic surface.

A second risk management issue concerning ball fields is screening and protected areas. If you have ever been to a baseball game, you have probably noticed the screens that hang down to protect spectators from errant balls and thrown bats. People who sit behind screens have a reasonable expectation of safety. They do not anticipate being hit by objects coming from the field, whereas those who sit in the open often accept the risk of being hit, for example, by an object unintentionally propelled into the stands.

In the case of *Bellezzo v. State of Arizona* (1993),[3] a spectator was injured while attending a college baseball game. She was sitting in an open area not protected by a screen. The injury occurred when a foul ball flew into the stands and hit her. She subsequently sued the state and university for damages suffered as a result of their alleged negligence.

The appellate court found for the defendant, citing that it was not an unforeseeable, unreasonable risk to sit in an unscreened area and be hit by a ball. In other words, you pay your money and take your chances at a baseball game. If, however, she had been injured when sitting behind a screen with a hole in it and a ball flew through the hole and injured her, she would have had a better chance of prevailing on a negligence claim.

Courts have generally held that spectators assume the risk of being struck by a foul ball if sitting outside of a protected area. There may be circumstances, however, where a spectator does not assume the risk of being hit by a foul ball while sitting in an unprotected area. Can you think of any? Consider the following hypothetical.

During the summer, Sammy Slugger attended a Triple A baseball game with his wife and four children. They had driven 30 miles from their home and paid for the tickets at the gate before entering the game. Their seats were 20 rows up along the third base line. The seats behind home plate were protected by a screen, but Sammy's seat was far enough up the third base line that it was unprotected. Sammy loved baseball and was enjoying the game with his family. Sammy also enjoyed watching the antics of the team mascot and eating and drinking the food and beverages offered at the game. The peanut vendor, a stadium employee, was a true favorite of the fans. Instead of walking along each row and distributing bags of peanuts by hand, this vendor had a unique method of selling peanuts. He would walk along the row beneath the spectators and throw bags of peanuts to whomever called for them. He would also throw a tennis ball with a carved hole in it to the hungry spectator, who would place money inside the ball and return it to the vendor. In the sixth inning of the game, the peanut vendor passed in front of Sammy and spotted a fan who wanted a bag. The fan was sitting several rows up and behind Sammy and his family. The vendor heaved the bag of peanuts as he always did but on this occasion he slipped on a piece of ice and lost control of this throw. The bag flew through the air but fell short of its intended mark. Instead, the bag hit Sammy squarely in the chest. Sammy reached down to retrieve the bag and at that instant felt as if he had been struck by a sledgehammer. Unknown to Sammy, a player had fouled a ball directly in Sammy's direction. Distracted, Sammy had not even seen it coming. He was rushed to the emergency room of the local hospital for treatment of his serious injury. Sammy, though still a fan of baseball, brings suit against all parties he believes to be responsible for his misfortune.

Do you believe that Sammy assumed the risk of being hit by the foul ball? Why? Would your opinion change if Sammy was distracted by a mascot, or was sitting in a lounge area in the outfield without a clear view of the field?

By sitting in a protected area (e.g., behind a screen), a spectator expects protection and generally cannot be held to have assumed the risk of being hit by objects coming from the playing field. Therefore, it would be wise for ball field supervisors to ensure that protective screens are strong enough to protect spectators and are free of rips, tears, and holes. Regular inspection and proper maintenance should be sufficient to accomplish this goal.

The location of screens is also important and should be a part of the risk management plan. At public softball fields, players and spectators walking outside the field are sometimes injured by balls that leave the confines of the park. Therefore, it is important for a ball field manager to consult with design experts to determine the best location for protective screening. Behind home plate is not the only area where errant balls can injure those outside the field.

A third risk management issue concerns fencing. The scenario described at the beginning of this section raised the issue of negligent maintenance relevant to outfield fences. Outfield fences are often designed to protect players by preventing them from encountering other hazards. However, often it is the fence itself that becomes the hazard and results in injury and subsequent litigation. Several recent cases illustrate the liability that can result when a participant is injured when he collides with an outfield fence.

In the case of *University of Texas Pan Amer. v. Valdez* (1993),[4] a college student-athlete was injured when he ran into an outfield fence while attempting to catch a long fly ball. He claimed that the school was negligent because there was no warning track to indicate the fence's location during play. The jury found the school to be 60% at fault, thus awarding the student 60% of the total award. On appeal, however, the school won on immunity grounds.

The case of *Pool v. City of Shreveport* (1992),[5] poses a different set of facts. Pool was injured when he collided with an outfield fence. In this case, a sign on the field indicated that the outfield fence was 300 feet from home plate, when in fact it was only 276 feet from home plate. The plaintiff contended that the city was negligent in providing an inaccurate distance indicator, which he claimed was the cause of his accident. Both the trial court and the appellate court held for the city. One reason cited is that the marker is intended for the benefit of the batter and not the outfielder. As a recreation manager, you should always be ready to expect the unexpected in your risk-management planning.

Safety measures relevant to fencing should be considered by field supervisors. One such measure would be to use fences that are flexible enough to allow injury-free collisions with them. It would also be wise to install plastic sleeves on protruding sections of fence to protect players from being impaled or cut. Cases exist where ballplayers have won lawsuits for injuries resulting from impalement by a fence.

Last, for unfenced ball fields that comprise a multitude of recreational softball fields, safety measures should be put in place. For example, it has been suggested that a safety zone be established that would extend for a specified distance in the outfield to provide safety from outside hazards. A ball hit into the safety zone would be out of play. This would encourage outfielders to slow down before nearing hazards further out.[6]

A fourth area of concern for a ball field manager is the lighting system. Two court cases raise liability issues from entirely different perspectives. The first involved a softball player who collided with a metal light post on the city parks and recreation department's field. After much time and expense, the city finally won the case on grounds that the pole was an obvious danger, and the plaintiff had voluntarily assumed the risks involved in the construction of the field.[7] To avoid participant injury and litigation such as this, it is suggested that light poles in or near the field of play should be properly padded and/or surrounded by flexible fencing.[8]

Another important issue relevant to lighting has been raised in case law. This issue is the adequacy of the light generated. In the case of *Kloes v. Eau Claire Cavalier Baseball Assoc. Inc.* (1992),[9] a pitcher was struck and injured by a batted ball on a field maintained by the city of Eau Claire. Kloes, the injured pitcher, complained the lighting was too dim for him to react in time to avoid being hit by the ball. The city had received complaints that the lighting was dim and uneven. The appeals court sent the case back to the trial court to determine whether the lighting was adequate and whether the pitcher contributed to his own negligence in any way.

Although the adequacy of lighting might appear to be completely subjective, standards are available. The adequacy of lighting can be determined, in part, by the level of competition and subsequent risk. Additionally, the unit of measurement for lighting is termed footcandles (FC), which can be determined for each field, based on the type of use and skill level of the players.[10] Sport administrators would be wise to determine the amount of lighting adequate to maintain a reasonably safe nighttime ballpark.

Proper grounding of lighting systems is the final risk management concern discussed. Lighting systems must be properly grounded to prevent electric shock. When a softball player in Texas flipped a switch to the field, a bare wire caused a short that sent 480 volts of electricity through the switch gear. The fact that the light pole was grounded saved his life and doubtless a very large lawsuit.[11]

There exist certain telltale signs that may indicate to a ball field supervisor that electrical grounding problems exist. These signs include broken or heavily painted conduits, loose-fitting conduit connectors or ground terminals, improperly bonded panels, lack of separate grounding connectors and ungrounded extension cords.[12] A ball field supervisor should be trained to look for these signs.

Ball field facility owners, managers, and supervisors must be cognizant of design and maintenance features that generate the potential for liability. Lawsuits in this area do not seem likely to disappear any time soon. However, if reasonable precautions are taken and due care is given to the maintenance and upkeep of the facility, the cost and trauma of litigation can be decreased. As mentioned, adequate attention to turf management, lighting, screens, and fencing will be of tremendous value in managing risk and will ensure a safe and enjoyable recreation experience for participants and spectators.

SECTION 2: EQUIPMENT

In addition to the duty to provide safe facilities, managers, coaches, teachers, and supervisors also have a duty to provide adequate safety equipment to sports participants. This once again comes down to the standard of care that supervisors of sport activities are required to meet. Knowing when to provide certain types of equipment and what type to provide is the duty of sport supervisors. Providing equipment that is free of manufacturing and design defects is the duty of the maker and seller of sports equipment.

Often, suits involving injury due to inadequate equipment will involve both the sport supervisor and the equipment manufacturer and seller. The supervisor will be named as the party responsible for the negligent selection and provision of improper equipment, while the maker and seller of the product will be sued for the defect in their product. If the manufacturer has the resources to mount a successful defense, attention will be focused on the supervisor and the school or organization for whom they work. Therefore, it is incumbent upon sport supervisors to meet or exceed standard of care when it comes to selecting and providing the proper equipment for their players.

To maintain a safe program, a coach, teacher, or recreation supervisor needs to know the type of equipment players will need for a given sport.

For example, in most contact sports, protective equipment is essential. The best possible protective equipment should be determined and requested. This means keeping up to date on current trends in equipment for the type of activity you coach or supervise. Records should be kept of these requests to prove that you have made a good faith effort to meet the applicable standard of care to your players. The following cases illustrate the duty that is imposed on sport supervisors to provide adequate equipment to their players. The first case shows how a good faith effort can be made to meet this duty, while the second case demonstrates what can happen when the proper equipment is not provided.

In the case of *Berman v. Philadelphia Board of Education* (1983),[13] 11-year-old Brad Berman was playing in a school hockey league. Games were played after school in the elementary school gymnasium, and the league was supervised by the school's physical education teacher. The players were provided with hockey sticks made with wooden shafts and plastic blades, but were not given face guards or any type of protective equipment. The supervisor had, on numerous occasions, asked the school board for protective equipment but was refused. He also instructed the players that raising sticks above the waist and other types of rough play were not permitted.

During one of the games, a player on the other team had control of the puck and was making a move on offense. Brad held his ground in an attempt to defend his goal. The other player went for a shot and struck the puck hard. On his follow through, his stick went up and struck Brad in the mouth, smashing his teeth. Several teeth were cut in half. It was an extremely painful injury. To repair his teeth required a substantial amount of expensive dental work. Brad's parents brought suit against the board of education, claiming negligence in failing to provide players with mouth guards. The Bermans won the case in the trial court, and the school board appealed.

The school board argued that there was no rule or regulation that required floor hockey players to wear mouth guards. Therefore, they argued, there was no duty on the part of the school board to provide this sort of protective equipment. The court of appeals disagreed with this argument. They looked at evidence that showed that the league supervisor knew mouth injuries were an inherent risk in the sport   He also had requested that the school purchase protective equipment for the players. He was never provided with such equipment. This evidence tended to relieve the supervisor of liability and place the liability on the school board.

Providing the proper protective equipment in football is a key concern for sport supervisors.

Also, the court rejected the argument that since there was no rule mandating the wearing of mouth guards, there was no duty to provide them. The court noted that the school board, knowing the risk of mouth injury in floor hockey, should have imposed its own rule requiring protective equipment. The standard of care is to provide for the safety and welfare of the students. The court held that regardless of the lack of a rule mandating mouth guards, the school board breached its duty to provide for the safety of the students. Thus, the court found that the board had breached its duty of care and was liable for negligence.

In the case of *Leahy v. School Board of Hernando County* (1984),[14] Leahy was a freshman in high school and had tried out for the football team. Equipment was issued on the first day of practice, but there were not enough helmets to go around. Leahy was one of the players who did not get a helmet. He was not told to do anything different from what the other players did, even though he did not have a helmet. On the second day of practice, the coach told Leahy to participate in an agility drill. In this drill, a dozen or so players were positioned on their hands and knees in a row. They all had helmets.

Leahy was put in a line and told to go up to the first lineman in the row, hit him on the shoulders, then fall to the ground and roll. He was to do this with each player in the row. The coaches stood to the side and watched once the drill had started. After several players with helmets did the drill, it was finally Leahy's turn. The drill by this time had become rowdy. Leahy went up to the first lineman and slapped his shoulders. In response, the lineman raised up quickly and slammed his helmet into Leahy's face.

Leahy broke several teeth and injured his face in the collision. His parents, on Leahy's behalf, sued the school board, claiming it was negligent in failing to provide their son with equipment that would have prevented the injury. Leahy lost his case in the trial court. The court granted the school board a directed verdict, which meant that a jury was not given the opportunity to hear the facts and reach a verdict. Leahy appealed the case.

The appellate court disagreed with the trial court, reversed its decision, and ordered a new trial. The appellate court held that the school board had a duty to its players to supply the proper equipment. The court noted that since helmets were used as protective devices, a jury could reasonably conclude that the school district did not meet the applicable standard of care in providing for the safety of Leahy.

There was no evidence presented that the coach or school gave precautionary instructions to Leahy about playing without a helmet or that his participation in practice would have limits. The court also left the question of whether it was foreseeable that Leahy would be injured by participating in the drill without a helmet to the jury in the new trial.

Sometimes budget constraints make it difficult or impossible to have state-of-the-art equipment. However, where the only equipment available is old and/or potentially unsafe, it becomes very important for the sport supervisor to be aware of potential hazards associated with the equipment and to warn participants of these hazards. This is particularly important when the hazards are not obvious or readily apparent.

Consider the following hypothetical:

Twelve-year-old Sammy Bigfoot was attending a city-run summer day camp. Sammy signed a waiver prior to participation in the camp program. One of the activities at camp was soccer. The soccer field had been set up in the outfield of an old softball park. Temporary soccer goals were set up at each end of the make-shift field. The goals were smaller than regulation size and relatively unstable. The camp program, however, had to make do with the equipment they had due to budget constraints. Sammy loved soccer and would get very excited whenever someone would score a goal. His enthusiasm was contagious, and everyone enjoyed having Sammy in the program. The soccer program had run smoothly thus far. The greatest concern was that someone would injure a leg or ankle from the uneven surface of the outfield. Therefore, the counselors were instructed to warn the children to be careful when running on certain parts of the field. One day, Sammy was involved in a particularly close and exciting game. They had played for 30 minutes and the score was tied at two apiece. Sammy's team took possession of the ball and moved it down field toward the opponent's goal. A teammate passed the ball to Sammy who dodged one defender and kicked with all his might. The ball slipped past the goalie and into the net. Sammy was beside himself with joy. He ran around the field and hugged every one of his teammates. He then went over to the goal and in an instant of pure excitement, leaped up and grabbed the top crossbar of the goal. His joy turned to fear as his weight caused the goal to tilt forward; sending Sammy forcefully to the ground. The crossbar landed on top of Sammy, who lay motionless on the ground. Sammy suffered several broken ribs, a fractured cervical disk, and emotional trauma as a result of the accident. Sammy and his parents sue all parties they believe to be responsible for his injury.

Baseball bases should meet appropriate safety specifications.

Do you feel the counselors/camp are liable for Sammy's injuries? Why or why not? What does the Consumer Product Safety Commission tell us regarding guidelines for soccer goal safety?

The manufacturer or seller of defective equipment is usually named as a defendant in a lawsuit when a defective product is the cause of an injury. This gets into an area of the law known as product liability. Product liability "refers to the legal liability of product manufacturers and sellers to compensate buyers, users, and even bystanders, for damages or injuries suffered because of defects in goods purchased."[15] Product liability, like negligence, is in the category of tort law.

You are probably aware of the litigation involving breast implants in the 1990s. This is a good example of product liability. Surveys indicate that the most common product-related injuries involve toys and sports and recreation equipment. A study released by RAND in 1989 showed that these injuries accounted for 17% of all product-related injuries. These injuries occur to people during leisure activities.[16] Product liability, therefore, is important for sports and recreation professionals to understand.

The doctrine of strict liability is closely associated with product liability. In product liability cases, the manufacturer and seller are strictly liable when their product is sold in an unreasonably dangerous condition and someone is injured by the product. This means that an injured person, to prevail in court, only needs to show that a defective product caused his injury. At one time, persons injured by a product had to convince the court (judge or jury) that a manufacturer or seller of a defective product was negligent. Thus, the four elements of negligence had to be proved. Now, however, strict liability applies to product liability cases.

Manufacturers and sellers can be found strictly liable for a product that enters the stream of commerce due to a defect caused by the manufacturing process or due to a defect in the design of the product. The following case provides an example of a product that had a defective design. It was hazardous even for the type of activity for which it was intended.

In the case of *Hauter v. Zogarts* (1975),[17] Fred Hauter had been given a golf training device from his wife as a Christmas present. It was called the golfing gizmo and was manufactured and sold by Zogarts. The gizmo consisted of two metal spikes, an elastic cord, a cotton cord, and a regular golf ball. The elastic cord was tied to a cotton cord in the center and stretched between the spikes. The ball was attached to one end of the cotton cord. The other end of the cotton cord was attached to the middle of the elastic cord. Once set up, the player could hit the ball with all his might and, if hit correctly, the ball would spring out and return to the player's feet. The instruction booklet made clear that the gizmo was completely safe, and a ball would never spring back and hit the player.

One day, after having used the gizmo about a dozen times previously, Fred decided to hit some balls using the device. He set it up in an open area in his front yard. He then pulled out a seven iron and took a full swing. The ball powered forward, the cord extended, and then sprung back. Fred fell to the ground and was rendered unconscious. When he regained his senses, he realized that the ball had hit him in the head. He had been hit on the temple and was seriously injured. His family sued Zogarts for, among other things, strict liability in tort for the defective design of the product. The Hauters won their case in the trial court. The court ordered a judgment notwithstanding the verdict.[18] Zogarts appealed this judgment.

Fred did not remember what happened due to his head trauma resulting from the injury. Experts were therefore brought in to provide opinion as to how the injury occurred. Everyone was in agreement that Fred had probably hit underneath the ball and caught his club on the elastic cord. This caused the ball to loop over the club and strike Fred in his temple. Zogarts did not mount an argument that the gizmo was not defective in its design. The appellate court, therefore, had an easy time deciding that strict liability existed.

In their jurisdiction (the state of California), a defectively designed product renders the manufacturer and seller strictly liable. The record showed that it was easy to entangle a club in the cord while using the gizmo under normal conditions. Also, the possibility of injury was great when this happened. This was enough to show that the product had been designed defectively. Also, the defect was the proximate cause of Fred's injuries. Therefore, Zogarts was held to be strictly liable and guilty of negligence based on the defective design of the product.

Strict liability is an important legal concept to remember when a sport injury occurs due to a defectively designed or manufactured product. The sport or recreation manager, however, should not feel he will be overlooked should a piece of sporting equipment injure a participant. If the product has been altered since the time it left the store, liability could attach to the person or organization who provided the equipment for use. A sound risk management plan pertaining to athletic facilities and equipment should be implemented and followed by the wise coach, manager, or sport supervisor.

SECTION 3: SECURITY ISSUES IN RECREATION, SPORTS, AND TOURISM

Providing a safe and secure facility is essential to avoiding legal liability. This book has already discussed how property owners and operators can be held liable through the concept of premises liability if persons are injured on their property. The concept of premises liability can also be used to establish liability on the part of sport or recreation facility operators if persons are injured while using or attending their facilities. This is true even when the harm is not caused by the owners or operators, but by third parties. Accordingly, sport and recreation facility operators need to understand the importance of providing quality security services in order to avoid legal liability.

The first issue that needs to be understood is how liability can be established against the owners and operators of sport and recreation facilities for the actions of others. Generally, a person does not owe a duty to protect others from the acts of third parties or to warn said individuals that they are endangered by third party action. However, a duty may arise if either a special relationship exists between the actor and the third person that imposes a duty upon the actor to control the third person's conduct, or if a special relation exists between the actor and the person that needs protection. A special relation does exist between landowners and those who use their premises.

Owners or operators of sports stadiums or arenas, like any other owner or operator of premises, are under a duty to exercise reasonable care under the circumstances to prevent harm to participants and spectators of activities that take place in their facilities.[19] So what type of duty is owed by facility owners and operators to those who use their facilities? After all, it would be unreasonable to expect them to be the insurers of their patrons' safety in terms of preventing all possible harm caused by third parties. Instead, Section 344 of the Restatement (Second) of Torts[20] and the courts have uniformly agreed that facility owners and operators only owe a duty to protect customers from the foreseeable acts of third parties.

Foreseeability is a difficult concept to define. However, the existence of foreseeability is essential for a plaintiff to prevail in a case against owners and operators of sport and recreation facilities for the actions of third parties. *Hayden v. University of Notre Dame* (1999)[20] provides a good example of how courts may find third-party action foreseeable. In Hayden, Letitia Hayden brought suit against the University of Notre Dame after spectators injured her while she was attending a football game at Notre Dame's football stadium. Hayden and her husband, both season ticket holders, were seated in the south end zone of the stadium behind the goalpost. During the second quarter of the football game, one of the teams kicked the ball into the stands near Hayden. Several spectators lunged for the ball and one of them struck Hayden, knocking her down and injuring her shoulder.

The court in Hayden found that there were several prior incidents involving fans being bumped or injured by other fans who were attempting to retrieve footballs. The court placed emphasis on Mrs. Hayden's testimony in which she stated that she had attended Notre Dame football games for many years and during this period she had witnessed balls landing in the seats near her many times. Furthermore, Hayden testified that she had witnessed fans jumping to retrieve balls on numerous occasions. Her husband also testified that the netting used to prevent balls from flying into the stands only worked about 50% of the time. When the netting did not work, the ball would fly into the stands and a scramble for the ball would ensue. He went on to state that he was even jostled by scrambling fans on several occasions. Finally, he stated that ushers were aware that fans were being jostled in scrambles for loose balls, however, the ushers did not aggressively attempt to retrieve the balls. Accordingly, the court found that Notre Dame should have foreseen that injuries were likely to result from the actions of third parties lunging for balls kicked into the end zone seating area. Thus, Notre Dame owed a duty to protect Hayden from such injury.

Terrorism

September 11, 2001, drastically and permanently changed the United States. The tragic events of that day have made American life more complicated and uncertain. This is true even for those who work in the sports and recreation industry, and especially true for those who own or operate sport and recreation facilities. What was once unimaginable and unforeseeable is now reality and this new foreseeable terrorism threat carries with it legal implications for those who own or operate sport and recreation facilities.

Terrorism is defined as the use of force or violence against persons or property in violation of the criminal laws of the United States for purposes of intimidation, coercion, or ransom. Terrorists typically use threats to create fear among the public, to try to convince citizens that their government is powerless to prevent terrorism, and to get immediate publicity for their causes. Acts of terrorism may include both threats and actions of terrorism, including assassinations, bombings, and the use of chemical, biological, and nuclear weapons.

In the post-9/11 society, American sport remains a symbolic target of terrorism based on its association with the globalization of the American economy and culture.[22] As such, sport and recreation venues carry an increased risk of terrorist attack. To assist facility managers, the International Association of Assembly Managers (IAAM) in cooperation with the U.S. Department of Homeland Security (DOHS) offers a free Terrorism Awareness Training Course. This four-hour course focuses exclusively on stadiums and arenas to assist security personnel in recognizing and preventing terrorist activity.[23] Further, representatives from the NFL, NHL, MLB, NBA and NCAA collaborated with the IAAM and produced the *Best Practices Guide*, which provides measures that can be taken by facility managers to protect against terrorism.

In the event of a terrorist attack on a sport venue, imposing liability on the owners and operators of sports stadiums and arenas for the actions of terrorists may seem unfair. Certainly, the terrorists are the ones to blame for their actions. However, it is also certain that the victims of terror will not be able to recover from the terrorists to any material degree.[24] Accordingly, victims of terrorism will look to others for compensation. If a sports facility is the target of a terrorist attack, then there is a possibility that the facility's owners and operators could be sued. Therefore, it is critical that sport and recreation facilities take reasonable measures to guard against terrorism. Facility managers must keep abreast of what other facilities are doing, monitor potential terrorism threats, and adopt security measures similar or identical to those proposed by the *Best Practices Guide*. Failure to take the appropriate measures could result in liability if a facility does fall prey to a terrorist attack.

Discussion Questions

1. Does the manager of a sports facility have any responsibility when fans are injured as a result of fighting in the stands? What type of situation may change that responsibility?

2. Docs the sports facility manager have any liability when a player trips over a protruding sprinkler head in the out-of-bounds area in a playing field? Explain.

3. What local activities or facilities may be the target of domestic or foreign terrorism?

4. Define the concept of forseeability. Name three activities where forseeability is an important safety consideration? Explain.

Notes

1. *Foley v. City of La Salle*, 608 N.E.2d 964 (III. App. 1993).
2. The discussion of ball field turf issues draws heavily upon a presentation of these issues by Perry, F. (1994, Jan.). Cover all your bases. *Athletic Business*, 5460; Proulx, C., (1994, May). Ideas on evaluations for sports turf management. *Park/Ground Management 911*; Kniley, S. (1994, Sept.). The turf game. *Athletic Business* 5660; and Milner, Ed. (1994, April). Choosing the best synthetic surface for your facility. *Athletic Management*, 18-20.
3. *Bellezzo v. State of Arizona*, 851 P.2d 847 (Ariz. App. 1993).
4. *University of Texas Pan Amer. v. Valdez*, 869 S.W.2d 446 (Tex. App. 1993).
5. *Pool v. City of Shreveport*, 607 So.2d 861 (La. App. 1992).
6. Berg, R. (1993). Building a safer ballpark. *Athletic Business*, 9.
7. *Ferraro v. Town of Huntington*, 609 N.Y.S.2d 36 (App. Div. 2 Dept. 1994).
8. Perry, F. (1994 Jan.). Cover all your bases. *Athletic Business*, 54-60.
9. *Kloes v. Eau Claire Cavalier Baseball Assoc., Inc.*, 487 N.W.2d 77 (Wis. App. 1992).
10. Lindstrom,C., (1994). All lighting systems are not created equal. *Scholastic Coach and Athletic Director*, 64-66.

11. This situation was illustrated in Rogers, J. (1994, Jan.). Safety considerations for sports lighting. *Athletic Business,* 58.
12. These conditions are described in McQuire, T. (1994, May). Proper grounding protects against injury, equipment damage. *Park/Grounds Management,* 8.
13. *Berman v. Philadelphia Board of Education,* 456 A.2d 545 (Penn. 1983).
14. *Leahy v. School Board of Hernando County,* 450 So.2d 883 (1984).
15. Black, H. C. (1979) *Black's Law Dictionary* (5th ed.). St. Paul, MN: West Publishing Co., p.1089.
16. Mergenhagen, P. (1995). Product liability: Who sues? *American Demographics,* 48-55.
17. *Hauter v. Zogarts,* 534 P.2d 377 (Cal. App. 1975).
18. A judgment notwithstanding the verdict, also called a JNOV or nonobstante verdicto, is a determination by the judge that one party should win the case (e.g., Fred Hauter in this case) after a verdict has already been decided in favor of the other party (e.g., Zogarts in this case). This judgment must follow a motion by the attorney for a directed verdict. This motion asks the judge to decide that their side has won the case since the other side doesn't have sufficient evidence to prevail in the case.
19. Hurst, R., Zoubek, P., & Pratsinakis, C. (2002). American sports as a target of terrorism: The duty of care after September 11th. *Sport and the Law Journal, 10*(1), 134-139.
20. Restatement (Second) of Torts. (1965). § 344.
21. *Hayden v. University of Notre Dame,* 716 N.E.2d 603 (Ind. App. 1999).
22. Tolbert, B. A. (2003, January 24). Playing it safe: NBA's security chief addresses New York City law alumni. UB Law Links. Retrieved May 28, 2004, from http://www.law.buffalo.edu/Alumni_And_Giving/ublaw_links/02-2003/default.asp?ll=5&f= NYCLunch.
23. IAAM. (2004). Department of Homeland Security presents terrorism awareness training course for stadiums and arenas. Retrieved May 28, 2004, from http://www.iaam.org/2004_meetings/DHS/DHS.htm.
24. Gash, J. (2003). At the intersection of proximate cause and terrorism: A contextual analysis of the (proposed) Restatement Third of Torts' approach to intervening and superseding causes. *Kentucky Law Journal, 91*(3), 523-612.

Chapter Twenty-Six

WARNINGS

A critical consideration in managing liability risk is communicating "the safety message" to those coming onto property, participating in an activity, or using a product. "Failure to warn" has been and will be a critical issue in the context of recreation, sports, and tourism litigation.

A failure to warn claim requires (1) a duty to warn, (2) a breach of that duty, and (3) actual damages or injury resulting from the breach of duty. A review of many "failure to warn" cases indicates the courts will look closely at whether the risk was open and obvious. A risk is considered open and obvious when its dangers are within the body of knowledge commonly known.[1] For example, a manager should not have to warn a person who is walking on a trail adjacent to a river not to jump into the swift water.

The failure to warn doctrine has very wide applicability. The doctrine may apply to products, training, activities, equipment, facilities, personnel actions, competitive sports, tourism activities, and other categories. As examples:

- **Products:** drugs or medical devices provided to the public should have adequate warning of product dangers or reactions.

- **Training:** should include critical instruction needed for safe participation.

- **Activities:** should warn about specific dangers associated with outdoor recreation activities.

- **Equipment:** should inform operators of equipment of the unique and dangerous characteristics of a particular piece of equipment.

- **Personal actions:** should notify employees they are being evaluated and subject to dismissal

- **Competitive sports:** should tell players that one member of the team tends to let the bat slip from his hands when batting

- **Tourism activities:** should tell tourist of the dangers of swimming in water contaminated with disease causing bacteria.

It is important to understand that giving warnings of known dangers is not a substitute for managing safe activities, and providing safe products, equipment, or facilities. Managers are expected to eliminate or reduce the potential for harm to participants from dangerous situations involving activities, products, equipment, and facilities. They have to do more than just warn about them.[2]

Effective Warning of Known Dangers

The following suggestions applicable to warnings may help reduce the risk of harm to participants if done correctly.

1. Use a "word" that makes people aware of dangerous conditions such as Danger, Warning, Caution...

2. State the nature of the hazard such as drowning hazard, submerged rocks, electrical shock hazard, and so forth.

3. Use colors that indicate danger such as yellow or red as appropriate and in relation to the setting.

4. Clearly indicate the degree of potential danger or injury such as death or severe injury.

5. Explain how to avoid the dangers (i.e. turn off power, avoid open flame in the area).

6. Provide illustrations depicting the situation if possible, in multiple language situations or international symbols where necessary or reasonable.

7. Use pictorials or other alert warning symbols (exclamation point) may be combined with the signal word to provide the user with a clear indication of the level of the hazard.

Figure 26.1. *Example of an Effective Warning Sign*

It is critical to determine what, how, and when to inform users of the non-obvious dangers involved in their activities. It is also important to determine who is responsible to warn the visitor, and who is coming onto the property or using the product that may not be familiar or knowledgeable about the possible hazards. The best of risk management plans can fail without effectively communicating the message to the target audience. This is particularly critical when children will be on the property, participating in an activity, or using the product.

Risk managers must also evaluate the background and education of the participant in regards to their skill and experience. A trained and experienced mountain climber might be held to have assumed the risk of climbing hazards, whereas a novice climber taking their first climbing lesson may not understand the risks without being warned beforehand.

If a recreation, sports, or tourism administrator wants to communicate a safety message to a target audience such as avalanche dangers, flash flooding, fire danger, contamination, and so forth, they must utilize the most effective means possible to reach the audience.

The risk manager needs to look at the lifestyle of the majority of participants of a particular activity. As an example, imagine that heavy snowfall during the night resulted in a snow avalanche danger. Most skiers are relatively young and have a tendency to listen to rock music radio stations while traveling. They will likely be traveling in an automobile or public transportation on their way to the ski area. The assumption that they will be listening to rock music is certainly not absolute or all-inclusive, but rather, generally true. Because there is a critical timing consideration, the effort should be to reach as many skiers as possible in the shortest of time...maybe starting with warnings broadcast by rock stations.

Contacting local rock music stations with the avalanche message would be the most likely means to reach a high percentage of the skiers and should be a first priority for receiving the avalanche message. Roadside signs along routes to the ski areas may be the second priority, but roadside posting of signs takes time and should be pre-planned with available sign backboards and pre-printed signs. Warning signs on roads going to the ski areas reach most of the skiers not listening to rock music stations.

Some media radio broadcast categories (formats) that can be used for warning specific segments of a public with safety issues include:

Types of radio stations matching target audience format:[3]

- Top 40—young audience with some broad appeal
- Freeform and progressive rock—young audiences
- AOR (album-oriented rock)—broad appeal
- Oldies, standards, and classic rock—older audience
- Classical, pop, easy-listening, jazz, dance—background music to other activities
- Alternative and modern rock—younger audience
- Country—broad appeal particularly in rural, southern, and western U.S.
- Urban (hip-hop/R&B)—young urban audiences
- Public radio formats—broad older appeal Community radio, local and limited appeal
- Dance music radio—broad limited appeal
- Sports format—sports enthusiasts
- News and talk—older audiences
- Business news—business-oriented audiences
- Religious music and talk—appeals to faith-oriented listeners

(broad assumptions made)

Television has a broad array of programming. It is sometimes difficult to get air time for warning messages, except for stories with significant news worthiness or those that depict unique and potentially critical conditions. Prior contact with television station managers, traffic reporters, sports reporters, weather reporters, and so on, may be critical to get air time during the prime time news or breaking into a broadcast schedule.

Other means of reaching large audiences through electronic communications may include the use of Twitter, blogs, and other electronic interactive programs.

When considering roadside signing, the message and means of communication must be professional. Roadside signs on state and national roads must meet national Roadside Signing National Standards.[4] These standards are designed to ensure visibility and effective communications.

In all cases there must be a balance between informing the public and protection of esthetic values. Intruding on privacy and damaging scenic beauty for the sake of communicating critical messages must be analyzed thoroughly. As an example, vandalizing a rock wall to write a safety message would be inappropriate while breaking down a hotel door when an active fire is discovered may well be an appropriate intrusion of privacy.

Preventive warnings are a good method to avoid tragedies. If signs ask visitors not to climb on a scenic overlook barrier fence the property manager may never know how many lives have been saved or spared from serious injuries. Risk surveys can determine what activity or facility presents the highest degree of risk. Communicating the potential dangers to the visitors is essential and reflects good stewardship.

Areas catering to children should be particularly sensitive to warning parents of the dangers ahead long before children (who have a tendency to run ahead of their parents) arrive at the danger. Signs warning that the springs ahead contain scalding water should be posted on the trail approaching the area as well as at the site of the hot springs. This is also true of overlooks, the intersection of trails with roads, natural water attractions, sudden drop offs, toxic plants (i.e., poison ivy) and the presence of dangerous animals. Managers should put themselves in the place of their visitors. They must ask themselves the question: "If I had my own children for the first time at this recreation site, what are the critical things I should I know to protect them from both the man-made and the natural environment?"

An overly exuberant manager may choose to warn the visitor of every possible danger they may face. This approach results in an excessive number of messages or signs that diminishes the importance of the most important messages. If a water source is contaminated and the non-potable water warning sign is intermixed with signs warning of high altitude exercise, splinters in wood rails, thistles, deer ticks, West Nile disease, dogs required to be on leashes, lock your car, and so on, the importance and critical nature of the contaminated water is lost in the morass of signs. It is not that the other issues are not important, but rather, contaminated water is a critical issue and clear and unencumbered notification must be given.

The design and location of signs and brochures is important. Sign letter size should be determined by the anticipated speed of the motor vehicle, bicycle, walker, and so forth. The following broad guidelines for highway sign letter size were developed by the USSC and the NHTSA[5]:

Letter Size	Traffic Speed	Maximum Viewing Distance in Feet	Distance Best Impact in Feet
4 inch	25-35 MPH	Less than 200	40
6 inch	35-45 MPH	Less than 300	60
8 inch	45-55 MPH	Less than 400	80
10 inch	65 MPH	Less than 500	100

In a recreation, sports, and tourism settings, signs are used to guide, regulate use, warn, and educate visitors. Always make certain that visitors can read the sign from appropriate distances. Signs and the vegetation that may surround them must be maintained. Signs in a state of disrepair are seldom taken seriously by the visitors. In country that has heavy snowfall, recognize that snow can cover important signs. In such areas, signs should be mounted above the anticipated snow level.

Signs should have contrasting colors for visibility. If possible, the sign colors should not distract from the surrounding environment. Earth tone colors usually complement the visual quality of the surrounding area. As an example, a sign along a trail in a forested environment that includes safety (bright) orange on a purple background may not be appropriate, while mustard colored letters on a natural wood background may be appropriate. Landscape architects will provide managers with excellent advice that will ensure visibility and scenic compatibility at the same time. Please note that federal and state regulatory road signs have mandatory color standards that cannot be changed for aesthetic and environmental coordination.

Other than bulletin boards or locations where visitors must stop, signs should be limited to a single message. Entry stations, ticket booths, and restrooms provide ideal locations for signs with multiple messages. If important messages are posted in restrooms on the back of doors (stalls), and above urinals and sinks, most visitors will have the opportunity to read the messages within 24 hours of visiting the facility.

The Musselman Case

The case of *Oberson v. USDA Forest Service* 514 F.3d 989 (2008), illustrates a need to warn of hidden dangers regardless of the protection afforded an organization through legislation or exculpatory documents. Oberson was the representative and caregiver for Brian Musselman, injured in the accident from which this case arose.

On February 25, 1996, a snowmobile accident involved Brian Musselman, an expert snowmobiler. He had joined friends to ride on snowmobile trails in Yellowstone National Park and Gallatin National Forest. After dark, he and his friends rode to a restaurant nine miles north of West Yellowstone, Montana. Musselman and three others rode on the Big Sky Trail, a groomed snowmobile trail managed by the U.S. Forest Service. They reportedly were running their snowmobiles competitively at speeds up to 60 mph.

At the restaurant, Musselman and his friends joined a group of some 20 people to cook steaks, drink beer, and tell stories. Musselman had at least three beers; others in the party drank more. The others consumed between four and eight beers. Upon leaving the restaurant around 10 p.m., some in the party were heavily impaired by alcohol. The plaintiff was not impaired and was fully able to operate his snowmobile.

No member of the group had previously traveled on the stretch of the Big Sky Trail immediately adjacent to the restaurant. The Forest Service had posted a speed limit of 45 mph on its Yellowstone-area trails, but was aware that snowmobilers regularly traveled this stretch of trail at speeds in excess of 60 mph. Musselman took off quickly from the restaurant and continued at a pace keeping him in front of the other riders. He was not exceeding 45 mph when he reached the accident site. The others approached the accident site at approximately 50-55 mph.

The stretch of trail approaching the accident site is flat and smooth for roughly a quarter of a mile. It then drops suddenly down a steep hill, the site of the accident. There it loses 17 feet of elevation over approximately 80 feet, an 11.5 degree pitch or 25% slope. At the time of the accident, there were no signs warning of the hill or instructing riders to slow down. Numerous witnesses suggested at trial that it was unusual for such a drop not to be signed and that a trail of such abrupt steepness was rare.

The plaintiff was the first rider to come to the hill, negotiating it safely and landing his snowmobile under control slightly off the trail. The next driver crashed his machine at the bottom. After the crash, the plaintiff got off his machine for reasons unknown, although the district court found that he was likely trying to help the crashed driver or warn the approaching riders of the drop. As Musselman stepped on the trail, two other snowmobiles came flying over the hill side by side. One of the riders hit the plaintiff's head, causing catastrophic brain injuries. The injury left Musselman unable to swallow, speak, understand complex communication, or independently conduct activities of daily living.

The defendant Forest Service won the lower court (District Court) decision; however, upon appeal the court reversed the lower court decision. The defendant Forest Service argued that they were afforded federal discretionary power (immunity), alcohol was involved, and the snowmobiles were likely going faster than the posted speed. All that said, the court determined that the Forest Service cannot breech their responsibility to warn of dangerous conditions.

The Forest Service was deemed to have sole responsibility for identifying and correcting hazards on the Big Sky Trail. To identify hazards, the Forest Service engages in a process called "warranting." The program manager for the Gallatin National Forest described the process as "identifying the hazards that our average, prudent, reasonable rider would not expect based on a spectrum of users that we had out there." Forest Service employees identify hazards during warranting by riding the trail at 35 mph during the day. Upon identifying a hazard, the Forest Service closes the trail, corrects the hazard, or warns the user. The Forest Service does not warrant trails at night, on the assumption that reflectors and a rider's judgment as to the appropriate speed will provide sufficient protection.

Following the accident, in November 1996, the Forest Service re-warranted the trail, making several adjustments to the site of the accident. The Service realigned the approach to the hill, replacing the straight, flat approach with a curve leading through trees. Additionally, signs were added indicating the upcoming curve and subsequent hill. The warranting form also noted that the hill can "sneak up on a person" at night and that the hill's crown was scheduled for reduction.

Sixteen days before the Plaintiff's accident, two snowmobiles and a snow grooming machine were involved in an accident at the hill in question. The snowmobiles were traveling in clear weather at night, going 35-40 mph, which the investigation report characterized as too fast based upon the conditions. The two snowmobiles collided with the grooming machine immediately after coming over the crest of the hill. In a Forest Service re-creation following the accident, an observer 100 feet back from the hill could not see the grooming machine, equipped with two headlights and a flashing light on top, when it was at the bottom of the hill. Although the collision caused only minor damage to the involved machines and no personal injury, the investigation found that the accident could have resulted in serious injury to the riders.

The court concluded in the Oberson case that the Forest Service's failure to correct or warn of this hazard was not the type of discretionary decision that is shielded from tort liability.

This case differs from *Childers v. United States,* 40 F.3d 973 (9th Cir. 1995), where the decision not to post signs and to close portions of Yellowstone National Park were the result of policy decisions regarding how best to manage the park during winter. The court explained: "Unable to maintain all the trails in the park, cognizant that posting warning signs would inadvertently attract visitors to unmaintained trails, and unable to post signs throughout the park, NPS could only decide to close large portions of the park, or to keep the park open, provide visitors with information on the hazards, and take steps to discourage visitors from going to hazardous areas."

In its decision, the court stated, "The case before us is different. It is more nearly analogous to cases such as *Summers v. United States,* 905 F.2d 1212, 1215-16 (9th Cir.1990), holding the discretionary function did not protect the Park Service where it had failed to warn visitors of the danger of stepping on hot coals in a fire ring in the Golden Gate National Recre-

Grand Canyon of the Yellowstone, Wyoming: Childers v. United States

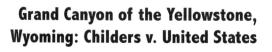

ation Area." The court found that "NPS's failure to identify and warn of the danger to barefoot visitors of hot coals on park beaches resembles more a departure from the safety considerations established in Service policies . . . than a mistaken judgment in a matter clearly involving [policy] choices." The court stated, "Here, the Forest Service knew of the hazard through its own investigation, which disclosed that sixteen days prior to Musselman's accident that the hill in question had been the site of a potentially serious collision between a snow grooming machine and two snowmobiles. In the absence of any evidence that the failure to post a warning or remedy the hazard was the product of a policy choice, we conclude that the discretionary function exception did not shield the Forest Service from liability."

Defendants also have some protection through state law. The majority of states have adopted a "sophisticated user doctrine" as a defense for Duty to Warn lawsuits. Simply stated, if the user or participant knew or should have known that there was a danger associated with the use of a product or participation in an activity, the "Sophisticated User" doctrine negates the duty to warn or a potential danger posed by the product or activity.[6] This defense centers on whether or not the plaintiff has or should have had advanced knowledge of the inherent dangers involved in their activity. The requirement to warn is also dependent upon whether the risks are open and obvious to the user. Those manufacturing firearms should not have to warn that firearms can cause injury or death.

Discussion Questions

1. List three recreation, sports, and tourism activities in your area and describe what type of warnings may be necessary to protect the user from reoccurring dangers. What methods would you use to warn the participant/visitor about the dangers?

2. List three sudden emergency situations that may occur in your area. Describe how you plan to warn the participants/visitors of new and significant dangers.

Notes

1. *Freas v. Prater Constr. Corp.,* 60 Ohio St.3d 6, 573 N.E.2d 27, 30 (Ohio 1991); *Livengood v. ABS Contractors Supply,* 126 Ohio App.3d 464, 710 N.E.2d 770, 772 (Ohio Ct. App. 1998); *Klauss v. Glassman,* 2005 WL 678984 at *3 (Ohio Ct. App. Mar. 24, 2005); *Gawloski v. Miller Bre Rogers v. Ingersoll-Rand Co.,* 144 F. 3d 841 (D.C. Cir. 1998); *Uniroyal Goodrich Tire Co. v. Martinez,* 977 S.W.2d 328 (Tex. 1998).) wing Co., 96 Ohio App.3d 160, 644 N.E.2d 731, 733 (Ohio Ct. App. 1994).

2. *Rogers v. Ingersoll-Rand Co.,* 144 F. 3d 841 (D.C. Cir. 1998); *Uniroyal Goodrich Tire Co. v. Martinez,* 977 S.W.2d 328 (Tex. 1998) also see *Restatement (Third) of Torts: Products Liability* [sections] 2 comment 1, which states that adequate warnings of a product's dangers are not a substitute for a reasonably safe design that would eliminate the hazards from the product.

3. National Association of Radio Broadcasters categories and from Wikipedia, the free encyclopedia 2010; note: not an all-inclusive listing.

4. As developed by the National Highway Traffic Safety Administration.

5. United States Sign Council and the National Highway Traffic Safety Administration.

6. Sungaila, M. C., & Mayer, K. C. (April 2009). *Defense Counsel Journal* pp. 196-205.

Chapter Twenty-Seven

PLAYGROUNDS

Introduction

The American people place great emphasis on the safety and well-being of their children. Examples of this concern are common. Automobile restraint devices for children and public outrage when a child is abused attest to this concern. Children often have trouble understanding when danger is present. They run and play with reckless abandon—without regard to cars speeding down a busy street or the dangers of climbing high structures. One place where children often fail to understand the dangers is playgrounds. Therefore, special care needs to be taken to ensure that playgrounds are safe places for children to go about the business of being children.

It seems that everywhere you turn, there is another playground. You see them at fast food restaurants, hotels, and resorts, on school grounds, and in public parks. Unfortunately, not every playground is built and maintained with the safety of children in mind. For example, the number of hospital emergency room visits due to playground injuries is greater than you might imagine. Each year, over 200,000 children need emergency room treatment due to playground injuries.[1] It is easy to see that given the sheer number of injuries, the potential for lawsuits is enormous. As a recreation professional managing playgrounds, you should know how to protect yourself from lawsuits by providing a safe play facility for those who use them. Knowing the standard of care that you will be held to is a good place to start.

SECTION 1: STANDARD OF CARE

The standard of care in a negligence action is determined by the courts in light of all the evidence in a particular case. When a negligence case comes before the court, the judges will look for standards set by authorities who have extensive knowledge about a given subject. The relevant guidelines and standards for playground safety are published and made available through professional organizations and regulatory agencies. These publications provide guidelines for practitioners such as coaches, teachers, hospitality managers, or recreation professionals. The people who create playground safety standards and guidelines are experts in such fields as engineering and recreation safety.

The standards for playground safety depend in part on guidelines created by the Consumer Products Safety Commission (CPSC) and the American Society for Testing and Materials (ASTM). However, these guidelines are not all that a court will consider in determining the standard of care. The standard of care is also influenced by the status of the user (e.g., invitee, licensee, trespasser), age of the child, precedent and statutory law, expert opinion, and various other factors. A description of the CPSC and the ASTM and a short history of their role in providing playground safety guidelines is important to show their impact on the standard of care in playground safety.[2]

The Consumer Products Safety Commission is an independent federal regulatory agency located in Washington, D.C. The commission is designed to bring together experts to work toward finding ways to protect consumers from potentially dangerous products. The agency has jurisdiction over numerous consumer products.[3] In 1974, people were becoming alarmed at the increasing number of injuries occurring on playgrounds, and petitioned the CPSC to develop mandatory safety standards for public playground equipment.

After coordinated efforts with the National Recreation and Park Association (NRPA),[4] and much hard work, the CPSC decided to abandon the plan to develop mandatory safety standards and instead published a set of guidelines for playground safety. Guidelines are not legal requirements, but instead serve as recommendations for decision makers to voluntarily follow. They can be used by the courts when determining whether the appropriate standard of care was met. In 1981, these guidelines—the first federal guidelines designed to provide for safer playgrounds—were published in the *Handbook for Public Playground Safety*.

The handbook, while going a long way toward setting a safety standard for playgrounds, still had some gaps and needed updating. For example, in the 1981 handbook, there were no maximum heights established for playground equipment. The safe height of equipment, as you can imagine, is something that is important to know. The severity of injury resulting from a fall from playground equipment is a function of the height of the equipment and the material making up the playground surface. Falls are a common safety hazard in playgrounds.

Playground equipment manufacturers felt the impact of the deficiencies in the handbook. Manufacturers bear an increased legal burden when their products result in injury. In many cases, they incur strict liability when an injury results from a product that does not meet the required standard. It is easy to imagine, therefore, the pressure playground manufacturers would face from litigation if they manufactured equipment without good, legally acceptable standards to follow.

The manufacturers therefore asked the American Society for Testing and Materials (ASTM) to develop a safety standard (rather than guidelines) for public playgrounds. The ASTM is an organization that develops standards for various products. It uses scientific tests to determine ways equipment can be manufactured and implemented to reduce injuries. The playground equipment manufacturers wanted one national standard that would reduce playground injuries and help prevent and defend against lawsuits.

In 1993, the first national standard for public playgrounds was published. This publication is entitled *F148793, Standard Consumer Safety Performance Specification for Playground Equipment and Public Use.* It was put together by experts such as designers, playground owners and managers, and equipment manufacturers, and sets forth standards for playground safety. The CPSC worked directly with the ASTM in developing these standards. The ASTM and CPSC provide periodic updates to the playground safety standards and guidelines.[5] Familiarity with these standards is essential for recreation professionals who manage and maintain playgrounds on their property. Revisions and updates to these publications are ongoing. The *CPSC Handbook for Public Playground Safety* is available online free of charge. The ASTM standards publication is available for a fee at www.astm.com.

Public Playground Safety Checklist[6]

1. Make sure surfaces around playground equipment have at least 12 inches of wood chips, mulch, sand, or pea gravel, or mats made of safety-rubber or rubber-like materials.

2. Check that protective surfacing extends at least six feet in all directions from play equipment. For swings, be sure surfacing extends, in back and front, twice the height of the suspending bar.

3. Make sure that tall structures are spaced at least nine feet apart.

4. Check for dangerous hardware, like open "S" hooks or protruding bolt ends.

5. Make sure spaces that could trap children, such as openings in guard-rails or between ladder rungs, measure less than 3.5 inches or more than nine inches.

6. Check for sharp points or edges in equipment.

7. Look out for tripping hazards, like exposed concrete footings, tree stumps, or roots.

8. Make sure elevated surfaces, like platforms and ramps, have guard-rails to prevent falls.

9. Check playgrounds frequently to see that equipment and surfacing are in good condition.

10. Carefully supervise children on playgrounds to make sure they are safe.

SECTION 2: PLAYGROUND SURFACES

Injuries to children occur frequently as a result of falls to hard surfaces from playground equipment. As mentioned, children do not often appreciate the danger associated with high places. Most children love to climb. This is why most of the playground equipment you see often includes something on which children can climb. Swings and slides are also standard equipment in most playgrounds. Some slides reach heights that would make most adults nervous. When you consider the height of playground equipment as a safety factor, you must also think about the ability of the playground surface to cushion a fall. As the next case illustrates, a fall to a hard surface could be life threatening.

In the case of *Salinas v. Chicago Park District* (1989)[7] an eight-year-old girl and her mother had decided to visit a city park and use the playground. There was no fee to use the facilities. The girl had developmental disabilities and had attended what her mother described as a "special" school when she was four years old. In the playground, there was a slide about five feet high with eight steps leading to a large circular platform on top. The child wanted to play on the slide, so she proceeded to climb the stairs to the platform from which she would slide down. Her mother watched her as she climbed to the fifth step and then turned to speak to a friend. When she turned back, her daughter was on the ground. The girl had fallen and struck her head on the asphalt surface below the slide. She later died of head injuries associated with the fall. Her parents sued the Chicago Park District for negligence in a wrongful death action. One claim the parents made was that the asphalt surface beneath the slide created a dangerous condition that the park department knew about, but which a child could not appreciate.

This case demonstrates the importance of the playground surface in the overall playground facility. The CPSC, which published the handbook providing guidelines for playground safety, warned not to install concrete or asphalt under aboveground playground equipment. Take some time to look around at the playgrounds in your community. Do you see any playgrounds with asphalt surfaces? You might even see asphalt surfaces covered with a thin carpet. This is problematic, since the danger of injury from a fall might be less obvious, because the hard surface is covered but offers little or no protection from a fall.

Common sense should tell you that a hard surface could result in death or serious injury from a fall. Can you think of any materials that could be used on the playground surface that could reduce the risk of serious injury when a child falls to the ground from playground equipment? Some materials that might work include wood mulch, sand, pads, or a plastic or synthetic material with cushioning properties. Surfacing technology continues to evolve and improve. Therefore, consult reputable playground manufacturers for information regarding the available types of playground surfacing.

When materials such as these are used, however, they must be given proper maintenance and upkeep. Think about what happens to sand when it rains or becomes wet and freezes. It becomes hard and uneven. Loose bulk surfaces such as those mentioned develop lumps and bare spots after having been walked on by the many tiny feet of children and exposure to wind and rain. Therefore, the playground surface must be regularly maintained and kept in a reasonably safe condition.

Consider the following hypothetical scenario:

Julie Slider and her mother were spending the morning at the local park in the playground area. Julie was eight years old and loved to play at this particular playground. Her favorite activity was sliding on the tall metal slide in the center of the play area. This made her mother nervous due to the height of the slide and the worn surface beneath the exit area, but she knew how much Julie loved to slide and couldn't bring herself to stop Julie from doing her favorite activity. She would usually walk over to the slide and watch Julie as she climbed to the top and slid to the bottom where she would be waiting.

But on this particular day, just as Julie began her climb to the top of the slide, she heard someone call her name. It was her friend from the neighborhood, so she felt obligated to turn and say a few words to her. It seemed like only a second or two had passed when she heard Julie scream and turned to see her lying on the ground beside the slide. While her mother was distracted, Julie had climbed to the top of the slide as usual and pushed off to begin her trip to the bottom. The hot July sun, however, had heated the slide to an unbearable temperature. Julie, in an attempt to escape the searing pain, rolled off the side of the slide about halfway down. She fell approximately 10 feet before colliding with a low fence that had been placed only a few feet from the slide. She then continued to the ground where her body met the hard-packed dirt playground surface. Julie suffered several broken ribs, a slight concussion, and a broken arm in the fall. She also suffered a great amount of emotional trauma. Her mother also claims she was damaged emotionally as a result of seeing her daughter in such a condition. She sues, on behalf of her daughter, all parties she believes to be responsible for this unfortunate incident.

What facts in this scenario might you use in an argument for liability on the part of the park? What arguments might you make in defense of the park? What amount of responsibility should the parent take for the incident? What should have been done to prevent this injury from occurring?

Risk management in the area of playground safety is essential. It should be the responsibility of every member of the agency or organization to be involved in the risk management process. Therefore, management should encourage all of its employees to look for potential safety hazards in the playgrounds and report these hazards in a timely manner. It is not difficult to take notice of sand or wood chips that have become hard-packed over time or bare spots that have formed beneath a slide or monkey bars because some sand has shifted. A secretary of a park department taking her lunch break on a park bench next to a playground, for example, could be on the lookout for playground safety hazards. If risk management is on every employee's mind, identification of hazards and the proper and consistent maintenance of playground surfaces should not be a problem. The result will be fewer tragic accidents from falls to hard playground surfaces and fewer lawsuits claiming that the park department was negligent in failing to warn of a dangerous condition that was not obvious to those who used the playground.

SECTION 3: THE PLAYGROUND SAFETY AUDIT

We have seen the problems that can arise when the type of playground surface is inadequate or the surface is improperly maintained. Other hazards associated with playgrounds include circumstances when a child's head becomes trapped in a piece of equipment, clothing becomes entangled (sometimes resulting in strangulation), or when sharp edges or protruding objects result in cuts and bruises. Another situation involves burns on playground equipment. When slides face in a southerly direction, they can heat to incredibly high temperatures. This can result in severe burns.

Given the problems that can arise, it doesn't take much imagination to understand the importance of maintaining safe playground facilities. The best way to keep a safe playground that meets the legal standard is to conduct a safety audit. A playground safety audit is the detailed and consistent examination of playground equipment. The audit has several important uses.

First, it is used to identify and test design flaws and life-threatening or serious hazards. Second, it is used to assist in developing a schedule of when to replace pieces of playground equipment. Third, it is used to show that the agency had a plan to meet current safety standards. In other words, it could be used to show that the standard of care was met in a negligence lawsuit. Finally, an audit can be used to serve the obvious function of preventing serious playground injuries.

An audit consists of three components. The first component is the identification and testing of hazards. The *CPSC Handbook* is a useful guide to understanding and implementing testing procedures. It contains guidelines for almost every piece of playground equipment you could imagine. These guidelines are often complemented with figures and illustrations. As an example, we will look at the guidelines for rungs of ladders and hand-gripping components from the handbook.

Whereas the steps of stairways and stepladders are used only for foot support, the rungs of rung ladders are used for both foot support and for hand support by a climbing child since rung ladders generally do not have handrails.

Rungs are generally round in cross section and should have a diameter or maximum cross sectional dimension between 0.95 and 1.55 inches.

Other components intended to be grasped by the hands such as the bars of climbers should also have a diameter or maximum cross sectional dimension between 0.95 and 1.55 inches. To benefit the weakest child in each age group, a diameter of 1.25 inches is preferred. All rungs should be secured in a manner that prevents them from turning.

As you can see, the guidelines contained in the handbook are very thorough and quite technical. Other issues addressed in the handbook include, in part, guidelines on how to reduce or prevent such hazards as sharp points, angles that produce head entrapment, tripping hazards, and hazards associated with suspended hazards or platforms. This handbook, along with a thorough understanding of current ASTM standards, should be an integral part of your playground safety audit.

The second component of an audit is an evaluation of the degree of danger posed by each piece of playground equipment. This is a component of any risk management process. Some of the dangers associated with playground equipment are quite serious. For example, falls to hard surfaces, head entrapment, strangulation, and cuts from sharp edges are a few that should raise concern. As you know, the greater the potential for a severe injury, the greater the likelihood of costly litigation resulting from the injury. Therefore, it would make sense that the potentially severe hazards are addressed first and with the most consideration.

Once the degree of danger has been established, the third component, the process of determining whether to repair or remove the hazard, can be considered. For example, if a piece of equipment is in such condition that it is considered to pose a high level of danger, then it must be removed immediately if it cannot be repaired. An obvious example would be a sharp piece of metal on a slide that could cut a child who comes in contact with it. Priority levels can be established based upon the degree of danger posed by the equipment after hazards have been identified. Medium to high levels of danger and low levels of danger can be established as classifications with the former given greater priority when budget considerations are made.

Everyone from playground supervisors to administrators should be trained to identify safety hazards on playgrounds. To conduct the playground safety audit, special teams should be trained for the job. Those who conduct the audit should be able to follow at least the minimum training guidelines. For example, the auditor should be able to read and write clearly, and have the ability to physically climb on the equipment. Also, the person doing the audit should be able to work with minimal supervision. Finally, he or she should have training in current safety guidelines. The person should fully understand the *CPSC Handbook* and ASTM standards and how to implement the testing procedures.

The audit and playground inspections should be conducted frequently and with consistency. Inspections should be conducted weekly to identify hazards, routine maintenance tasks (litter removal, vandalism repair, surface checks, etc.) should be performed several times a week, and a comprehensive audit should be conducted on a reasonable schedule. The methods used to conduct the audit should be consistent each time it is performed. Also, the methods used should meet or exceed the standards put forth by the CPSC, the ASTM, and/or those implemented by other agencies. The advice of a professional in risk management can also help you to meet the standards that are acceptable to the courts.

Finally, everything done during the audit should be documented. The most faded ink is better than the best memory and could mean everything in a court of law. The audit should document the identified hazards and the test results. Also, the level of danger each hazard poses and when it was removed or repaired needs to be documented. A physical map of the playground area included with the testing and other documents would be helpful. Documentation is sometimes time-consuming and tedious, but is necessary if the audit is to serve its purpose of demonstrating whether the organization had met the standard of care when a lawsuit arises.

The case of *City of Miami v. Ameller* (1985)[9] illustrates the need for an audit. In this case, a young boy was playing on the monkey bars at a city park. He was climbing across the bars, lost his grip, and fell to the concrete surface below. A cushioning material is recommended by the CPSC for areas under pieces of elevated playground equipment. The boy was injured and sued the park department. The court felt that the park had a responsibility to provide for the public safety and welfare. This meant that it was required to meet playground industry standards as well as their own. The court reasoned that a failure to meet these standards would result in a breach of the duty owed by the park to the public.

This case illustrates the importance of conducting an audit. Suppose this case occurred today. A proper audit would identify the hazard (the concrete surface below the monkey bars), and use the CPSC guidelines set forth in the handbook to test and implement the correct surfacing material. This would likely reduce the probability and severity of injury to children.

It is also a good idea, as a park and recreation professional managing play areas, to be certified in playground safety. The NRPA has created the National Playground Safety Institute (NPSI). The NPSI has experts in playground safety who have drawn upon sources such as the *CPSC Handbook*, ASTM standards, and other relevant materials. Through their efforts, they have developed an invaluable body of practical information on playground safety.

Because of their expertise in this area, the NPSI has been approved by the National Certification Board of the NRPA to provide certification. They conduct seminars, provide course materials, and administer the certification exam. If you meet the requirements, you will become a Certified Playground Safety Inspector (CPSI). To attain this goal, a recreation professional must complete a comprehensive training program on playground hazard identification and risk management methods. Once the course has been successfully completed, the CPSI exam can be taken at the available time and location.

Those seeking credentials include administrators, managers, designers, supervisors, and teachers. The certification must be renewed every three years to keep up with the rapid changes that take place in playgrounds. Certification is a good idea, because it provides those who have achieved it with knowledge of playground standards, which are critical, as we have seen from the previous cases, when defending against lawsuits and ensuring that children have a fun and safe place to play.

Discussion Questions

1. Where can a park manager find the publication that establishes the standards for playground equipment?

2. Is there a guide as to the minimum age a child can play in a park without parental or adult supervision? Do you believe there should be a standard? Explain?

3. How long does an agency have to fix a broken piece of play equipment once they learn it is damaged or dangerous?

Notes

1. United States Consumer Product Safety Commission.
2. Information concerning the type of products over which the CPSC has jurisdiction can be found at their website (www.cpsc.gov).
3. This discussion draws heavily on an excellent presentation of the subject in Wallach, F., (1995). Playgrounds: The long trail. *Parks and Recreation,* 6067.
4. The National Recreation and Park Association is an organization that serves professionals and citizens dedicated to parks, recreation, and conservation through various programs and publications.
5. The most current updates can be found by visiting the CPSC website at www.cpsc.gov.
6. Consumer Products Safety Commission. (2001). Public Playground Safety Checklist, CPSC Document#327.
7. *Salinas v. Chicago Park District,* 545 N.E.2d 184 (III. App. 1989).

8. This information is quoted directly from the *Handbook for Public Playground Safety.* Pub. No. 325. U.S. Consumer Product Safety Commission, Washington, D.C.

9. *City of Miami v. Ameller*, 472 So.2d 728 (Fla. App. 1985).

Chapter Twenty-Eight

AQUATICS

Introduction

Most of us have spent warm summer days relaxing beside a swimming pool and enjoying its cool and refreshing water. Swimming pools are immensely popular and come in many different shapes and sizes. Given their popularity, it is necessary for most public recreation agencies, country clubs, hotels, many private recreation providers, and even theme parks to provide some form of aquatic facility for their patrons. Thus, as a recreation provider or hospitality professional, you need to be aware of the issues that face those who manage swimming pools and aquatic facilities.

The legal issues are especially important due to the nature of swimming and diving activities. When evaluating risk in the management of swimming pools, it is necessary to think about the type of risk that will most likely be encountered. Usually, when a pool-related accident occurs, it is severe. It is easy to think of types of severe injuries that occur in and around pools. Diving accidents often involve broken necks and limbs, while drownings are an all-too-common tragedy. A drowning or injury resulting in paralysis could lead to a lawsuit that could be devastating to your organization.

Therefore, the manager of an aquatics facility has a great deal of responsibility. When you understand the severity of the risk involved, it is easy to see that a good risk management plan is essential. A key part of that plan is to understand and adhere to the appropriate standard of care for an aquatics facility. The standard of care comes from various sources and is discussed throughout the remainder of this chapter.

SECTION 1: STANDARD OF CARE

Suppose that a drowning occurs at a hotel or resort. The survivors will most likely sue, claiming that the hotel and hotel management was somehow negligent. Their cause of action would probably be wrongful death. At trial, the court would try to determine if the hotel management took reasonable care to protect its swimming pool patrons. If reasonable care was taken, it would have met the standard of care and not be held negligent.

The standard of care is of central importance in a negligence action. It will depend on several things. First, the standard owed will depend on the jurisdiction or place where the injury occurred. Why is the place where the injury occurred so important? It is because the laws of the state or locality might define the standard. For example, what if the pool where the drowning occurred was Olympic-sized and there was only one lifeguard on duty? Next, suppose that the state legislature had passed a law that a minimum of three lifeguards is required to guard an Olympic-sized pool. Suppose also that a city ordinance required three lifeguards at a pool of this size. These laws would be central to the plaintiff's legal claim.

The potential severity of risk in aquatics is high.

In addition to municipal and state laws, local administrative regulations play a role in determining the standard of care in a negligence case. The Department of Health and Social Services, for example, sometimes provides regulations governing public pool safety. On the local front, many public health agencies have instituted control programs whose goal is to ensure that swimming pools are kept safe and that health standards are maintained.

Another source for swimming pool facility standards are those set forth by industry groups. You will recall that guidelines for playground safety have been established in much the same manner. These standards, however, do not have the weight of law and should be treated as such. Care should be taken to make sure that your own standards are high enough for a court to find that you have met the applicable standard of care for swimming pool safety. In other words, the trade association or industry group may have failed to create standards that were reasonable to prevent injury. The following case illustrates this point.

In the case of *King v. National SPA and Pool Institute, Inc.* (1990),[1] a man was killed when he dove from a diving board into his pool and hit his head on the bottom. The pool was manufactured by a company that complied with the trade association's minimum standards for the size and dimensions of the pool. The man's wife sued the trade association. The court held that the trade association had a duty to exercise reasonable care when it set swimming pool design standards. In this case, the standards set forth by the trade association were questionable. An aquatics administrator should draw on information from as many sources as possible to set the highest standard possible for their aquatic facility.

Standards for pool managers in various contexts will be discussed throughout this chapter. Lifeguards, for example, must meet certain requirements as set forth in statutes or municipal ordinances that require certification by various lifeguard certification programs. These programs help provide for the safety of swimming pool patrons and reduce lawsuits. Whatever aspect of aquatic facility management that is involved, the applicable laws, regulations, and ordinances must be looked up and understood by the manager or risk management coordinator.

SECTION 2: DUTY TO SUPERVISE THE ACTIVITY-LIFEGUARDS

You will find lifeguards at many public and private pools. They have the enviable task of sitting poolside on hot summer days while everyone else toils in cramped offices or other places that aren't nearly as much fun. The job of a lifeguard, however, is very important. It is his or her job to protect and supervise swimmers and come to the rescue of those in trouble. So it is important that lifeguards be properly trained so they will know what to do in the case of an emergency. If trouble comes up and the lifeguard is not prepared for it, then injury or death of a swimming pool patron may result. Another likely result is a lawsuit against the lifeguard and everyone involved in the supervision and control of the pool and its personnel. The following case illustrates what can happen when lifeguards fail to meet a reasonable standard of care.

In the case of *Barnett v. Zion Park District* (1996),[2] a 10-year-old boy was enjoying the swimming pool operated by the Zion Park District. He had climbed the ladder to a diving board and had walked out to the end when he slipped and hit his head on the top of the diving board. He then fell unconscious into the pool and sank to the bottom of the deep end. Several other swimmers saw this and went to the lifeguards for help. One lifeguard, when told of the situation, replied to the plea for help with indifference. The lifeguard responded that the child had been with a group that had been causing trouble, said that the boy was all right and they were only playing, then turned away. Another lifeguard was approached by a different swimmer who was met with equal indifference.

The swimmer then ran to the lifeguard shack and summoned help. The boy was pulled from the water but it was too late—he was dead. The boy's mother sued the park district for the negligence of the lifeguard staff. She claimed that the lifeguards exhibited willful and wanton misconduct in the way they handled the situation.

Consider also the case of *Phillips v. Southeast 4-H Educational Center, Inc., et al.* (1999),[3] where a 32-year-old man drowned while swimming laps at a pool operated by the defendant. On the day of the incident, two certified lifeguards were on duty. One of the lifeguards was the pool's senior lifeguard and manager. The patron was swimming laps both above and below the water. After swimming several laps underwater, he stood up in the shallow end and then sat underwater. The lifeguard noticed bubbles coming to the surface. When the bubbles stopped, the guard was in the water within "moments." The swimmer was pulled from the water and immediately given CPR. The other guard called for emergency response personnel. The rescue squad arrived in 10 minutes, during which time CPR was administered continuously. The swimmer was pronounced dead on arrival at the hospital. The wife of the deceased sued the defendant for negligence. Central to her case was the theory that the lifeguards were negligent in not recognizing that her husband was unconscious sooner, and if they had, he could have been saved. In particular, she claimed that the lifeguards breached the "10/20-second rule." It was claimed the breach occurred since the lifeguard waited a minute before effecting a rescue after noticing the bubbles had stopped. The court did not agree, and held that the plaintiff did not demonstrate proof of causation. Judgment was for the defendant.

These cases illustrate the need for a qualified lifeguard staff. Lifeguards should pass a lifesaving certification course and be trained and oriented with respect to the specific facility in which they will work. Even though the cases do not address the issue of their certification, their training and orientation to the facility is clearly suspect.

The need for lifeguards who are qualified to perform the tasks that will keep swimming pool patrons safe led to the establishment of lifesaving certification programs. Certification programs are currently administered by a number of organizations of which the primary ones are: the American Red

Cross, Jeff Ellis and Associates (an aquatics risk management company), the Young Men's Christian Association (YMCA), and the Boy Scouts of America. Some municipal laws and regulations require that lifeguards be certified by one or more of these organizations. These programs change continuously to keep pace with current trends and standards, so it is best to contact these organizations directly to find out about their certification requirements.

In addition to certification, lifeguards should be managed and supervised properly. Proper management of a lifeguard staff will provide lifeguards with the tools and information to meet and exceed the relevant standards. The obvious result of meeting or exceeding standards is a reduction in liability. Put yourself in the shoes of an aquatics facility manager. Then, from a management perspective, using what you have learned from the cases, personal experience, and common sense, ask yourself what issues you would want to address. The following, though not exhaustive, is a list of issues to consider.

1. Does the pool have the correct number of lifeguards for the facility? The applicable standards should be reviewed to see if the number of lifeguards is sufficient for the size of the pool. One or two lifeguards may not be able to adequately guard a large pool.

2. Are the lifeguards trained and supervised to anticipate and deal with problems that might arise at their particular location? For example, do they know about the thunderstorms that pass over like clockwork every summer afternoon?

3. Are the lifeguard stands located in positions where the entire pool area can be observed, and are the lifeguards instructed to stay in these areas while on duty?

4. Are lifeguards given sufficient time out of the sun so that they are not fatigued from overexposure to the point that they cannot pay adequate attention to the pool?

5. Are lifeguards taught to recognize the potential dangers associated with toys brought into the pool area and which toys should not be allowed?

6. Has an ongoing training program been implemented so that the lifeguards are kept up to date on current trends and standards?

7. Are first-aid and emergency medical equipment available, and do the lifeguards know how to use it?

8. Have the lifeguards been taught the proper procedures for handling an emergency and provided with communication devices such as handheld radios or telephones?

9. Do the lifeguards have emergency phone numbers so that emergency medical care can be summoned quickly in a serious emergency?

Consider the case of *Cater v. City of Cleveland* (1998).[4] In this case, a 12-year-old boy died from complications incurred as the result of a near drowning at a municipal indoor swimming pool. On the day of the incident, there were four Red Cross certified lifeguards on duty. The boy was at the pool during open swim which lasted from 1 to 4:30 p.m. One of the lifeguards patrolled the deck, two were stationed in lifeguard chairs (a high chair and a folding chair) at the deep end, and one in a lifeguard chair at the shallow end. At 3 p.m., the guard on patrol and a guard stationed at the deep end decided to take a lunch break. The break was unauthorized, because it was against policy to leave during open swim. This left one guard in the high lifeguard chair at the deep end and one in a guard chair at the shallow end. The guard in the chair later testified that it was difficult to see due to glare from the sun reflecting off a glass-paneled wall directly behind his chair. At 3:40 p.m., swimmers in the deep end yelled to the guards that someone was at the bottom of the pool. The two guards pulled the boy from the water and began CPR. The pool manager was nearby when he heard a whistle blown by the guard and rushed over to assist with the resuscitation attempts. Several employees were told to call 911 but were unable to get through since they were unaware that they had to dial a "9" first to get an outside line. The paramedics arrived at 4:10 p.m., 30 minutes after the boy was pulled from the water. He was taken to the hospital where he later developed acute bronchial pneumonia and died.

The boy's parents brought suit claiming that the defendant had provided negligent supervision. The city prevailed in the lawsuit in the trial court and again upon appeal. The decisions were based on the applicable statute that provided immunity to a governmental entity where injury or death resulted "from the exercise of judgment or discretion in determining whether to acquire, or how to use, equipment, supplies, materials, personnel, facilities, and other resources unless the judgment or discretion was exercised...in a wanton or reckless manner." R.C.2744.03(A)(5). The court held that the pool management had not acted in a reckless or wanton manner.

The Supreme Court reversed this decision. The court held that immunity was not absolute, and that reasonable minds could differ as to whether the city acted in a wanton or reckless manner in its use of personnel, facilities, and equipment. In particular, the court found it appalling that the city had no policy in place or training regarding the making of 911 calls. The city had admitted they had failed to train their employees in the use of the phone to make 911 calls. Second, the court found that the two lifeguards who left the pool to eat lunch created a dangerous condition by reason of their absence. Testimony revealed the near drowning occurred within five to 15 feet of the lifeguard chair in the deep end of the pool left empty by the absent lifeguard. Third, the court addressed the issue of glare, which allegedly obstructed the lifeguard's view of the deep end of the pool. The court held that it was for the trier of fact to determine whether the city, which knew about the glare problem at the pool, created an unreasonable risk of harm by not correcting the problem. Given these issues, the court remanded the case to the trial court for a new trial.

The following case illustrates the importance of having the correct number of lifeguards for the facility. It also demonstrates where the standards governing the number of lifeguards can be found. A statute or municipal (city) ordinance might hold the key in determining the standard a court will use when deciding whether a pool operator will be found to be negligent. A thorough knowledge of these laws should be obtained either by the pool operator or through the services of a professional risk manager so that the applicable standards can be met.

In the case of *Cassio v. Creighton University* (1989),[5] a 31-year-old man went for a swim in the Creighton University swimming pool. He was performing scuba diving exercises. With all his scuba gear on, he swam laps for 30-45 minutes. Then he moved to the deep end where he would swim to the bottom of the pool and surface repeatedly. There was only one lifeguard on duty at the time. She was talking to her supervisor when it was noticed that something was terribly wrong. A girl was standing at the deep end looking down into the water with a shocked expression on her face.

The lifeguard and the supervisor jumped up and ran to the deep end of the pool. They looked in the water and saw the man lying motionless on the bottom. The lifeguard dove in and swam to the bottom of the deep end. She reached the unconscious man and attempted to carry him to the surface, but he was too heavy. She came to the surface and gave her account of the situation. Another man who had been using the weights in the adjacent area saw what was happening and dove into the pool. He was able to bring Cassio to the surface. The man had turned a bluish color, which indicated he had a lack of oxygen in his blood. CPR was administered to no avail. Cassio was pronounced dead on arrival at the hospital.

The Cassio family sued the university, claiming that Creighton was negligent in failing to provide adequate supervision of the pool area on the date Cassio died. The family argued that there should have been more than one lifeguard on duty at the time of Cassio's death, since a city law required two lifeguards to be on duty at all times at a pool as large as Creighton's. On the day that Cassio died, there was only one lifeguard on duty. The supervisor had only come in to talk for a few minutes. The case was appealed all the way to the state supreme court. The court found the issue of the insufficient number of lifeguards to be relevant to the case. On other issues, however, the case was sent back for a new trial.

In addition to municipal and state laws governing pool safety, certain administrative regulations might apply. The following case illustrates where administrative regulations were brought into play following the drowning-death of a child at a municipal swimming pool.

In the case of *Johnson v. City of Darlington* (1991),[6] an eight-year-old boy was spending the afternoon swimming at the outdoor city swimming pool. Three lifeguards were on duty that day, but none were at their stations. One was talking with some friends in the far corner of the complex, the second was talking with friends outside the fence surrounding the pool, while the third was standing at the edge of the pool on the far end.

While the lifeguards were away from their posts, the boy slipped beneath the surface and drowned. The boy's parents sued the city claiming that the lifeguards were negligent in failing to properly supervise the pool area. His parents lost the case. They argued that health code regulations that governed safety at public pools were violated, and this violation would defeat governmental immunity provided by the state recreational use statute.

The court gave consideration to the administrative regulations as setting the standard of care for this case. Since, however, they were determined not to carry the same weight as state laws, the city, prevailed in the lawsuit. Pool managers should be familiar with both administrative regulations and state and local laws that address swimming pool safety. Then, standards should be set at or above whichever rule is the more stringent. A good risk management plan would include thoroughly researching all the laws and rules that apply to swimming pools.

Consider the following hypothetical scenario:

One hot summer day, Homer Swimson was enjoying the day at his outdoor university pool. Homer had paid to use the pool as part of his student activity fee for the summer semester. It was a clear and sunny day, with about 50 people swimming or lounging about in the warm sun. There were only two lifeguards on duty that day due to an illness of one and another who had quit without notice the day before to spend some time at home before the semester began. Homer had been playing pool at his fraternity house and partaking in some of the previous night's liquid refreshments before heading over to the pool. He had slept for about an hour in a lounge chair by the side of the pool and awoke feeling somewhat groggy and very hot. He looked around the pool and noticed some of his friends nearby. Homer then stumbled to the side of the pool and decided to dive into the cool water. It was not the deep end, but he had dived many times before in shallow water and never had any problems. So he stepped forward and dove into the cool, inviting water. Homer recalls the surprise he felt when his head met the bottom of the pool and then the blackness that followed. On the surface, one of his friends noticed that Homer had been under water for what seemed to be longer than normal. He ran to the lifeguard station and told the guard that his friend might be in trouble. The lifeguard told him not to worry; his friend was probably just playing a joke on him. He then ran to the other lifeguard and told her of the situation. She ran immediately to where Homer had entered the pool and pulled him from the water. He was given CPR and revived but not before suffering some brain damage. Homer was also paralyzed from the waist down as a result of his injury. His parents sue on Homer's behalf all parties they feel to be responsible for his condition.

What do you think are the key issues in this scenario when considering liability on the part of the school and pool management? Do you feel the school should be held liable, or is Homer responsible for his own actions? Why?

Waterparks

Pools come in many shapes and forms, and the popularity of novel aquatic facilities such as wave pools and waterslides is evident. Waterslides, for example, have enjoyed tremendous success and are now quite common. Many theme parks and hotels boast waterslides as their main attraction. Waterslides are a lot of fun. Some waterslides allow you to travel at fast speeds through winding tubes until you are dumped into a pool of water below. You experience a rush of adrenaline as you pick up speed while cruising down the slide. You also depend on the person operating the slide to make sure that no one is too close in front or behind you so that you do not crash into anyone. You also want to know what dangers to look out for, especially if it is your first time on the slide. A headfirst slide, for example, into a shallow pool below could be disastrous. Therefore, adequate supervision is very important. As with pool lifeguards, waterslide operators must be well trained and supervised. The following case shows what can happen when proper supervision is not provided.

In the case of *Volcanic Gardens Management Co. v. Beck* (1993)[7] Beck was using the waterslide at Wet' N Wild Water World. She had never been on a waterslide but thought it would be fun. She took her five-year-old daughter in her arms, sat on an innertube, and took off. As she was traveling down the slide, she lost her innertube and was sliding without it. She had just made it to the point where the slide entered the pool at the bottom when she felt a sharp pain in her back. Unknown to her, a young boy was traveling down the slide on an innertube just behind her. When she hit the pool at the bottom, the boy's feet slammed into her back and he toppled over her. She developed multiple fractures in her vertebrae and suffered temporary paralysis. She sued the company that managed the waterpark and won.

Her lawsuit claimed that the park was negligent in failing to properly supervise the boy who ran into her and in failing to warn her that the boy was traveling so close behind her on an innertube. It turned out that the attendant on duty at the slide failed to warn her that she could lose her innertube or that she could be bumped from behind. Also, the park made no effort to separate the patrons by spacing them at intervals so that they would not collide with each other. Further, it was revealed that patrons often lost their innertubes and they often collided with one another.

Based on the facts of the case, the court concluded that the waterpark did not meet the standard of providing ordinary care to its patrons. Since there were past incidents of collisions between patrons, and the waterpark knew about them, it had a duty to eliminate or reduce the risk associated with people colliding into one another. Since the waterpark did nothing to reduce the risk of collisions, of which it was aware, the court found it guilty of negligence in failing to provide adequate supervision of the patrons using the waterslide.

This case provides insight on how to reduce the risk of liability in waterslide facilities. Can you think of measures the waterpark could have taken to manage its legal risk in this instance? Some ideas are outlined below. As you read them, think of any you might add to the list.

1. The standard of care in providing for the safety of the participants must be established. In particular, the intervals at which waterpark patrons should be spaced when using the slide should be determined.

2. The type of equipment used should meet a reasonable standard of care. Are innertubes used at other waterparks with a reasonable degree of safety? The waterpark should not continue to use the innertubes if they have been the cause of past accidents.

3. A standard should be set and maintained for the type of sliding that is done. If activities such as tandem sliding or headfirst sliding have resulted in injury, this should not be allowed.

4. A waterpark should provide warnings of potential dangers of which the waterpark patrons might not be aware. The warnings could be placed on signs or given verbally. Remember that if a substantial number of patrons are foreign speaking, give the warnings in that language or use international symbols.

5. The waterpark should document the number and type of accidents and injuries that arise. If they are too frequent or severe, changes should be made to eliminate the problems.

SECTION 3: DUTY TO PROVIDE SAFE PREMISES

In addition to providing properly trained and managed lifeguards, another standard that must be addressed concerns the safety of the pool and surrounding area. This gets into an area of law known as premises liability. A pool can be supervised properly, but if someone misjudges the depth of the pool and dives headlong into shallow water and fractures his back, a lawsuit might still arise. There are quite a few lawsuits that have been filed against pool owners and pool manufacturers after people have dived into shallow water and been injured.

If you own a private pool or manage a pool for public use, you need to know whether your pool is designed safely and whether adequate warnings are in place. Knowing how to prevent diving injuries is often not so clear. Perhaps it might seem obvious that diving into shallow water would be dangerous. The following case illustrates how at least one court has taken this view.

In the case of *Glittenberg v. Doughboy Recreational Indus* (1992),[8] Glittenberg had decided to go for a swim in his neighbor's pool. His neighbors had an aboveground pool in their back yard that was seven and one-half feet deep at its deepest point and three and one-half feet deep at its most shallow point. The pool had a redwood deck and fence surrounding it. The pool was simple with no diving board, ladder, depth markings, or signs warning of the depth. He had been swimming in the pool twice before and felt that it was okay to dive in shallow water, since he thought he knew what he was doing.

Glittenberg stepped off the side of the pool and dived headfirst into the inviting cool water. His head struck the pool bottom, and he suffered permanent paralysis. He sued both his neighbors and the company who manufactured the pool. He felt that someone should have warned him that it was dangerous to dive in the shallow pool. He lost the case.

The court held that there is no duty to warn of open and obvious dangers. It concluded that the risk of diving in shallow water was an open and obvious danger. All properties of the pool were knowable or known. The court rejected the argument that someone diving into shallow water could not know how water will act upon the human body and therefore should be warned of the possibilities of injury.

Additionally, the court concluded that ignorance of how hydrodynamic forces act upon the body when diving is no excuse. The court stated, "The fact that most individuals do not understand how the laws of physics operate during a dive no more alters the perceived danger in the use of this product than failure to understand the medical reasons why a cut with a knife that severed a major artery could lead to death or catastrophic injury."[9] In other words, common sense should tell you it is dangerous to dive in shallow water.

The appellate court decision in *Blagg v. Illinois F.W.D. Truck and Equipment Company* established the following standards for similar cases: 1. the settlement agreement did not fairly and reasonably allocate the damages between husband and wife, 2. The settlement cannot circumvent the workers compensation and no part of the loss of consortium award can be used to reimburse a lien, 3. the wife's recovery for loss of consortium is limited by the physical injure caused by the spouse's comparative negligence, and 4. it is necessary to remand to the trial court because the possible comparative negligence was not examined in the court's approval of the settlements.

In the case of *Erickson v. Muskin Corp.* (1989),[10] on a hot summer afternoon, plaintiff and his wife decided to go swimming at a neighbor's pool. The neighbors had an above-ground oval pool that was between three and one-half to four and one-half feet deep. It was deeper at the ends because of an expandable liner on the pool's bottom. As the afternoon wore on, plaintiff decided to try something that looked like fun. He spotted an innertube floating in the pool and asked someone to move it closer to him. The man then sprang forward and dove through the inner tube.

By passing through the innertube at such an extreme angle, he could not pull out of the dive and crashed head-first into the bottom of the pool. Plaintiff suffered a compression fracture in his fifth cervical vertebrae and became a permanent quadriplegic. He and his wife sued the swimming pool manufacturer, among others, for negligent failure to warn of a dangerous condition. The jury in the trial court found that the pool was unreasonably dangerous due to a lack of warning of the dangers involved in diving into it. On appeal, the verdict was reduced on the finding that, among other things, Lance was a 25-year-old college graduate, he assumed the risk of injury when he dived through an innertube into shallow water.

Although this defense is available, should it be relied upon completely at the expense of implementing a sound risk management program? The answer is "certainly not!" There is increasing evidence that the dangers of shallow water diving are not easy to recognize in many cases. It has been convincingly argued that it is not always easy to accurately judge the water's depth. With the number of diving injuries per year reaching five figures,[11] it might just be that the dangers of diving are not so obvious.

To avoid the tragic outcomes illustrated by the previous cases, certain measures should be taken to avoid or reduce the risk of lawsuits and maintain a safe facility. These measures take a common-sense approach but are very important. Can you think of any more to add to the list?

1. Post accurate depth markers at the appropriate intervals.

2. The pool floor should be designed with the appropriate colors so that water depth can be best estimated by the diver.

3. Post "Danger—No Diving" signs where conditions dictate that a dive would be too dangerous to attempt (e.g., above-ground pools or shallow water.) The signs should be in a language or pictures so that people who speak foreign languages can understand them and be specific as to the relevant dangers where appropriate.[12]

4. If possible, diving instruction classes should be given to educate people about the proper way to dive. Swimming and diving classes should address safe diving methods.

5. Swimmers need to be warned not to mix alcohol and swimming—especially diving. Education on the effects of alcohol is important to reinforce this point.

Many hotels and recreation facilities have removed diving boards from their pool areas because of the liability associated with diving. They also often post "swim at your own risk" and "no diving" signs to provide warnings to their patrons. If diving is to be allowed, the pool should meet or exceed the standards for a safe depth. Think about the depth that would provide for safety and whether supervision should be provided.

In addition to diving accidents, another area of concern for pool owners and operators involves children. Drowning is a leading cause of injury-related death among children, and numerous lawsuits have sprung from these unfortunate deaths.[13]

One area where the issue of drowning occurs involves children in unguarded pools. The question arises as to whether liability can exist where there is no lifeguard but the pool is open for use. Consider the following case.

In *Turner v. Parish of Jefferson, Houma Motels, et al.* (1998),[14] a 12-year-old girl drowned in a Holiday Inn swimming pool. There were no lifeguards at the pool. The young girl was with her basketball team, who was participating in a regional tournament. Her parents were not with her on this particular trip. She was under the supervision of volunteer coaches. After completing the tournament game on Saturday, the team had dinner and arrived back at the hotel at about 9 p.m. The pool closed at 10 p.m. Upon their return to the hotel, the group went to the Holidome pool for a swim. Testimony revealed there were approximately 30 to 50 people in the pool. The pool was crowded with children swimming and playing. It was very loud in the pool area. A swimmer testified that he saw the girl playing tap ball with a group of children in water that was a little below her shoulders. He also saw her go into the six-foot depth area on several occasions to retrieve the ball. She eventually left the game to swim elsewhere. The other swimmer stayed to play the game of tap ball. On one occasion the ball was knocked into the six-foot deep area. The swimmer retrieved the ball and walked back. He stepped on something that he thought was a toy. The water was cloudy and he could not see the bottom. A few seconds later he had to retrieve the ball again and decided to see what he had stepped on earlier. It was the girl on the bottom of the pool. He dove under and brought her to the surface, where she was given CPR. The coach ran to find someone to call 911. Efforts to save the girl were unsuccessful. Evidence revealed there were no hotel employees or security personnel monitoring activities around the pool at the time of the drowning. The hotel manager on duty was also not in the area.

The girl's parents brought a wrongful death suit against the hotel and other named parties. Part of their claim was that the hotel was negligent in failing to provide a lifeguard. The court held that the hotel breached its duty to maintain the premises in a reasonably safe and suitable condition. A central component of this duty was to have supervision given the number of children known to be using the pool. The hotel knew that there would be many children staying at the hotel that weekend for the basketball tournament. They also had reason to believe, from prior experience, that the pool would be crowded with children. Even with this knowledge, the hotel failed to employ a temporary lifeguard or staff someone with water safety training to monitor the pool area. Additionally, with the knowledge of potential crowding in and around the pool area, the hotel neither possessed nor posted a requirement relative to pool capacity. Further, there was not a safety rope at the deep end, depth markers at the deep end were not displayed, and the water was cloudy. Given these facts and circumstances, the court found the defendant negligent.

When a child enters a pool after hours (e.g., by climbing a low fence) and is injured, a whole new area of law comes into play. This area of law is referred to as "attractive nuisance." An attractive nuisance is a man-made condition that is dangerous to children and attracts them to it. A swimming pool is considered by most courts to be an attractive nuisance. It is obviously dangerous to a small child given the possibility of drowning.

Suppose that you manage the pool at a city park. It is completely surrounded by a six-foot-high fence. There is also a metal gate with a latch that is locked with a padlock. One very hot and busy day in midsummer, the staff person in charge of closing the pool inadvertently fails to shut the padlock completely, and it doesn't lock. A child from the adjacent neighborhood comes by on his bike a few minutes later and decides to look through the fence into the pool area. He tries the lock and pulls it from the latch and enters the pool. He climbs upon the diving board in the deep end of the pool and walks to the end. He jumps up and down on the flexible board a few times. On the next jump, he trips and falls into the water. He cannot swim and drowns with no one there to rescue him.

The most likely outcome would be a negligence suit by the parents of the deceased child against the park and the pool manager. The parents would most likely make an attractive nuisance claim. They would claim that the city failed to take reasonable precautions to protect children from the dangerous unoccupied pool. They would argue that it was indeed an attractive nuisance, since one would expect children to be attracted by the pool and want to come there to play.

Inadequate fences are often the reason children are able to enter an unsupervised pool area. State and city codes often regulate the height offences surrounding pools. They should be high enough to discourage people from climbing over them. In addition to the height of a fence, it must also have gates that prevent people from entering. To prevent children from entering the pool area after hours, gates should be self-closing and self-latching. If a wading pool is present, it should be enclosed by an additional fence with a self-closing gate. Finally, gates that provide access to the pool facility should be located at the shallow end of the pool.

The swimming pool shell and deck are areas where the frequency of injury can be high if not properly maintained. The pool shell is the part of the pool that holds the water. It can present problems if it has formed cracks or has an otherwise irregular surface. Cracks sometimes form in the winter when there has been a dramatic change in the temperature. Cracks can create problems with water loss from the pool and can also cause cuts and abrasions in feet and hands. This can result in the immediate problem of lawsuits from injured swimmers and problems associated with water contamination from blood-borne pathogens.

The pool deck must also be properly maintained. Cracks in the surface or indentations where water is held can result in trip and fall injuries that often give rise to lawsuits. To prevent this from happening, a proper drainage system should be in place that drains water away from the pool. Also, the walking surface should be clean and have a nonslip surface. Cracks should be filled and repaired and an additional nonslip surface should be installed around the pool rim. A good risk management plan will address all the foreseeable problems that could arise on the premises.

SECTION 4: DUTY TO PROVIDE SAFE EQUIPMENT

In addition to the premises, courts impose a duty on pool owners and operators to keep swimming pool equipment in a reasonably safe condition. If a swimmer is injured and he brings suit, it is the judge or jury who decides what is reasonable under the circumstances. The violation of a city code might find the pool operator negligent per se where the defendant is guilty of negligence based solely on the fact that an injury occurred and he or she violated a city regulation.

However, even if a code regulating pool equipment is complied with, liability might still exist if the court finds that the equipment was not kept in a reasonably safe condition. Suppose that you manage an aquatic facility. In the midst of performing tedious mid-afternoon paperwork, you receive an urgent call from a frantic lifeguard. A child's arm has become trapped in an underwater drainage pipe.

Ordinarily, this would not have happened, because there was a fastened grill cover attached to the pipe as required by statute. Over time, however, the bolts connecting the grill had loosened and it had slipped off. Proper maintenance would have ensured that the grill was securely fastened to the pipe. Thus, even though the grill cover was there as required by statute, it was not properly maintained. In a negligence suit by the child or his parents, the fact that the drain was improperly maintained would be an important factor in the case even though the city had met the statutory requirement of having a cover for the drain.

Therefore, proper maintenance and inspection programs should be initiated that keep pool equipment in compliance with the applicable city codes. These programs should also ensure that the equipment is in the best possible shape. The following is a list of equipment that bears special attention from a risk management perspective.

1. **Drains:** Drains should be covered and not be of the type that allow suction where hair, arms, feet, and legs can get caught and trap a swimmer under water.

2. **Safety equipment:** Emergency rescue equipment such as safety ropes, rescue tubes, ring buoys, and backboards should be in good working order and easy to access. Also, a first aid kit with all essential contents should be on hand.

3. **Floating lane dividers:** Proper tension should be kept on the lines so that swimmers do not get strangled or caught in them.

4. **Ladders and handrails:** These devices provide a safe means of entering and exiting the pool and should be located in areas where they will be both accessible and safe.

5. **Underwater lights and heating devices:** These should be properly placed and maintained to avoid the risk of burns or electrocution.

6. **Overhead lights:** Overhead lights can give pool patrons the opportunity to use pool facilities when it is dark. Lights should be of sufficient power to allow the lifeguards and swim staff to adequately supervise the pool area. They must also be carefully positioned so that the hazards associated with breakage and electrical shock can be avoided or minimized.

7. **Diving boards:** Diving boards must meet all the current applicable standards for safety. These standards can be found in places such as municipal and state codes, the National Swimming Pool Institute, and the NCAA. Diving boards should be permanent structures with parts that are in proper and safe working order. They should also have side rails to prevent someone from falling to the pool deck. Mounting bolts should be checked for corrosion and tightened if loose. Also, the base of the board should be checked for hairline fractures. A proper ongoing maintenance and inspection program is necessary to accomplish this task. Finally, the configuration and depth of the pool must be correct for the type and size of board used. This is especially important when adding or changing a diving board.

8. **Electrical installations:** Great care must be taken to prevent the risk of electrical shock in aquatic facilities. Many states and/or localities have adopted rules that address this issue. The substance of these laws is often adopted from the National Electrical Code (Article 680).

9. **Pool water:** Pool water must be properly sanitized so that organisms harmful to people are destroyed. Pool water should be free of harmful organisms or algal blooms that cloud the water. The dangers of harmful bacteria in the water are obvious, and cloudy water makes it difficult for swimmers and divers to judge the water's depth. The other side of the coin is that too much chemical concentration in the water, while often solving the former problem, can create others. A balance must be met. Therefore, regulations are often in place to ensure the proper type and amount of chemicals are used. The American Public Health Association generally sets the standard for water purity and the tests that determine if the standards have been met. These standards are often adopted by the state and local health department and contained in their health codes.[15] Often, it is required that pool managers keep daily records of the tests and observations they make and file these with the health department. "These records indicate clearness of the water, disinfection, and other routine treatment of the water, the number of people using the facilities on a given day, and, occasionally, diseases or injuries occurring on the premises."[16]

The manager of an aquatics facility must be aware of the rules and legal responsibilities that must be met. If the standards and requirements outlined in the codes and laws are followed, the safety and enjoyment of the facility will be enhanced, and the risk of successful litigation against your organization might be reduced.

Notes

1. *King v. National Spa and Pool Institute, Inc.,* 570 So.2d 612 (Ala. 1990).
2. *Barnett v. Zion Park District,* 665 N.E.2d 808 (Ill. 1996).
3. *Phillips v. Southeast 4-H Educational Center, Inc., et al.,* 510 S.E.2d 458 (Va. 1999).
4. *Cater v. City of Cleveland,* 697 N.E.2d 610 (Ohio 1998).
5. *Cassio v. Creighton University,* 446 N.W.2d 704 (Neb. 1989).
6. *Johnson v. City of Darlington,* 466 N.W.2d 233 (Wis. 1991).
7. *Volcanic Gardens Management Go. v. Beck,* 863 S.W.2d 780 (Tex. App. 1993).
8. *Glittenberg v. Doughboy Recreational Indus.,* 491 N.W.2d 208 (Mich. 1992).
9. *Glittenberg v. Doughboy Recreational Indus.,* 491 N.W.2d 208, 215 (Mich. 1992).
10. *Erickson v. Muskin Corp.,* 535 N.E.2d 475 (Ill App. 1989) overruled by *Blagg v. Illinois F.W.D. Truck & Equipment Company,* 143 Ill. 2d 188, 572 N.E. 2d 920 (1991 Ill)
11. The U.S. Consumer Products Safety Commission.
12. The general rule is that if at least 25% of persons using the facility speak a foreign language, the signs need to be written in that language also.
13. Baker, S. F., & Wailer, A. E. (1989). *Childhood injury state by state mortality facts.* Baltimore, The Johns Hopkins Injury Prevention Center.
14. *Turner v. Parish of Jefferson, Houma Motels, et al.,* 721 So.2d 64 (La. App. 5 Cir. 1998).
15. American Jurisprudence, 7 Am Jur Trials 645, Swimming Pool Accidents; West Publishing Co.
16. Ibid. at 658.

Discussion Questions

1. What recreation pursuit results in the most deaths each year in the United States?

2. Name at least two programs that are recognized as nationally certified lifeguard training programs.

ABOUT THE AUTHORS

John O. Spengler, J.D., Ph.D., is an associate professor in the Department of Tourism, Recreation and Sport Management at the University of Florida. Dr. Spengler teaches and conducts research in risk management and liability issues in sport and recreation, and policy issues relevant to physical activity and health promotion in school and park settings. Dr. Spengler's research on policy and legal issues relevant to the joint and shared use of sport and recreation facilities in schools and parks, and physical activity in parks, has been funded by the Robert Wood Johnson Foundation. He is the author of four textbooks, two book chapters, and numerous articles on the subjects of law, policy, and risk management in sport and physical activity. Dr. Spengler is a Fellow with the Research Consortium of the American Alliance for Health, Physical Education, Recreation and Dance, and past president of the American Association for Physical Activity and Recreation (AAPAR) Safety and Risk Management Council. He also has been recognized in "Who's Who Among America's Teachers," and has received several teaching awards, including the 2002 and 2009 University of Florida College of Health and Human Performance "Teacher of the Year" award. He has presented at numerous professional conferences, meetings, and webinars to grantees, students, military personnel, lawyers, practitioners, sport and recreation professionals, health advocates, policy makers, and researchers.

Bruce Hronek is a professor emeritus at Indiana University. He has recently retired, having taught and conducted research in recreation, tourism, and sports related subject areas in the Department of Recreation, Sports, and Tourism Studies for 22 years. He is a senior fellow in the Eppley Institute for Public Lands at Indiana University. Hronek worked for the United States Forest Service for 33 years in various positions throughout the United States. Hronek is a consultant for individuals and organizations regarding recreation, sports, and tourism legal matters. He has conducted seminars nationally and internationally on legal liability, philanthropy, recreation, sports, tourism, and natural resource management.

He received his B.S. in forestry at the University of Idaho, received a master's degree in business administration from Western International University, in Phoenix, Arizona, and a law degree (MLS) from Antioch Law School, now Clark law school at the University of the District of Columbia in Washington D. C.

He is the author or co-author of five books and numerous articles on risk management in recreation, sports, tourism, and natural resource management. Hronek has numerous teaching and performance awards including two University Teaching Excellence Awards, two University Trustees Teaching Awards, and performance-based awards for working in Federal Service.

INDEX